DuckDB in Action

Get the eBook FREE!
(PDF, ePub, Kindle, and liveBook all included)

We believe that once you buy a book from us, you should be able to read it in any format we have available. To get electronic versions of this book at no additional cost to you, purchase and then register this book at the Manning website.

Go to https://www.manning.com/freebook and follow the instructions to complete your pBook registration.

That's it!
Thanks from Manning!

DuckDB in Action

MARK NEEDHAM
MICHAEL HUNGER
MICHAEL SIMONS
FOREWORD BY MARK RAASVELDT
AND HANNES MÜHLEISEN

MANNING
SHELTER ISLAND

Manning Publications Co.
20 Baldwin Road
PO Box 761
Shelter Island, NY 11964

Development editor: Rhonda Mason
Technical editor: Jordan Tigani
Review editor: Radmila Ercegovac
Production editor: Kathy Rossland
Copy editor: Christian Berk
Proofreader: Melody Dolab
Technical proofreader: Dirk Gomez
Typesetter and cover designer: Marija Tudor

ISBN 9781633437258
Printed in the United States of America

To Rainer and Stefan
—Michael Simons

I dedicate this book to all the people who are suffering in the world from injustice, poverty, war, and disease. It is a shame that humanity wastes its future and the planet on greed for wealth and power instead of working together to create a better world for all. I will donate most of the royalties from this book to charities helping to make the world a better place.
—Michael Hunger

brief contents

contents

foreword

Welcome, dear reader, to this book about DuckDB. It feels somewhat surreal to write a foreword for this book about DuckDB because it seems like everything has happened so quickly. The world of data management systems moves slowly—software projects started in the 70s are still in strong positions on the market.

It has only been a few short years since we sat at the Joost bar in Amsterdam one evening in 2018 and decided we were going to build a new system. We had been toying with the idea previously but had been hesitant, as we knew it was a daft idea. The common wisdom is that it takes "ten million dollars" to make a new database system successful. But we decided on an equally daft plan: we would create a new kind of data management system—one that had never been built before—an in-process analytical system. Maybe the usual rules did not apply to this new kind of system. After some more beers, we had pretty much decided on the first rough draft of DuckDB's architecture. The very next day, we started hacking.

Only a year later, in 2019, we opened up our repository and started telling people about it. We showed our first demo of DuckDB at the 2019 SIGMOD conference, coincidentally in Amsterdam. Since we co-organized the conference, we snuck stickers in the goodie bags in an early attempt at a type of viral marketing. At the same time, we also opened up the source code repository to the public. The "duck was out of the bag," so to speak.

But thousands of open source projects are started every day, and the vast majority will—regrettably or not—never gain any traction. This was also our expectation—that, most likely, nobody was going to care about our "DuckDB." But an amazing thing happened: little by little, the stars on the GitHub repository started to accumulate. We think this came about because of another design goal of DuckDB: ease of use. We had observed that the prevailing sentiment in data systems seemed to have been that the world should be grateful to be allowed to use the hard-won results of database systems research and the systems we build. We had observed a worrying effect, however: the results of decades of research were simply being ignored because they were hard to use. In somewhat of a paradigm shift for data systems, one design goal of DuckDB was to make it as easy to use as possible and to fix some of the biggest gripes we had heard from practitioners.

Somehow, people seem to have noticed. Big popularity gains came from activity on the social network formerly known as Twitter and most notably from regularly being featured on Hacker News. Now DuckDB is downloaded millions of times each month and used everywhere from the biggest companies to the smallest embedded devices. MotherDuck offers practitioners a hosted version but in DuckDB style and with a strong local component. Heck, people are even writing books about DuckDB.

We're glad that Mark and the two Michaels are the ones who bring this book to you. It's an honor for us that such an excellent team is writing this book. They are experts in explaining challenging data technology to developers in a fun, engaging, but still deeply competent way. We hope you enjoy this book and, of course, that you enjoy working with DuckDB.

—MARK RAASVELDT AND HANNES MÜHLEISEN
CREATORS OF DUCKDB, 2023

preface

This book covers DuckDB—a modern, fast, embedded analytical database. It runs on your machine and can easily process many gigabytes of data from a variety of sources, including JSON, CSV, Parquet, SQLite, and Postgres. DuckDB integrates well into the Python and R ecosystems and allows you to query in-memory data frames without copying the data. You don't need to spin up cloud data warehouses for your day-to-day data processing anymore; you can just run DuckDB on your data, locally or in the cloud.

With DuckDB, you can solve your relational data analytics tasks without friction. It is really user friendly and easy to learn. Best of all, you can use it embedded in your Python environments and applications, much like SQLite. We strongly believe that we hit the sweet spot in teaching DuckDB, covering its CLI-embedded mode, Python integrations, and capabilities for building data pipelines as well as processing data—all while also guiding readers through a painless deep-dive into modern SQL with DuckDB.

While we all are longtime data expert practitioners and educators, we come from different corners of this spectrum—graph, real-time columnar, and relational databases—yet we all find something of value in DuckDB that we think is worth speaking about. We enjoy using DuckDB a lot, both outside our expertise but also as a useful tool in our respective areas of work.

acknowledgments

Thanks go out to Jordan Tigani, cofounder and CEO of MotherDuck, who was our technical editor. His diligent work and feedback made our examples and writing a lot better. Big thanks also to all the other technical reviewers who diligently worked through the chapters and left their feedback, especially to Marcos Ortiz, Georg Heiler, and Jacob Matson for reviewing the original proposal, and to Dirk Gomez for checking all the code.

The writings and explanations by Mark Raasveldt, Hannes Mühleisen, and Alex Monahan helped us a lot, teaching us more about the inner workings of DuckDB, the ideas behind it, and some SQL gymnastics we had no idea were possible before. Thank you!

Many thanks to Ryan Boyd and Mehdi Quazza. They not only gave valuable feedback but helped us a lot in making more people aware of the book.

We also thank the editing team at Manning, especially Rhonda Mason and Jonathan Gennick, for dealing so positively with us, and Christian Berk for his diligent copy editing and fast feedback loop. Michael Hunger and Michael Simons are happy about our colleagues at Neo4j, who may have raised an eyebrow or two but have enough self-confidence to acknowledge that both the graph and relational approach can coexist. DuckDB has been influential for us when thinking about empathy for users of our software.

To all the reviewers—Andrej Abramušić, Abhilash Babu Jyotheendra Babu, Anjan Bacchu, Chris Bolyard, Thiago Britto Borges, Nadir Doctor, Didier Donsez, Dirk Gómez, Simon Hewitt, Andrew Judd, Madiha Khalid, Simeon Leyzerzon, Noel Llevares, Sebastian Maier, Eli Mayost, Sumit Pal, Anup K. Parikh, Sasha Sankova, William Jamir Silva, Ganesh Swaminathan, Mary Anne Thygesen, Rohini Uppuluri, Ankit Virmani, Wondi Wolde, and Heng Zhang—your suggestions helped make this a better book.

And, of course, a book such as this, written in addition and parallel to the duties at work, takes a toll on spare time and private lives. We thank our families for their continuous support of our crazy ideas.

about this book

We didn't want to write a reference book (that's what the docs are for), but rather, to share the excitement and joy we experienced when working with DuckDB so that you'll learn something new on every page, while having the same fun we had when writing. The book is fast-paced, information-rich, hands-on, and informative, with easy-to-understand and practical examples.

Who should read this book

The ideal reader for this book is a data engineer, data scientist, or developer who is interested in analyzing existing structured data efficiently without having to set up infrastructure. They should be familiar and comfortable with command-line tools and preferably some Python. We will cover a lot of SQL, starting with simple clauses and working our way toward advanced, analytical statements. DuckDB is available on all major operating systems and does not require any installation process; downloading and running the executable is enough. Our chapter on MotherDuck, the serverless analytic platform, requires creating an account if you want to try it out.

How this book is organized: A road map

We start with a gentle introduction to DuckDB in chapters 1 and 2, presenting its use cases and its place in modern data pipelines. First, we will make sure you are able to use the DuckDB CLI before we proceed with an introduction to SQL in chapter 3. We will cover the basic clauses and statements before entering the world of advanced data analysis with SQL in chapter 4, using advanced aggregations, window functions, recursive SQL, and more. Of course, we will include the vendor-specific, developer-friendly extensions that DuckDB brings to the table.

DuckDB has many facets to it, with one of them being the fact that it does not force its persistence storage upon you. We spend the whole of chapter 5 discussing how you can actually use the SQL engine on top of many different file formats for your purpose, without ingesting the data into tables.

Chapter 6 will dive deep into DuckDB's Python integration before we move to the cloud with MotherDuck in Chapter 7.

After that, we will have all the tools ready to build effective data pipelines (chapter 8) and deploy data applications (chapter 9).

In chapter 10, we will take a step back and discuss some considerations for large datasets and apply what we've learned so far.

DuckDB not only offers a CLI and a fantastic Python integration but also Java, C, C++, Julia, Rust, and many other language integrations. In the appendix, we will have a look at these, especially how to use DuckDB from Java.

About the code

This book contains many examples of source code both in numbered listings and in line with normal text. In both cases, the source code is formatted in a `fixed-width font like this` to separate it from ordinary text. Sometimes, code is also **`in bold`** to highlight code that has changed from previous steps in the chapter, such as when a new feature is added to an existing line of code.

In many cases, the original source code has been reformatted; we've added line breaks and reworked indentation to accommodate the available page space in the book. In rare cases, even this was not enough, and listings include line-continuation markers (➡). In those cases, you might need to remove an extra space introduced by that marker to make the code work or fix long URLs.

Additionally, comments in the source code have often been removed from the listings when the code is described in the text. Code annotations accompany many of the listings, highlighting important concepts.

You can get executable snippets of code from the liveBook (online) version of this book at https://livebook.manning.com/book/duckdb-in-action. The complete code for the examples in the book is available for download from the Manning website at https://www.manning.com/books/duckdb-in-action, and from GitHub at https://github.com/duckdb-in-action/examples.

liveBook discussion forum

Purchase of *DuckDB in Action* includes free access to liveBook, Manning's online reading platform. Using liveBook's exclusive discussion features, you can attach comments to the book globally or to specific sections or paragraphs. It's a snap to make notes for yourself, ask and answer technical questions, and receive help from the author and other users. To access the forum, go to https://livebook.manning.com/book/duckdb-in-action/discussion. You can also learn more about Manning's forums and the rules of conduct at https://livebook.manning.com/discussion.

Manning's commitment to our readers is to provide a venue where a meaningful dialogue between individual readers and between readers and the author can take place. It is not a commitment to any specific amount of participation on the part of the authors, whose contribution to the forum remains voluntary (and unpaid). We suggest you try asking the authors some challenging questions lest their interest stray! The forum and the archives of previous discussions will be accessible from the publisher's website as long as the book is in print.

about the authors

MARK NEEDHAM

Mark is a product marketing engineer at ClickHouse, where he creates short-form videos and writes blog posts about real-time data warehouses. He also works on developer experience, simplifying the getting-started experience by making product tweaks and improvements to the documentation.

Mark has worked in the data infrastructure field for the last decade, first at Neo4j on graph databases and then at StarTree on real-time analytics with Apache Pinot. He has been blogging about his experiences with writing software for the last 15 years at markhneed ham.com and has created many short educational videos on data and AI topics at https://www.youtube.com/@learndatawithmark.

He tweets as @markhneedham.

MICHAEL HUNGER

Michael Hunger has been passionate about software development for more than 35 years. For the last 14 years, he has been working on the open source Neo4j graph database, filling many roles, most recently as head of product innovation and developer product strategy. Before joining Neo4j, he consulted in large Java projects and wrote his fair share of SQL code for Oracle, Informix, and MySQL databases. He also created the Jequel SQL DSL in 2006, which was later merged into similar efforts.

As a developer, Michael enjoys many aspects of programming languages, tools, and technologies, learning new things every day, participating in exciting and ambitious open source projects, and contributing to and writing software-related books and articles. His interests span Java, Kotlin, GraphQL, Graph Databases, Generative AI, and modern data analytics. Michael has spoken at numerous conferences and helped organized several of them. His efforts got him accepted to the Java Champions program; he's been writing a bi-monthly column on "Effective Java" for the Java SPEKTRUM print magazine for more than 12 years. Michael helps kids learn to program by running weekly girls-only coding classes at local schools.

You can find more about Michaels's writing and projects on his blog at https://www.jexp.de.

MICHAEL SIMONS

Michael Simons is a Java champion and senior staff software engineer at Neo4j and has been working professionally as a developer for more than 20 years. In his role at Neo4j, he is a vital part of Neo4j's integration into the broader Java ecosystem.

Before entering the graph space, he worked in the German utility sector, using SQL to compute and predict energy usage for large German transport grid operators and energy producers, way before analytical databases became more mainstream. To this day, he enjoys using the declarative nature of SQL (and, of course, Cypher) to ask machines for answers instead of instructing them to produce a result.

Michael is a known speaker at conferences, bridging Java and databases—relational and graph alike—for many years. Michael is the author of the bestselling book *Spring Boot 2* and co-author of *arc42 by Example*, a book about software architecture documentation. He also writes a blog at info.michael-simons.eu.

In the spare time that is left, Michael still dreams about becoming an amateur athlete, and when he isn't training for the next marathon, he uses DuckDB to document his progress at biking.michael-simons.eu/history.

about the cover illustration

The figure on the cover of *DuckDB in Action* is "Paisanne Dequito," or "A peasant woman from Quito," taken from a collection by Jacques Grasset de Saint-Sauveur, published in 1788. Each illustration is finely drawn and colored by hand.

In those days, it was easy to identify where people lived and what their trade or station in life was just by their dress. Manning celebrates the inventiveness and initiative of the computer business with book covers based on the rich diversity of regional culture centuries ago, brought back to life by pictures from collections such as this one.

An introduction
to DuckDB

This chapter covers

- Why DuckDB, a single node in-memory database, emerged in the era of big data
- DuckDB's capabilities
- How DuckDB works and fits into your data pipeline

We're excited that you've picked up this book and are ready to learn about a technology that seems to go against the grain of everything that we've learned about big data systems over the last decade. We've had a lot of fun using DuckDB, and we hope you will be as enthused as we are after reading this book. This book's approach to teaching is hands-on, concise, and fast paced and will include lots of code examples.

After reading the book, you should be able to use DuckDB to analyze tabular data in a variety of formats. You will also have a handy new tool in your toolbox for data transformation, cleanup, and conversion. You can integrate it into your Python notebooks and processes to replace pandas DataFrames in situations where they are not performing. You will be able to build quick applications for data analysis using Streamlit with DuckDB. Let's get started!

1.1   *What is DuckDB?*

DuckDB is a modern embedded analytics database that runs on your machine and lets you efficiently process and query gigabytes of data from different sources. *Embedded databases* run within another process, like your application or notebook, and are not accessed over a network. DuckDB was created in 2018 by Mark Raasveldt and Hannes Mühleisen, who, at the time, were researchers in database systems at Centrum Wiskunde & Informatica (CWI)—the national research institute for mathematics and computer science in the Netherlands.

The founders and the CWI spun DuckDB Labs off as a startup to further develop DuckDB. Its engineering team focuses on making DuckDB more efficient, user friendly, and better integrated.

The nonprofit DuckDB Foundation governs the DuckDB Project by safeguarding the intellectual property and ensuring the continuity of the open source project under the MIT license. The foundation's operations and DuckDB's development are supported by commercial members, while association members can inform the development road map.

While DuckDB focuses on the local processing of data, another startup, Mother-Duck, aims to extend DuckDB to a distributed, self-serve analytics system that can process data in the cloud and on the edge. It adds collaboration and sharing capabilities to DuckDB and supports processing data from all kinds of cloud storage.

The DuckDB ecosystem is quite broad, allowing many people and organizations to create integrations and generally useable applications as well as get excited about its possibilities. Fortunately, the DuckDB community is very helpful and friendly—you can find them on Discord (https://discord.duckdb.org/) and GitHub (https://github.com/duckdb/duckdb). The documentation is comprehensive and detailed enough to answer most questions.

DuckDB lets you process and join local or remote files (e.g., from cloud buckets or URLs) in different formats, including CSV, JSON, Parquet, and Apache Arrow, as well as several databases, like MySQL, SQLite, and Postgres. You can even query pandas or Polars DataFrames from your Python scripts or Jupyter notebooks. A diagram showing conceptually how DuckDB is typically used is shown in figure 1.1.

Unlike the pandas and Polars DataFrame libraries, DuckDB is a real analytics database, implementing more efficient data-processing mechanisms that can handle large volumes of data in seconds. With its SQL dialect, even complex queries can be expressed more succinctly. Its expressiveness allows you to handle more operations inside a single database query, avoiding multiple executions, which would be more costly.

The architecture of the core database engine is the basis for efficient processing and memory management. You can see a diagram showing the way that a query is processed in figure 1.2.

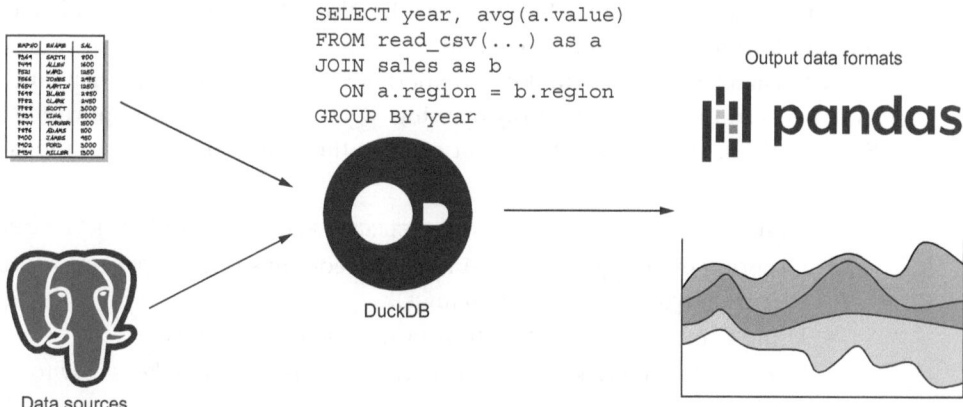

Figure 1.1 **DuckDB and other tools in the ecosystem**

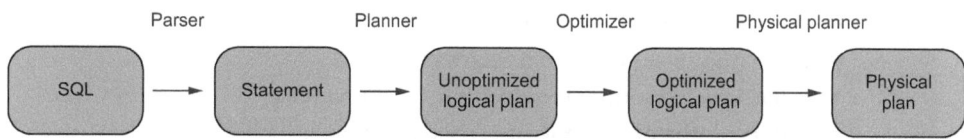

Figure 1.2 **A high-level overview of DuckDB's query-processing pipeline**

We can see that DuckDB processes queries the same way as other databases, with an SQL parser, query execution planner, and query runtime. The query engine is *vectorized*, which means it processes chunks of data in parallel and benefits from modern multicore CPU architectures. DuckDB supports several extensions that add new capabilities to the system, as well as user-defined functions, and has a variety of user interfaces, including a CLI, API, and lower-level integration into other systems, like data processing libraries.

1.2 Why should you care about DuckDB?

DuckDB makes data analytics fast and fun again, without the need to set up large Apache Spark clusters or run a cloud data warehouse just to process a few hundred gigabytes of data. Accessing data from many different sources directly and running the processing where the data resides without copying it over the wire makes your work faster, simpler, and cheaper. This not only saves time, but also a lot of money, and reduces frustration.

For example, we recently had to process AWS access log files residing in S3. Usually, we would run AWS Athena SQL queries against the compressed JSON files. This tends to get expensive, with a large part of the cost being based on the amount of data scanned by the analytics service. Now we can instead deploy DuckDB to an EC2 VM and query the files close to the data for a fraction of the cost, as we only pay for the VM, not for the processed data volume.

With DuckDB, you can run lots of experiments and validate your ideas and hypotheses quickly and locally, all simply by using SQL. In addition to supporting the ANSI SQL standard, DuckDB's SQL dialect extends the standard with innovations like the following:

- Simplifying SELECT * queries with SELECT * EXCLUDE() and SELECT * REPLACE()
- Ordering by and grouping results by ALL columns (e.g., GROUP BY ALL saves the user from typing out all field names)
- Using PIVOT and UNPIVOT to transpose rows and columns
- The STRUCT data type and associated functions, which make it easy to work with complex nested data

We are excited about DuckDB because it helps to simplify data pipelines and data preparation, allowing more time for the actual analysis, exploration, and experimentation.

In this book, we hope to convince you of the following about DuckDB:

- It is faster than SQLite for analytical workloads.
- It is easier to set up than a Spark cluster.
- It has lower resource requirements than pandas.
- It doesn't throw weird Rust errors like Polars.
- It is easier to set up and use than PostgreSQL, Redshift, and other relational databases.
- It is faster and more powerful for data transformations than Talend.

1.3   *When should you use DuckDB?*

You can use DuckDB for all analytics tasks that can be expressed in SQL and work on structured data (i.e., tables or documents) as long as your data is already available (not streaming) and data volumes don't exceed a few hundred gigabytes. Its columnar engine can deal well with both wide tables with many columns as well as large tables with many rows. DuckDB can process a variety of data formats, as previously outlined, and can be extended to integrate with other systems.

As the data doesn't leave your system (local or privacy-compliant hosting), it's also great for analyzing private data, like health information, home automation data, patient data, personal identifying information, financial statements, and similar datasets.

Here are some examples of some common analysis tasks that DuckDB is well placed to solve:

- Analyzing log files where they are stored, without needing to copy them to new locations
- Quantifying personal medical data about one's self, such as a runner might do when monitoring heart rates
- Reporting on the power generation and consumption using data from smart meters

- Optimizing ride data from modern transport operations for bikes and cars
- Preprocessing and pre-cleaning of user-generated data for machine learning training

A great use of DuckDB is for more efficiently processing data that is already available in pandas or Polars DataFrames because it can access the data directly without having to copy the data from the DataFrame representation. The same is true for outputs and tables generated by DuckDB. These can be used as DataFrames without additional memory usage or transfer.

1.4 When should you not use DuckDB?

As DuckDB is an analytics database, it has minimal support for transactions and parallel write access. Therefore, you couldn't use it in applications and APIs that process and store input data arriving arbitrarily.

The data volumes you can process with DuckDB are mostly limited by the main memory of your computer. While it supports spilling over memory (out-of-memory processing) to disk, that feature is aimed more at exceptional situations, where the final portion of processing won't fit into memory. In most cases, that means you'll have a limit of a few hundred gigabytes for processing, with not all of it needing to be in memory at the same time, as DuckDB optimizes loading only what's needed.

DuckDB focuses on the long tail of data analytics use cases, so if you're in an enterprise environment with a complex setup of data sources, tools, and applications processing many terabytes of data, DuckDB might not be the right choice for you. DuckDB does not support processing live data streams that update continuously. Data updates should happen in bulk by loading new tables or large chunks of new data at once. DuckDB is not a streaming, real-time database; you would have to implement a batching approach yourself by setting up a process to create mini-batches of data from the stream and store those mini-batches somewhere that could then be queried by DuckDB.

1.5 Use cases

There are many use cases for a tool like DuckDB. Of course, the most exciting is when it can be integrated with existing cloud, mobile, desktop, and command-line applications and do its job behind the scenes. In these cases, it would be the equivalent of the broad usage of SQLite today, only for analytical processing instead of transactional data storage. When analyzing data that shouldn't leave the user's device, such as health, training, financial or home automation data, an efficient local infrastructure comes in handy. The local analytics and preprocessing also reduce the volume of data that has to be transported from edge devices, like smart meters or sensors.

DuckDB is also useful for fast analysis of larger datasets, such as log files, where computation and reduction can be done where the data is stored, saving high data transfer time and costs. Currently, cloud vendors offer expensive analytics services, like BigQuery, Amazon Redshift, and AWS Athena, which charge by processed data volume to process this kind of data. You can replace many of those uses with scheduled cloud functions processing the data with DuckDB. You can also chain those processing functions by writing out intermediate results to cloud storage, which can then also be used for auditing.

For data scientists, using DuckDB's state-of-the-art query engine can make data preparation, analysis, filtering, and aggregation more efficient than using pandas or other DataFrame libraries—and all of this without leaving the comfortable environment of a notebook with Python or R APIs. This will put more advanced data analytics capabilities in the hands of data science users so that they can make better use of larger data volumes while being faster and more efficient. We will show several of these later in the book. Also, the complexity of the setup can be greatly reduced, removing the need to involve a data operations group.

A final exciting use case will be the distributed analysis of data between cloud storage, the edge network, and the local device. This is, for instance, currently being worked on by MotherDuck, which allows you to run DuckDB both in the cloud and locally.

1.6   *Where does DuckDB fit in?*

This book assumes you have some existing data that you want to analyze or transform. That data can reside in flat files like CSV, Parquet, or JSON, or another database system, like PostgreSQL or SQLite. For the book, we provide example data in the book's GitHub repository: https://github.com/duckdb-in-action/examples.

Depending on your use case, you can use DuckDB transiently to transform, filter, and pass the data through to another format (figure 1.3). In most cases, though, you will create tables for your data to persist it for subsequent high-performance analysis. When doing that, you can also transform and correct column names, data types, and values. If your input data is nested documents, you can unnest and flatten the data to make relational data analysis easier and more efficient.

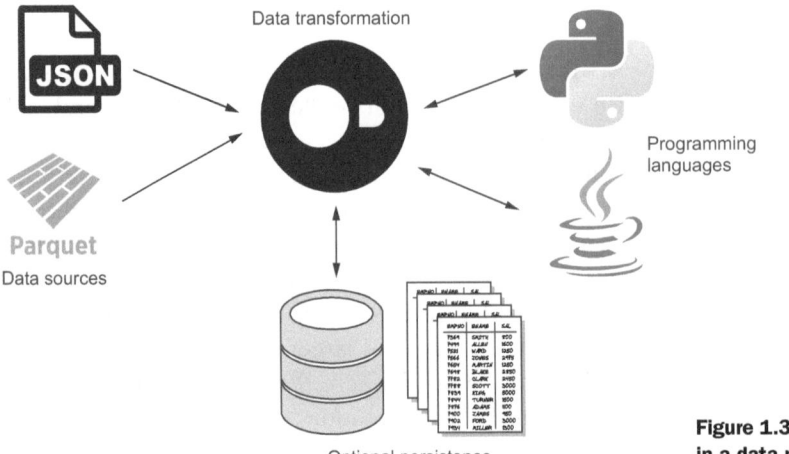

Figure 1.3   **Using DuckDB in a data pipeline**

In the next step, you need to determine which SQL capabilities or DuckDB features can help you perform that analysis or transformation. You can also perform *exploratory data analysis* (EDA) to quickly get an overview of the distribution, ranges, and relationships in your data.

After getting acquainted with the data, you can proceed to the actual analytics tasks. Here, you will build the relevant SQL statements incrementally, verifying at each step that the sample of the results produced matches your expectations. At this stage, you might create additional tables or views before using advanced SQL features, like window functions, common table expressions, and pivots. Finally, you need to decide which way the results are consumed: by turning them into files or databases again, serving them to users through an application or API, or visualizing them in a Jupyter notebook or dashboard.

1.7   Steps of the data processing flow

In the following sections, we will describe some specific aspects of DuckDB's architecture and feature set at a high level to give you an overall understanding and appreciation. We have ordered the sections in the sequence of how you would use DuckDB, from loading data to populating tables and writing SQL for analysis to visualizing those results, as shown in figure 1.4.

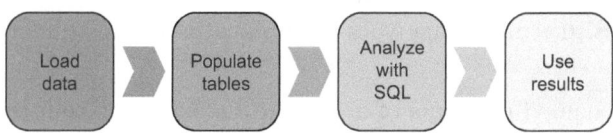

Figure 1.4   The data processing flow

1.7.1   Data formats and sources

DuckDB supports a large number of data formats and data sources, and it lets you inspect and analyze their data with little ceremony. Unlike other data systems, such as SQL Server, you don't need to first specify schema details up front. When reading data, the database uses sensible defaults and inherent schema information from the data, which you can override when needed.

> **NOTE**   With DuckDB, you can focus more on the data processing and analysis you need to do and less on upfront data engineering. Because it is an open source project built by practitioners, there is a lot of emphasis on usability—if something is too hard to use, someone in the community will propose and submit a fix. And if the built-in functionality does not reach far enough, there's probably an extension that addresses your needs (e.g., geospatial data or full-text search).

DuckDB supports a variety of data formats:

- CSV files can be loaded in bulk and parallel, and their columns are automatically mapped.
- DataFrames' memory can be handled directly by DuckDB inside the same Python process without the need to copy data.
- JSON formats can be destructured, flattened, and transformed into relational tables. DuckDB also has a JSON type for storing this type of data.
- Parquet files, along with their schema metadata, can be queried. Predicates used in queries are pushed down and evaluated at the Parquet storage layer to reduce the amount of data loaded. This is the ideal columnar format to read and write for data lakes.
- Apache Arrow columnar-shaped data can be read via Arrow Database Connectivity (ADBC) without data copying and transformations.
- Accessing data in cloud buckets, like S3 or GCP, reduces transfer and copy infrastructure and allows for cheap processing of large data volumes.

1.7.2 Data structures

DuckDB handles a variety of tables, views, and data types. For table columns, processing, and results, there are more data types available than just the traditional data types, like string (varchar), numeric (integer, float, and decimal), dates, timestamps, intervals, Boolean, and binary large objects (BLOBs).

DuckDB also supports structured data types like enums, lists, maps (dictionaries), and structs:

- *Enums*—Indexed, named elements of a set that can be stored and processed efficiently.
- *Lists or arrays*—These hold multiple elements of the same type, and there are a variety of functions for operating on these lists.
- *Maps*—Efficient key–value pairs that can be used for keeping keyed data points. They are used during JSON processing and can be constructed and accessed in several ways.
- *Structs*—Consistent key–value structures, where the same key always has values of the same data type. That allows for more efficient storage, reasoning, and processing of structs.

DuckDB also allows you to create your own types and database extensions, which can provide additional data types. DuckDB can also create virtual or derived columns that are created from other data via expressions.

1.7.3 Developing the SQL

When analyzing data, you usually start by gaining an understanding of the shape of the data. Then, you work from simple queries to creating more and more complex ones from the basic building blocks. You can use DESCRIBE to learn about the columns and data types of your data sources, tables, and views. Armed with that information, you can get basic statistics and distributions of a dataset by running count queries, count(*), globally or grouped by interesting dimensions like time, location, or item type. That gives you some good insights into what to expect from the data available.

DuckDB even has a SUMMARIZE clause (https://duckdb.org/docs/guides/meta/summarize.html) that gives you statistics per column:

- count
- min, max, avg, and std (deviation)
- approx_unique (estimated count of distinct values)
- percentiles (q25, q50, q75)
- null_percentage (part of the data being null)

To write your analytics query, you can start working on a subset of the data by using LIMIT or by only looking at a single input file. Start by outlining the result columns that you need (these may sometimes be converted—e.g., for dates using strptime). Those are the columns you would group by. Then, apply aggregations and filters to your data as needed. There are many different aggregation functions available in DuckDB (https://duckdb.org/docs/sql/aggregates.html), from traditional ones, like min, avg, and sum, to more advanced ones like histogram, bitstring_agg, list, or approximations like approx_count_distinct. There are also advanced aggregations, including percentiles, entropy or regression computation, and skewness. For running totals and comparisons with previous and next rows, you would use window functions aggregation OVER (PARTITION BY column ORDER BY column2 [RANGE …]). Repeatedly used parts of your analytics statement can be extracted into named common table expressions (CTEs) or views. Often, it also helps for readability to move parts of the computation into subqueries and use their results to check for existence or do some nested data preparation.

While you're building up your analytical statement, you can check the results at any time to make sure they are still correct and you've not taken an incorrect detour. This takes us to our next and last section on using the results of your queries.

1.7.4 Using or processing the results

You've written your statement and gotten the analytics results quickly from DuckDB. Now what?

It would be useful to keep your results around (e.g., by storing them in a file or a table). Creating a table from your results is straightforward with CREATE TABLE <name> AS SELECT …. DuckDB can write a variety of formats, including CSV, JSON, Parquet, Excel, and Apache Arrow. It also supports other database formats, like SQLite, Postgres, and others, via custom extensions. For smaller results sets, you can also use the DuckDB CLI to output the data as CSV or JSON.

But because a picture tells more than 1,000 rows, often the preferred choice is data visualization. With the built-in bar function, you can render inline bar charts of your data. You can also use command-line plotting tools, like youplot, for some quick results in your terminal.

In most cases, though, you would use the large Python and JavaScript ecosystem to visualize your results. For those purposes, you can turn your results into DataFrames, which then can be rendered into a variety of charts with matplotlib; ggplot in Python; ggplot2 in R; or d3, nivo, or observable in JavaScript. A visual representation showing this is provided in figure 1.5.

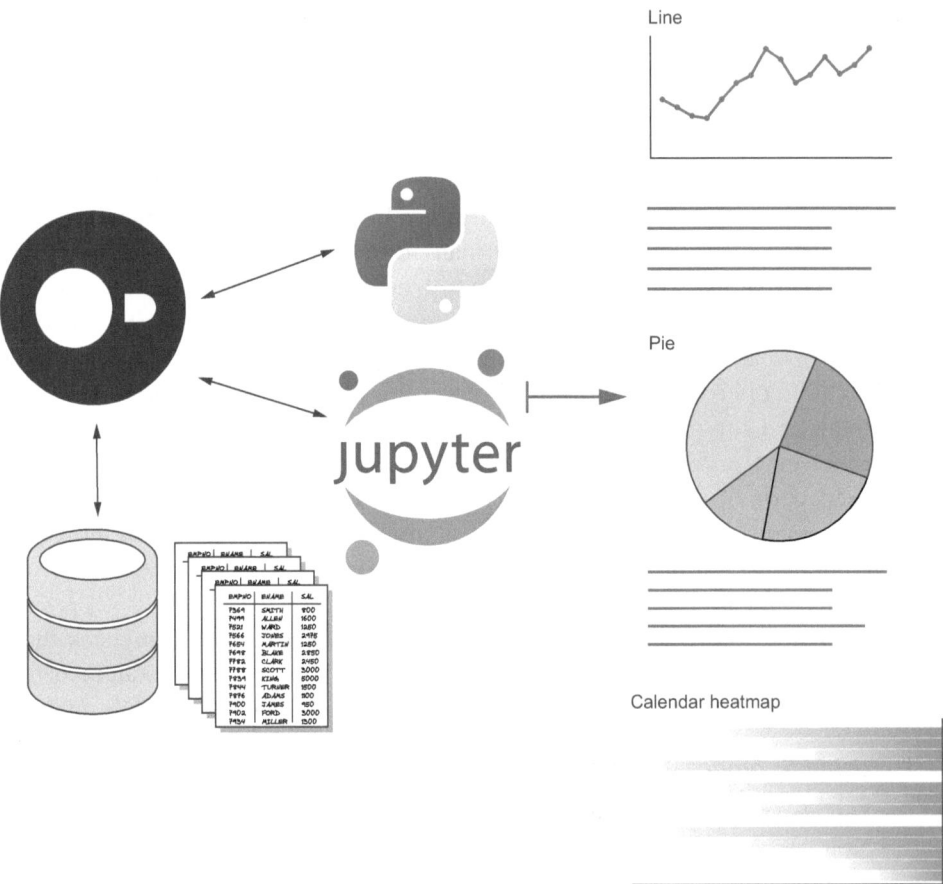

Figure 1.5   Visualizing data in a dashboard or Jupyter Notebook

As DuckDB is so fast, you can serve the results directly from your queries on the data via an API that web, command-line, or mobile clients can consume. You only really need a traditional client–database server setup if your source data is too big to move around and your results are comparatively small (much less than 1% of the volume).

Otherwise, you can embed DuckDB into your application (e.g., built with Streamlit) or dashboarding tool and have it run on local raw data or a local DuckDB database.

Summary

- DuckDB is a newly developed analytical database that excels at in-memory processing.
- The database supports an extended dialect of SQL and gains new capabilities with extensions.
- DuckDB can read a variety of formats natively from local and remote sources.
- The integration in Python, R, and other languages is seamless and efficient.
- As an in-process database, it can process data efficiently without copying.
- In addition to the traditional data types, DuckDB also supports lists, maps, structs, and enums.
- DuckDB provides a lot of functions on data types and values, making data processing and shaping much easier.
- Building up your SQL queries step by step after learning about the shape of your data helps you stay in control.
- You can use the results of your query in a variety of ways, from generating reports and visualizing in charts to outputting in new formats.

Getting started with DuckDB

Now that we have an understanding of what DuckDB is and why it came into prominence in the early 2020s, it's time to get familiar with it. This chapter will be centered on the DuckDB *command-line interface* (CLI). We'll learn how to install it on various environments, before learning about the its built-in commands. We'll conclude by querying a remote CSV file.

2.1 Supported environments

DuckDB is available for a range of different programming languages and operating systems (Linux, Windows, and macOS) both for Intel/AMD and ARM architectures. At the time of writing, there is support for the command line, Python, R, Java, JavaScript, Go, Rust, Node.js, Julia, C/C++, ODBC, JDBC, WASM, and Swift. In this chapter, we will focus on the DuckDB command line exclusively, as we think that is the easiest way to get you up to speed. The DuckDB CLI does not require a separate server installation, as DuckDB is an embedded database, and in the case of the CLI, it is embedded in the CLI executable.

The command-line tool is published to GitHub releases, and there are a variety of packages for different operating systems and architectures. You can find the full list on the installation page: https://duckdb.org/docs/installation/index.

2.2   Installing the DuckDB CLI

The installation is a "copy to" installation, meaning no installers or libraries are needed. The CLI consists of a single binary named duckdb. Let's learn how to go about installing DuckDB.

2.2.1   macOS

On macOS, the official recommendation is to use the Homebrew (https://brew.sh) package installer, as shown in the following listing.

> **Listing 2.1   Installing DuckDB on macOS via Homebrew**

```
/bin/bash -c "$(curl -fsSL https://raw.githubusercontent.com/\
Homebrew/install/HEAD/install.sh)"          ◁─── This is only necessary to install the
                                                 Homebrew package manager itself—
brew install duckdb                              don't run it if you already have it.
```

2.2.2   Linux and Windows

There are several different packages available for Linux and Windows, depending on the particular architecture and version that you're using. You can find a full listing on the GitHub releases page (https://github.com/duckdb/duckdb/releases). In the following listing, we learn how to get the DuckDB CLI running on Linux with an AMD64 architecture.

> **Listing 2.2   Getting DuckDB running on Linux**

```
wget https://github.com/duckdb/duckdb/releases/download/v0.10.0/\
duckdb_cli-linux-amd64.zip          ◁─── Don't forget to update this link to the latest
unzip duckdb_cli-linux-amd64.zip         version from the GitHub releases page
./duckdb -version                        (https://github.com/duckdb/duckdb/releases).
```

2.3   Using the DuckDB CLI

The simplest way to launch the CLI is as follows—and yes, it's that short, and it's quick:

```
duckdb
```

This will launch DuckDB and the CLI. You should see something like the following output:

```
v0.10.0 20b1486d11
Enter ".help" for usage hints.
Connected to a transient in-memory database.
Use ".open FILENAME" to reopen on a persistent database.
```

The database will be transient, with all data held in memory. It will disappear when you quit the CLI, which you can do by typing .quit or .exit.

2.3.1 SQL statements

You can enter or paste SQL statements directly in the command line and end them with a semicolon and a newline. While there is no semicolon, you can enter newlines. They will be executed directly and output the results in compact table format. You can change the output formats as explained in section 2.5.1. For longer running operations, a progress bar will be shown. The following listing provides a simple example selecting a few constant values.

Listing 2.3 A simple select statement

```
select v.* from values (1),(3),(3),(7) as v;
```

By default, it will be printed in a tabular format:

```
┌───────┐
│ col0  │
│ int32 │
├───────┤
│     1 │
│     3 │
│     3 │
│     7 │
└───────┘
```

2.3.2 Dot commands

In addition to SQL statements and commands, the CLI has several special commands that are only available in the CLI: the special dot commands. To use one of these commands, begin the line with a period (.) immediately followed by the name of the command you wish to execute. Additional arguments to the command are entered, space separated, after the command. Dot commands must be entered on a single line, and no whitespace may occur before the period. No semicolon is required at the end of the line in contrast to a normal SQL statement or command.

Some of the most popular dot commands are described as follows:

- .open closes the current database file and opens a new one.
- .read allows reading SQL files to execute from within the CLI.
- .tables lists the currently available tables and views.
- .timer on/off toggles SQL timing output.
- .mode controls output formats.

- `.maxrows` controls the number of rows to show by default (for `duckbox` format).
- `.excel` shows the output of next command in spreadsheet.
- `.exit`, `.quit` or `ctrl-d` exit the CLI.

A full overview can be retrieved via `.help`.

2.3.3 CLI arguments

The CLI takes in arguments that can be used to adjust the database mode, control the output format, or decide whether the CLI is going to enter interactive mode. The usage is `duckdb [OPTIONS] FILENAME [COMMANDS]`.

Some of the most popular CLI arguments are described as follows:

- `-readonly` opens the database in read-only mode.
- `-json` sets the output mode to `json`.
- `-line` sets the output mode to `line`.
- `-unsigned` allows for the loading of unsigned extensions.
- `-s COMMAND` or `-c COMMAND` runs the provided command and then exits. This is especially helpful when combined with the `.read` dot command, which reads input from the given filename.

The following is an example that demonstrates how the CLI can be parameterized to output the results of a query as JSON:

```
duckdb --json -c 'select v.* from values (1),(3),(3),(7) as v;'
```

```
[{"col0":1},
{"col0":3},
{"col0":3},
{"col0":7}]
```

To get a list of the available CLI arguments, call `duckdb -help`.

2.4 DuckDB's extension system

DuckDB has an extension system used to house functionality that isn't part of the core of the database. You can think of extensions as packages that you can install with DuckDB.

DuckDB comes preloaded with several extensions, which vary depending on the distribution that you're using. You can get a list of all the available extensions, whether installed or not, by calling the `duckdb_extensions` function. Let's start by checking the fields returned by this function.

Listing 2.4 The format of `duckdb_extensions` output

```
DESCRIBE
SELECT *
FROM duckdb_extensions();
```

The `duckdb_extensions` function returns, among other information, the name of the extension and whether it is installed and actually loaded:

```
| column_name    | column_type |
|   varchar      |   varchar   |
|----------------|-------------|
| extension_name | VARCHAR     |
| loaded         | BOOLEAN     |
| installed      | BOOLEAN     |
| install_path   | VARCHAR     |
| description    | VARCHAR     |
| aliases        | VARCHAR[]   |
```

Let's check which extensions we have installed on our machine:

```
SELECT extension_name, loaded, installed
from duckdb_extensions()
ORDER BY installed DESC, loaded DESC;
```

The results of running the query are as follows:

extension_name varchar	loaded boolean	installed boolean
autocomplete	true	true
fts	true	true
icu	true	true
json	true	true
parquet	true	true
tpch	true	true
httpfs	false	false
inet	false	false
jemalloc	false	false
motherduck	false	false
postgres_scanner	false	false
spatial	false	false
sqlite_scanner	false	false
tpcds	false	false
excel	true	
15 rows		3 columns

You can install any extension by typing the INSTALL command followed by the extension's name. The extension will then be installed in your database but not loaded. To load an extension, type LOAD followed by the same name. The extension mechanism is idempotent, meaning you can issue both commands several times without running into errors.

NOTE   Since version 0.8 of DuckDB, the database autoloads installed extensions if it can determine they are needed, so you might not need the LOAD command.

By default, DuckDB cannot query files that live elsewhere on the internet, but that capability is available via the official httpfs extension. If it is not already in your distribution, you can install and load the httpfs extension:

```
INSTALL httpfs;
LOAD httpfs;
```

This extension lets us directly query files hosted on an HTTP(S) server without having to download the files locally, and it supports S3 as well as a few other cloud storage providers. We can then check where that's been installed by entering the following:

```
FROM duckdb_extensions()
SELECT loaded, installed, install_path
WHERE extension_name = 'httpfs';
```

You should see this output:

loaded	installed	install_path
boolean	boolean	varchar
true	true	/path/to/httpfs.duckdb_extension

We can see that this extension has now been loaded and installed and also view the location where it's been installed.

2.5   *Analyzing a CSV file with the DuckDB CLI*

We're going to start with a demonstration of the CLI for a common task for any data engineer—making sense of the data in a CSV file! It doesn't matter where our data is stored, be it on a remote HTTP server or cloud storage (S3, GCP, or HDFS), DuckDB can now process it directly without having to do a manual download and import process. As the ingestion of many supported file formats, such as CSV and Parquet, is parallelized by default, it should be lightning quick to get your data into DuckDB.

We went looking for CSV files on GitHub and came across a dataset containing the total population figures for several countries (https://mng.bz/KZKZ). We can write the following query to count the number of records:

```
SELECT count(*)
FROM 'https://github.com/bnokoro/Data-Science/raw/master/'
    'countries%20of%20the%20world.csv';
```

If we run this query, we should see the following output indicating we've got population data for over 200 countries:

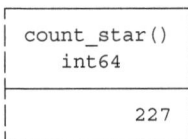

```
| count_star() |
|    int64     |
|--------------|
|          227 |
```

If, as is the case here, our URL or filename ends in a specific extension (e.g., .csv), DuckDB will automatically process it. But what if we try to automatically process a short link of that same CSV file?

```
SELECT count(*)
FROM 'https://bit.ly/3KoiZR0';
```

Running this query results in the following error:

```
Error: Catalog Error: Table with name https://bit.ly/3KoiZR0 does not exist!
Did you mean "Player"?
LINE 1: select count(*) from 'https://bit.ly/3KoiZR0';
```

Although it's a CSV file, DuckDB doesn't know that because it doesn't have a .csv suffix. We can solve this problem by using the read_csv_auto function, which processes the provided URI as if it was a CSV file, despite its lack of .csv suffix. The updated query is shown in the following listing.

> **Listing 2.5   Specifying the format of a remote file**

```
SELECT count(*)
FROM read_csv_auto("https://bit.ly/3KoiZR0");
```

This query will return the same result as the query that used the canonical link from which the format could be deduced.

2.5.1   *Result modes*

For displaying the results, you can choose between different modes using .mode <name>. You can see a list of available modes by typing .help mode.

Throughout this chapter, we've been using duckbox mode, which returns a flexible table structure. DuckDB comes with a series of different modes, which broadly fit into two categories:

- *Table based*—These types of modes work well with few columns and include duckbox, box, csv, ascii, table, list, and column.
- *Line based*—These types of modes work well with many columns and include json, jsonline, and line.

There are some others that don't fit into those categories, including html, insert, and trash (no output).

Our first query counted the number of records in the CSV file, but it'd be interesting to know what columns it has. Many columns would get truncated if we were to use the default mode, so we're going to change to line mode before running the query:

```
.mode line
SELECT *
FROM read_csv_auto("https://bit.ly/3KoiZR0")
LIMIT 1;
```

Changing to
line mode

The results of running this query are shown in the following listing.

Listing 2.6   A result in `line` mode

```
Country = Afghanistan
                        Region = ASIA (EX. NEAR EAST)
                    Population = 31056997
                Area (sq. mi.) = 647500
       Pop. Density (per sq. mi.) = 48,0
    Coastline (coast/area ratio) = 0,00
                 Net migration = 23,06
  Infant mortality (per 1000 births) = 163,07
             GDP ($ per capita) = 700
                  Literacy (%) = 36,0
             Phones (per 1000) = 3,2
                    Arable (%) = 12,13
                     Crops (%) = 0,22
                     Other (%) = 87,65
                       Climate = 1
                     Birthrate = 46,6
                     Deathrate = 20,34
                   Agriculture = 0,38
                      Industry = 0,24
                       Service = 0,38
```

As you can see from the output, `line` mode takes up a lot more space than `duckbox`, but we've found it to be the best mode for doing initial exploration of datasets that have plenty of columns. You can always change back to another mode once you've decided on a subset of columns you'd like to use.

The dataset has lots of interesting information about various countries. Let's write a query to count the number of countries and find the maximum population average area across all countries. This query only returns a few columns, so we'll switch back to `duckbox` mode before running the query:

```
.mode duckbox
SELECT count(*) AS countries,
       max(Population) AS max_population,
       round(avg(cast("Area (sq. mi.)" AS decimal))) AS avgArea
FROM read_csv_auto("https://bit.ly/3KoiZR0");
```

countries	max_population	avgArea
int64	int64	double
227	1313973713	598227.0

So far, no tables have been created in the process, and we've just touched the tip of the iceberg of demonstrating what DuckDB actually can do. While the previous examples have all been run in interactive mode, the DuckDB CLI can also run in a noninteractive fashion. It can read from standard input and write to standard output. This makes it possible to build all sorts of pipelines.

Let's conclude with a script that extracts the population, birth rate, and death rate in countries in Western Europe and creates a new local CSV file containing that data. We can either .exit from the DuckDB CLI or open another tab before running the following command:

```
duckdb -csv \
 -s "SELECT Country, Population, Birthrate, Deathrate
     FROM read_csv_auto('https://bit.ly/3KoiZR0')
     WHERE trim(region) = 'WESTERN EUROPE'" \
 > western_europe.csv
```

The first few lines of western_europe.csv can be viewed with a command-line tool or text editor. If we use the head tool, we can find the first six lines—the header and five rows of data—like this:

```
head -n6 western_europe.csv
```

The output would then look like table 2.1.

Table 2.1   The first six lines of western_europe.csv, showing population, birth rate, and death rate of some countries in Western Europe

Country	Population	Birthrate	Deathrate
Andorra	71,201	8,71	6,25
Austria	8,192,880	8,74	9,76
Belgium	10,379,067	10,38	10,27
Denmark	5,450,661	11,13	10,36
Faroe Islands	47,246	14,05	8,7

We can also create Parquet files, but for that, we can't pipe the output straight into a file with a Parquet extension. Instead, we can use the COPY ... TO clause with the filename as the destination, as shown in the following listing.

Listing 2.7   Writing explicitly to a Parquet file

```
duckdb \
-s "COPY (
     SELECT Country, Population, Birthrate, Deathrate
     FROM read_csv_auto('https://bit.ly/3KoiZR0')
     WHERE trim(region) = 'WESTERN EUROPE'
   ) TO 'western_europe.parquet' (FORMAT PARQUET)"
```

You could then view the contents of the Parquet file using any Parquet reader, perhaps even DuckDB itself!

```
duckdb -s "FROM 'western_europe.parquet' LIMIT 5"
```

The results will be the same as those in table 2.1.

Config file for repeated configuration and use

Repeated configuration and usage can be stored in a config file that lives at $HOME/ .duckdbrc. This file is read during startup, and all commands in it—both dot commands and SQL commands—are executed via one `.read` command. This allows you to store both the configuration state of the CLI and anything you might want to initialize with SQL commands.

An example of something that might go in the duckdbrc file is a custom prompt and welcome message when you launch DuckDB, like this:

```
-- Duck head prompt
.prompt 'O> '
-- Example SQL statement
select 'Begin quacking now '||cast(now() as string) as "Ready, Set, ...";
```

Summary

- DuckDB is available as a library for Python, R, Java, JavaScript, Julia, C/C++, ODBC, WASM, and Swift.
- The CLI supports additional dot commands for controlling outputs, reading files, built-in help, and more.
- With `.mode`, you can use several display modes, including `duckbox`, `line`, and `ascii`.
- You can query CSV files directly from an HTTP server by installing the `httpfs` extension.
- You can use the CLI as a step in any data pipeline, without creating tables, by querying external datasets and writing results to standard out or other files.

Executing SQL queries

Now that you've learned about the DuckDB CLI, it's time to tickle your SQL brain. We will be using the CLI version of DuckDB throughout this chapter. However, all the examples here can be fully applied from within any of the supported environments, such as the Python client, the Java JDBC driver, or any of the other supported language interfaces.

In this chapter, we will quickly go over some basic and necessary SQL statements and then move on to more advanced querying. In addition to explaining SQL basics, we'll also be covering more complex topics, including common table expressions and window functions. DuckDB supports both of these, and this chapter will teach you how to build queries for doing the best possible in-memory online analytical processing (OLAP) with DuckDB.

To get the sample up and running, you should have an idea about data ingestion with DuckDB, as discussed in chapter 2, especially how to ingest CSV files and deal with implicit (automatic) or explicit column detection. Knowledge of the data types presented in chapter 1 will also be helpful. If you want to go straight to querying data, please jump to section 3.4.3, in which we discuss SQLs SELECT statement in detail. We think it's better to start by defining tables and structures first, populating them with data, and then querying them, rather than making up queries on generated or nonexistent data.

3.1 A quick SQL recap

SQL queries are composed of several statements, which are in turn composed of clauses. A *command* is a query submitted to the CLI or any other of the supported clients. Commands in the DuckDB CLI are terminated with a semicolon. Whitespaces can be used freely in SQL commands. You have the option to either align your commands beautifully or type them all in one line—it doesn't matter which you choose. SQL is case-insensitive for keywords and identifiers.

Most statements support several clauses that change their behavior, most prominently the WHERE, GROUP BY, and ORDER BY clauses. WHERE adds conditions on which rows are included in the final result, GROUP BY aggregates many values into buckets defined by one or more keys, and ORDER BY specifies the order of the results returned.

Next, we will demonstrate how to use each of the statements and clauses relevant to your analytical workloads using a real-world example: energy production from photovoltaics. The aim of this example is to provide you with concrete details on each of the concepts so that you leave with an understanding of how they are applicable in your own workloads.

3.2 Analyzing energy production

Energy consumption and production have been the subjects of OLAP-related analysis for a while. Smart meters measuring consumption in 15-minute intervals have been available to many industries—such as metal processing and large production plants—for some time now and have become quite standard. These measurements are used to price the consumed energy, forecast consumption, and more.

With the rise of smart monitoring systems, detailed energy readings are now available in private households as well, becoming more mainstream each year. Imagine you have a photovoltaic grid and smart meter installed at your house. You want to be able to plan your electricity usage a bit or forecast an amortization of your grid, the same way large industries can. To do so, you don't have to go into a full time-series database and a live dashboard. Hopefully, DuckDB and the examples we use throughout this chapter provide a good starting point for creating your own useful reports.

The dataset we are going to use in the following examples is available from the U.S. Department of Energy under the name Photovoltaic Data Acquisition (PVDAQ; https://mng.bz/9d6o). The dataset is documented on GitHub (https://github.com/openEDI/documentation/blob/main/pvdaq.md). The National Renewable Energy Laboratory from the Department of Energy also offers a nice, simple API for getting the partitioned CSV/Parquet files via PVDAQ (https://developer.nrel.gov/docs/solar/pvdaq-v3/). Access is free and requires little personal information. The dataset is published under the Creative Commons Attribution license (http://opendefinition.org/licenses/cc-by/). Parts of the dataset are redistributed unchanged for ease of access in this chapter with the sources of this book.

NOTE Why are we storing measurements in quarter-hour intervals when modern sensors produce much finer measurements? A period of 15 minutes turned out to be fit enough for the aforementioned purposes, such as pricing and buying smart intervals, while simultaneously small enough to be handled with ease in most modern relational systems. The power output or consumption is measured in units of watts (W) or kilowatts (kW) and is typically sold using kilowatt-hours (kWh). These 15-minute intervals can be easily converted from W to kWh, while remaining accurate enough for good production charts. In most cases, you want to smooth the values on at least an hourly basis—peaks and dips due to clouds are often irrelevant. Reviewing a weather forecasting chart and using daily measurements generally provides a good base interval, as this accounts for weekends and bank holidays and smooths out small irregularities.

3.2.1   *Downloading the dataset*

We will use DuckDB's `httpfs` extension to load the data without going through CSV files. To install it, run `install httpfs; load httpfs;` in your DuckDB CLI. We'll be working with the following data files:

- *https://oedi-data-lake.s3.amazonaws.com/pvdaq/csv/systems.csv*—This file contains the list of all PV systems the PVDAQ measures.
- *Readings for systems 10, 34, and 1,200 from 2019 and 2020*—The URLs all follow the schema discussed in the forthcoming text (please change the `system_id` and `year` URL parameters accordingly). You'll need an API key to access them—we are using DEMO_KEY.

The URLs used to get the data are described as follows, with the API key, system ID, and year all supplied via query string parameters:

```
https://developer.nrel.gov/api/pvdaq/v3/data_file?api_key=DEMO_KEY
&system_id=34&year=2019
```

If you can't access those URLs for any reason, the source code of this book contains a database export under the name `ch03_db`, which has the complete dataset. You can import it into a fresh database by using the following commands:

```
duckdb my_ch03.db
import database 'ch03_db';
```

> **TIP** Another option is to use a remote database on motherduck.com via `ATTACH 'md:_share/duckdb_in_action_ch3_4/d0c08584-1d33-491c-8db7-cf9c6910eceb'` in your DuckDB CLI. While the shared example is read-only, it contains all data we used, and you can follow all examples that don't deal with insertion and the like. Chapter 12 will cover the services offered by MotherDuck in detail.

We picked this dataset for specific reasons: its domain is easy to grasp yet complex enough to introduce many analytical concepts backed with actual real-world needs. As with any analytical process, you will eventually run into inconsistent data. This is the case in some series in this dataset too.

If you don't use the ready-made database, don't worry yet about the necessary queries for ingesting the raw data—we will get there in a bit. In the upcoming sections, we will first discuss and create the database schema and then download the readings for several PV systems.

3.2.2 *The target schema*

DuckDB is a *relational database management system* (RDBMS). That means it is a system for managing data stored in relations. A *relation* is essentially a mathematical term for a table.

Each *table* is a named collection of rows. Each row of a given table has the same set of named columns, and each column is of a specific data type. Tables themselves are stored inside schemas, and a collection of schemas constitutes the entire database you can access.

> **NOTE** What is a *surrogate key*? To address rows in a table, a column with a unique value or a combination of columns that is unique over all rows is required. Such a column is usually referred to as the primary key. Not all data you can possibly store in a database has unique attributes. For example, using a person's name as their unique or primary key would be an awful choice. In such scenarios, database schema designers often introduce numerical columns based on a monotonous, increasing sequence or columns containing a *universally unique identifier* (UUID) as *surrogate keys*.

The schema for our dataset consists of a handful of tables (figure 3.1). These tables are normalized so that the supported joins can easily be demonstrated. The three tables we'll be working with are as follows:

- `systems`—This contains the systems for which production values are read.
- `readings`—This contains the actual readings taken for the systems.
- `prices`—This contains the prices for selling energy. Prices in our examples are measured in European cents per kilowatt-hour (cents/kWh), but using any unit per kilowatt-hour will work.

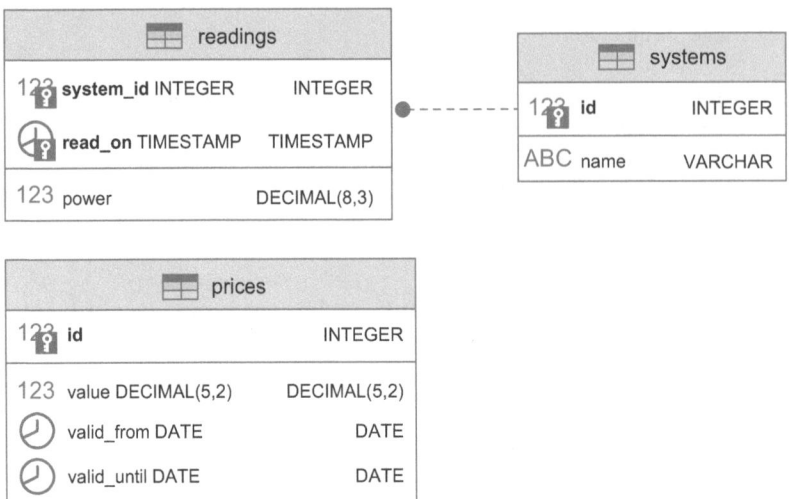

Figure 3.1   Energy consumption schema

The systems table uses the ID defined in the CSV set. We treat it as an externally generated surrogate key. Th prices table uses a SEQUENCE, and the readings table uses a *concatenated natural key* (the ID of the system they have been read from plus the timestamp at which they have been read).

3.3   *Data definition language queries*

We have already seen that you can query many sources with DuckDB without creating a schema containing tables first. DuckDB, however, is a full-fledged RDBMS, and we will use data definition language (DDL) queries to create our target schema prior to ingesting our dataset. New tables are created with the CREATE TABLE statement, and existing tables can be altered with the ALTER TABLE statement. If you don't need a table anymore, you will want to use DROP TABLE.

> **NOTE**   DuckDB supports the entire collection of data definition language clauses, but we only use a subset of them in this chapter for brevity's sake. Be sure to consult the statements documentation (https://duckdb.org/docs/sql/statements/overview) to see all the supported clauses.

3.3.1   *The CREATE TABLE statement*

Let's create the table for the systems we are going to monitor with the CREATE TABLE statement. You must specify the name of the table to create and the list of columns. Other options, such as modifiers to the whole statement, are optional. The column list is defined by the name of the column followed by a type and optional column constraints.

Listing 3.1   A basic CREATE TABLE statement

```
CREATE TABLE IF NOT EXISTS systems (
    id          INTEGER PRIMARY KEY,
    name        VARCHAR(128) NOT NULL
);
```

IF NOT EXISTS is an optional clause that makes the whole command idempotent, so it does not fail if the table already exists.

PRIMARY KEY makes this a mandatory column that serves as a primary, and therefore unique, key. An index will also be added.

This modifier makes the column a mandatory column (literal NULL values cannot be inserted).

In the previous examples, as well as upcoming examples that build upon the table created here, we have made use of various constraints: primary and unique keys as well as foreign keys. We do this not only to demonstrate the available options of the CREATE STATEMENT but also because we care about data integrity.

In DuckDB—as with almost any other database—constraints usually have a negative effect on performance when loading a huge amount of data, as the indexes that back those constraints must be recreated, respectively updated, and rules must be checked. If you don't need integrity checks, omit those constraints.

> **NOTE** DuckDB also offers a CREATE OR REPLACE TABLE statement. This will drop an existing table and replace it with the new definition. We prefer the IF NOT EXISTS clause, though, as we consider it safer than unconditionally dropping a table, since any potential data will be gone afterward.

The definition of the readings table looks slightly different. The table uses a composite primary key. This is a key composed of the reference column system_id, which points back to the systems table and the timestamp column containing the date and time the value was read. Such a primary key constraint cannot be directly defined with one of the columns but goes outside the column list.

Listing 3.2   Creating the readings table with an idempotent statement

```
CREATE TABLE IF NOT EXISTS readings (
    system_id   INTEGER NOT NULL,
    read_on     TIMESTAMP NOT NULL,
    power       DECIMAL(10,3) NOT NULL
                DEFAULT 0 CHECK(power >= 0),
    PRIMARY KEY (system_id, read_on),
    FOREIGN KEY (system_id)
                REFERENCES systems(id)
);
```

Here, several clauses are used to ensure data quality: a default value of 0 is assumed for the power readings, and since an additional column check constraint is used, no negative values are inserted.

This is how a composite primary key is defined after the list of columns.

Foreign key constraints are also table constraints and go after the column definitions.

Finally, we cover the prices table. The script for it actually contains two commands, as we are going to use an incrementing numeric value as the surrogate primary key. We do this by using a DEFAULT declaration with a function call to nextval(). This function takes the name of a sequence as input. Sequences are numeric values stored in the database outside table definitions. A sequence is created via CREATE SEQUENCE.

Listing 3.3 Creating the `prices` table with a primary key based on a sequence

```
CREATE SEQUENCE IF NOT EXISTS prices_id
    INCREMENT BY 1 MINVALUE 10;           ◁─┐ This creates a monotonous incrementing
                                             │ sequence, starting with 10.
CREATE TABLE IF NOT EXISTS prices (
    id            INTEGER PRIMARY KEY
                  DEFAULT(nextval('prices_id')),  ◁─┐ This uses the nextval() function as
    value         DECIMAL(5,2) NOT NULL,             │ a default value for the id column.
    valid_from    DATE NOT NULL,
    CONSTRAINT prices_uk UNIQUE (valid_from)  ◁─┐ This adds a unique table constraint
);                                              │ for the valid_from column.
```

Why don't we use `valid_from` as the primary key? In the initial application, we might be only dealing with selling prices, but in the future, we might be dealing with buying prices too. There are several ways to model that, such as using an additional table or introducing a `type` column to the `prices` table that specifies whether a certain value is a selling or buying price. Using `valid_from` as a primary key would prevent two prices with different types from being valid from the same date. Therefore, you would need to change a simple primary key to a composite one. While other databases might allow dropping and recreating primary and unique keys, DuckDB does not, so in this case, you would need to go through a bigger migration.

Additionally, updating the values of primary keys can be costly on its own, not only from an index perspective but also from an organizational one (e.g., if the column has already been used as a reference column for a foreign key). Every constraint is backed by an index, and changing values often requires a reorganization of that index, which can be slow and costly. Updating several tables in one transaction is a common source of errors, which often lead to inconsistencies. That danger is not present in the `readings` table, where we used the `timestamp` column as the primary key because the readings are essentially immutable.

> **TIP** Review the existing sequences in your database using SELECT sequence_name FRIN duckdb_sequences();.

3.3.2 *The ALTER TABLE statement*

Defining a schema is a complex task, and organizations usually put a lot of effort into it. However, you will rarely encounter a case in which a schema covers all eventualities and is completely correct from the start. Requirements change all the time. Having a requirement to capture the validity of a price, for example, makes an additional column necessary. In that case, use the ALTER TABLE statement:

Many DDL-related statements support an **IF NOT EXISTS** clause, which makes them less error-prone when working with existing schemas.

```
ALTER TABLE prices
ADD COLUMN IF NOT EXISTS valid_until DATE;    ◁─
```

Additionally, with ALTER TABLE, we can DROP and RENAME the column as well as RENAME the table. Some column options, such as default values, can be changed; however, adding, dropping, or changing constraints is not supported at the time of writing. If you want to do that, you'll need to recreate the table.

There are other ways to create tables, including *Create table as select* (CTAS). This is a shortcut that duplicates the shape of a table and its content in one go. For example, we could create a duplicate of the prices table like this:

```
CREATE TABLE prices_duplicate AS
SELECT * FROM prices;
```

We could also add a LIMIT 0 clause to copy the schema of a table without data or a WHERE clause with conditions to copy the shape together with some data.

3.3.3 The CREATE VIEW statement

The CREATE VIEW statement defines a view of a query. It essentially stores the statement that represents the query, including all conditions and transformations. The view will behave as any other table or relation when being queried, and additional conditions and transformations can be applied. Some databases materialize views, while others don't. DuckDB will run the underlying statements of a view if you query that view. If you find yourself running into performance bugs, you might want to materialize the data of a view in a temporary table using a CTAS statement. Any additional predicates that you use when querying a view inside the WHERE clause are oftentimes used as *pushdown predicates*. That means they will be added to the underlying query defining the view and will not be used as filters after the data has been loaded.

A view that is helpful in our scenario is one that gives us the amount of energy produced per system and per day in kWh. This view will encapsulate the logic to compute that value with the necessary grouping statements for us. Views are a great way to create an API inside your database. That API can serve ad hoc queries and applications alike. When the underlying computation changes, the view can be recreated with the same structure without affecting any outside application.

The GROUP BY clause is one of those clauses you hardly can go without in the relational world; we will explore exactly why it's so important later in the chapter. For this example, it is enough to understand that the GROUP BY clause computes the total power produced by system and day. The sum function used in the select list is a so-called aggregate function, aggregating the values belonging to a group.

Listing 3.4 Creating a view for power production by system and day

```
CREATE OR REPLACE VIEW v_power_per_day AS
SELECT system_id,
       date_trunc('day', read_on)       AS day,
       round(sum(power)  / 4 / 1000, 2)  AS kWh,
FROM readings
GROUP BY system_id, day;
```

It does not matter whether the underlying tables are empty for a view to be created, as long as they exist. While we did create the `readings` table, we haven't inserted any data yet, so querying the view with `SELECT * FROM v_power_per_day` will return an empty result for now. We will return to this view in section 3.4.1 and use it in several subsequent examples in this chapter and chapter 4.

3.3.4   *The DESCRIBE statement*

Perhaps universally, relational databases support the `DESCRIBE` statement to query the database schema. In its most basic implementation, it usually works with tables and views.

> **TIP**   Relational databases are based on the relational model and eventually relational algebra. The relational model was first described by Edgar F. Codd in 1970. In essence, all data is stored as sets of tuples grouped together in relations. A *tuple* is an ordered list of attributes—think of it as the column list of a table. A *table*, then, is the relation of a set of tuples. A *view* is also a relation of tuples, and so is the result of a query. Graph databases, in contrast to relational databases, store actual relations between entities. In this book, however, we use the term as defined in the relational model.

The `DESCRIBE` statement in DuckDB works not only with tables but also with everything else being a relation: views, queries, sets, and more. You might want to describe the `readings` table with `DESCRIBE readings;`. Your result should be similar to the following:

column_name varchar	column_type varchar	null varchar	key varchar	default varchar	extra int32
system_id	INTEGER	NO	PRI		
read_on	TIMESTAMP	NO	PRI		
power	DECIMAL(8,3)	NO		0	

Describing a specific subset of columns (a new tuple) selected from any table, such as

`DESCRIBE SELECT read_on, power FROM readings;`

yields the following:

column_name varchar	column_type varchar	null varchar	key varchar	default varchar	extra varchar
read_on	TIMESTAMP	YES			
power	DECIMAL(8,3)	YES			

Last but not least, describing any constructed tuple such as `DESCRIBE VALUES (4711, '2023-05-28 11:00'::timestamp, 42);` works the same:

column_name varchar	column_type varchar	null varchar	key varchar	default varchar	extra varchar
col0	INTEGER	YES			
col1	TIMESTAMP	YES			
col2	INTEGER	YES			

TIP Use the DESCRIBE statement in all scenarios in which you are unsure about the shape of the data. It works for all kinds of relations, local and remote files. The type of file being used affects how efficiently DuckDB can optimize the DESCRIBE statement. For example, remote files (e.g., files in Parquet format) can even be described very quickly, while files in CSV format often take longer to describe, as they don't carry a schema with them, and the engine needs to sample their content.

3.4   Data manipulation language queries

In the context of databases, all statements that insert, delete, modify, *and* read data are referred to as *data manipulation language* (DML). This section will first cover the INSERT and DELETE statements before going into querying data. We won't go into much detail on the UPDATE statement here. The beauty of SQL queries is that they compose very naturally, so everything you'll learn, for example, about the WHERE clause, also applies to the clause being used in INSERT, DELETE, UPDATE, and SELECT statements.

3.4.1   The INSERT statement

When creating data, the INSERT statement is used. Inserting data is a task ranging from simple "fire-and-forget" statements to complex statements mitigating conflicts and ensuring high-data quality. We start simple and naive by populating the price table we created in listing 3.3. An INSERT statement first specifies where you want to insert and then what you want to insert. The *where* is a table name—here, it is the prices table. The *what* can be a list of column values, but they must match the column types and order of the table. In our case, we're inserting one row with four values, two numeric and two strings, with the latter automatically being cast to a DATE:

```
INSERT INTO prices
VALUES (1, 11.59, '2018-12-01', '2019-01-01');
```

The preceding query is fragile in a couple of ways. First, relying on the order of columns will break your statement as soon as the target table changes. Also, we explicitly use the 1 as a unique key. If you were to execute the query a second time, it would rightfully fail, as the table contains already a row with the given key. The second row violates the constraint that a primary key must be unique:

```
D INSERT INTO prices
> VALUES (1, 11.59, '2018-12-01', '2019-01-01');
Error: Constraint Error: Duplicate key "id: 1" violates primary key
➥constraint. If this is an unexpected constraint violation please
```

➥double check with the known index limitations section in our
➥documentation (https://duckdb.org/docs/sql/indexes).

While the conflict could not have been prevented given the schema, we can mitigate it by using the nonstandard ON CONFLICT clause and just do nothing. The DO NOTHING clause targets the primary index by default (the id column, in this case). While still being fragile, this statement is at least now idempotent:

```
INSERT INTO prices
VALUES (1, 11.59, '2018-12-01', '2019-01-01')
ON CONFLICT DO NOTHING;
```

In this case, idempotency might be less useful than you think: you don't get an error, but you most likely won't get the expected result, either. In our example, a better solution would be to specify all columns we want to insert and avoid using an explicit value for the ID. Overall, we already defined a sequence and a default value for the column that generates IDs for us:

```
INSERT INTO prices(value, valid_from, valid_until)
VALUES (11.47, '2019-01-01', '2019-02-01'),
       (11.35, '2019-02-01', '2019-03-01'),
       (11.23, '2019-03-01', '2019-04-01'),
       (11.11, '2019-04-01', '2019-05-01'),
       (10.95, '2019-05-01', '2019-06-01');
```

There's another possible cause of failure: we defined a unique key for the validity date. On that error, we can actually react in a way that makes sense from a business perspective. We can insert or replace the value when a conflict on that key arises. In the following example, we use the new price to update the old one:

```
INSERT INTO prices(value, valid_from, valid_until)
VALUES (11.47, '2019-01-01', '2019-02-01')
ON CONFLICT (valid_from)           ◁──┐  As the table has multiple constraints (primary
  DO UPDATE SET value = excluded.value;    and unique keys), we must specify on which
                                            key the conflict mitigation shall happen.
```

We will revisit that topic in section 3.4.2.

Of course, it is possible to use the outcome of a SELECT statement as input for the INSERT statement. We will have a look at the anatomy of a SELECT statement shortly, but to complete the example, please use it as follows. Think of this statement as a pipeline to the INSERT clause. As shown in listing 3.5, it selects all the data from the file named prices.csv and inserts them in order of appearance (you can find that file inside the ch03 folder in this book's GitHub repository: https://github.com/duckdb -in-action/examples).

> **Listing 3.5   Inserting data from other relations**

```
INSERT INTO prices(value, valid_from, valid_until)
SELECT * FROM 'prices.csv' src;
```

Let's also fill the systems table and load the first bunch of readings before we go over the SELECT statement in detail. To be able to write the INSERT statement properly, we must understand what the CSV data looks like. We will make use of the fact that we can use DESCRIBE with any relation—in this case, a relation that is defined by reading the CSV file:

```
INSTALL 'httpfs';          ◁─┐  Installs the httpfs extension and loads
LOAD 'httpfs';               │  it so that we can access the URL

DESCRIBE SELECT * FROM
    'https://oedi-data-lake.s3.amazonaws.com/pvdaq/csv/systems.csv';
```

Without specifying any type hints, systems.csv looks like this for DuckDB:

column_name varchar	column_type varchar	null varchar	key varchar	default varchar	extra varchar
system_id	BIGINT	YES			
system_public_name	VARCHAR	YES			
site_id	BIGINT	YES			
site_public_name	VARCHAR	YES			
site_location	VARCHAR	YES			
site_latitude	DOUBLE	YES			
site_longitude	DOUBLE	YES			
site_elevation	DOUBLE	YES			

Using the system_id and system_public_name will do nicely for us. However, it turns out that there are duplicates in the file, which will cause our insertion to fail. The easiest way to filter out duplicates is by applying the DISTINCT keyword in the columns clause of the SELECT statement, as shown in the following listing. This ensures a unique set over all the columns we select.

Listing 3.6 Inserting a distinct set of rows from another table

```
INSTALL 'httpfs';
LOAD 'httpfs';

INSERT INTO systems(id, name)
SELECT DISTINCT system_id, system_public_name
FROM 'https://oedi-data-lake.s3.amazonaws.com/pvdaq/csv/systems.csv'
ORDER BY system_id ASC;
```

The systems in section 3.2.1 have been selected for specific reasons. We start with the dataset for system 34, as it suits our requirements to begin with (having readings in 15-minute intervals). It does have some inconsistencies to deal with: the power output is sometimes NULL (not present) or negative. We will use a CASE expression to default missing values to 0.

The URL does not clearly identify which type of file or structure is behind it for DuckDB (e.g., by using a familiar extension such as .csv or .parquet). To address this, we must use the `read_csv_auto` function (see the following listing), as the database won't be able to infer the correct file type.

> **Listing 3.7 Downloading and ingesting the first set of readings**

```
INSERT INTO readings(system_id, read_on, power)
SELECT SiteId, "Date-Time",
       CASE
           WHEN ac_power < 0 OR ac_power IS NULL THEN 0
           ELSE ac_power END
FROM read_csv_auto(
       'https://developer.nrel.gov/api/pvdaq/v3/data_file?' ||
       'api_key=DEMO_KEY&system_id=34&year=2019'
     );
```

A sample of the data for system 34 in 2019 we just ingested can be achieved with

```
SELECT * FROM readings WHERE date_trunc('day', read_on) = '2019-08-
    26' AND power <> 0;
```

The sample looks as follows:

| system_id | read_on | power |
int32	timestamp	decimal(10,3)
34	2019-08-26 05:30:00	1700.000
34	2019-08-26 05:45:00	3900.000
34	2019-08-26 06:00:00	8300.000
.	.	.
.	.	.
.	.	.
34	2019-08-26 17:30:00	5200.000
34	2019-08-26 17:45:00	2200.000
34	2019-08-26 18:00:00	600.000
51 rows (6 shown)		3 columns

Now that we've finally ingested some data into the readings table, the view `v_power_per_day` created in listing 3.4 also returns data. Remember, `v_power_per_day` creates daily groups and sums up their power values, as shown with the output of

`` `SELECT * FROM v_power_per_day WHERE day = '2019-08-26'` ``

The output is as follows:

| system_id | day | kWh |
int32	date	double
34	2019-08-26	716.9

If you don't remember the definition of the view, be sure to check it again. A view is a great way to encapsulate logic, such as by truncating the date to a day and aggregating the total value of readings on that day, such as in our example.

The query is essentially the same for 2020, apart from the URL parameter. Why don't we generate a list of filenames using the `range` function that acts as an inline table like this?

```
SELECT *
FROM (
    SELECT 'https://' || years.range || '.csv' AS v
    FROM range(2019,2021) years
) urls, read_csv_auto(urls.v);
```

While this query is theoretically correct, it does not (yet) work due to restrictions in how so-called table functions (see section 4.9) are implemented in DuckDB. At the time of writing, they only accept constant parameters. Furthermore, `read_csv` or `read_parquet` learn about their schema by looking at the input parameters and reading the given files, so there's a chicken-and-egg problem to be solved.

3.4.2 Merging data

Oftentimes, you find yourself with a dataset that contains duplicates or entries that already exist within your database. While you can certainly ignore conflicts, as shown in section 3.4.1, when your only task is to refine and clean new data, you sometimes want to merge new data into existing data. For this purpose, DuckDB offers the `ON CONFLICT DO UPDATE` clause, known as `MERGE INTO` in some other databases. In our example, we might have multiple readings from different meters for the same system and want to compute the average reading. Instead of doing nothing on conflict, we use a `DO UPDATE` now.

In listing 3.8, a random reading is inserted first, and then an attempt is made to insert a reading on the same time for the same device. The second attempt will cause a conflict, not on a primary key, but on the composed key of `system_id` and `read_on`. With the `DO UPDATE` clause, we specify the action to take when a conflict arises. The update clause can update as many columns as necessary, essentially doing a merge/upsert; complex expressions, such as a `CASE` statement, are allowed too.

Listing 3.8 Computing new values on conflict

```
INSERT INTO readings(system_id, read_on, power)
  VALUES (10, '2023-06-05 13:00:00', 4000);

INSERT INTO readings(system_id, read_on, power)      Here, the action
  VALUES (10, '2023-06-05 13:00:00', 3000)           is specified.
ON CONFLICT(system_id, read_on) DO UPDATE
SET power = CASE                                      Columns from the original dataset can
  WHEN power = 0 THEN excluded.power                  be referred to by the alias .excluded.
  ELSE (power + excluded.power) / 2 END;
```

NOTE DuckDB also offers INSERT OR REPLACE and INSERT OR IGNORE as short-hand alternatives for ON CONFLICT DO UPDATE and ON CONFLICT DO NOTHING, respectively. INSERT OR REPLACE, however, does not have the ability to combine existing values, as in the preceding example, nor does it allow you to define the conflict target.

3.4.3 *The DELETE statement*

There are some outliers in the data sources we're using. We imported a bunch of readings that are measured on different minutes of the hour, and we don't want them in our dataset. The easiest way to deal with them is to apply the DELETE statement and get rid of them. The following DELETE statement filters the rows to be deleted through a condition based on a negated IN operator. That operator checks the containment of the left expression inside the set of expressions on the right-hand side. date_part is just one of the many built-in functions of DuckDB dealing with dates and timestamps. This one (see the following listing) extracts a part from a timestamp—in this case, the minutes from the read_on column.

Listing 3.9 Cleaning the ingested data

```
DELETE FROM readings
WHERE date_part('minute', read_on) NOT IN (0,15,30,45);
```

Sometimes, you will know about quirks and inconsistencies like these upfront, and you won't have to deal with them after you ingest the data. With time-based data, as in our example, you could have written the ingesting statement utilizing the time_bucket function. We noticed that inconsistency only after importing and think it's worthwhile to point this out.

3.4.4 *The SELECT statement*

This section focuses on the SELECT statement and querying the ingested data. This statement retrieves data as rows from the database or, if used in a nested fashion, creates ephemeral relations. Those relations can be queried again or used to insert data, as we have already seen.

The essential clauses of a SELECT statement and their canonical order are shown in the following listing.

Listing 3.10 The structure of a SELECT statement

```
SELECT select_list
FROM tables
WHERE condition
GROUP BY groups
HAVING group_filter
ORDER BY order_expr
LIMIT n
```

There are more clauses, in both the standard and the DuckDB-specific SQL dialect, and we will discuss a couple of them in the next chapter as well. The official DuckDB documentation has a dedicated page to the SELECT statement (https://duckdb.org/docs/sql/statements/select), which we recommend using as a reference on how each clause of the SELECT statement is supposed to be constructed.

We think the following clauses are the most important to understand:

- FROM in conjunction with JOIN
- WHERE
- GROUP BY

They define the sources of your queries, filter both reading queries as well as writing queries, and, eventually, reshape them. They are used in many contexts in addition to querying data. Many other clauses are easier to understand, such as ORDER, which—as you'd expect—puts things in order.

THE SELECT AND FROM CLAUSES

Every standard SQL statement that reads data starts with the SELECT clause. The SELECT clause defines the columns or expressions that will eventually be returned as rows. If you want to get everything from the source tables of your statement, you can use the *.

> **NOTE** Sometimes, the SELECT clause is called a projection, choosing which columns to be returned. Ironically, the selection of rows happens in the WHERE clause.

The SELECT and FROM clauses complement one another, and we could pick either to explain first, or we could explain them together: the FROM clause specifies the source of the data on which the remainder of the query should operate, and for most queries, that will be one or more tables. If there is more than one table list in the FROM clause or the additional JOIN clause is used, we speak about joining tables together.

The following statement will return two rows from the prices table. The LIMIT clause we are introducing here limits the number of returned rows. It's often wise to limit the amount of data you get back in case you don't know the underlying dataset so that you don't cause a large amount of network traffic or end up with an unresponsive client:

```
SELECT *
FROM prices
LIMIT 2;
```

It will return the first two rows. Without an ORDER clause, the order is actually undefined and might differ in your instance:

id int32	value decimal(5,2)	valid_from date	valid_until date
1	11.59	2018-12-01	2019-01-01
10	11.47	2019-01-01	2019-02-01

The SQL dialect of DuckDB allows us to cut the previous code down to just FROM prices;. (Without the limit, it will return all rows, but that's OK, since we know the content of that table from section 3.4.1.)

THE WHERE CLAUSE

The WHERE clause allows you to filter your data by adding conditions to a query. Those conditions are built out of one or more expressions. Data selected using a SELECT, DELETE, or UPDATE statement must match those predicates to be included in the operations. This allows you to select only a subset of the data in which you are interested. Logically, the WHERE clause is applied immediately after the FROM clause or the preceding DELETE or UPDATE statement.

In our example, we can replace that arbitrary LIMIT with a proper condition that will include only the prices for a specific year (2000) by adding the following WHERE clause. Take note that we are using a DuckDB extension to SQL; in the case of a star-select, you can omit the SELECT * and just start with the FROM clause:

```
FROM prices
WHERE valid_from BETWEEN          ◁───┐  The BETWEEN keyword is shorthand
    '2020-01-01' AND '2020-12-31';    │  for x <= v AND v <= y.
```

Based on our example data, the query will return 11 rows:

| id | value | valid_from | valid_until |
int32	decimal(5,2)	date	date
15	8.60	2020-11-01	2023-01-01
17	8.64	2020-10-01	2020-11-01
.	.	.	.
.	.	.	.
.	.	.	.
25	9.72	2020-02-01	2020-03-01
26	9.87	2020-01-01	2020-02-01
11 rows (4 shown)			4 columns

THE GROUP BY CLAUSE

Grouping by one or more columns generates one row of output per unique value of those columns; it lets you group all rows that match those fields together. Then, the grouped values get aggregated via an aggregation function, such as count, sum, avg, min, or max, so that one single value for that group is produced. This can be useful when you want to do things like compute the average number of readings per day or the sum of the customers in each state. If the GROUP BY clause is specified, the query is always an aggregate query, even if no aggregations are present in the select list. DuckDB has a handy extension that lets you group your query by all columns that are not part of an aggregate function: GROUP BY ALL. Figure 3.2 demonstrates how a selection of rows is grouped by the column year as well as the results of applying the aggregates count, avg, min, and max to it.

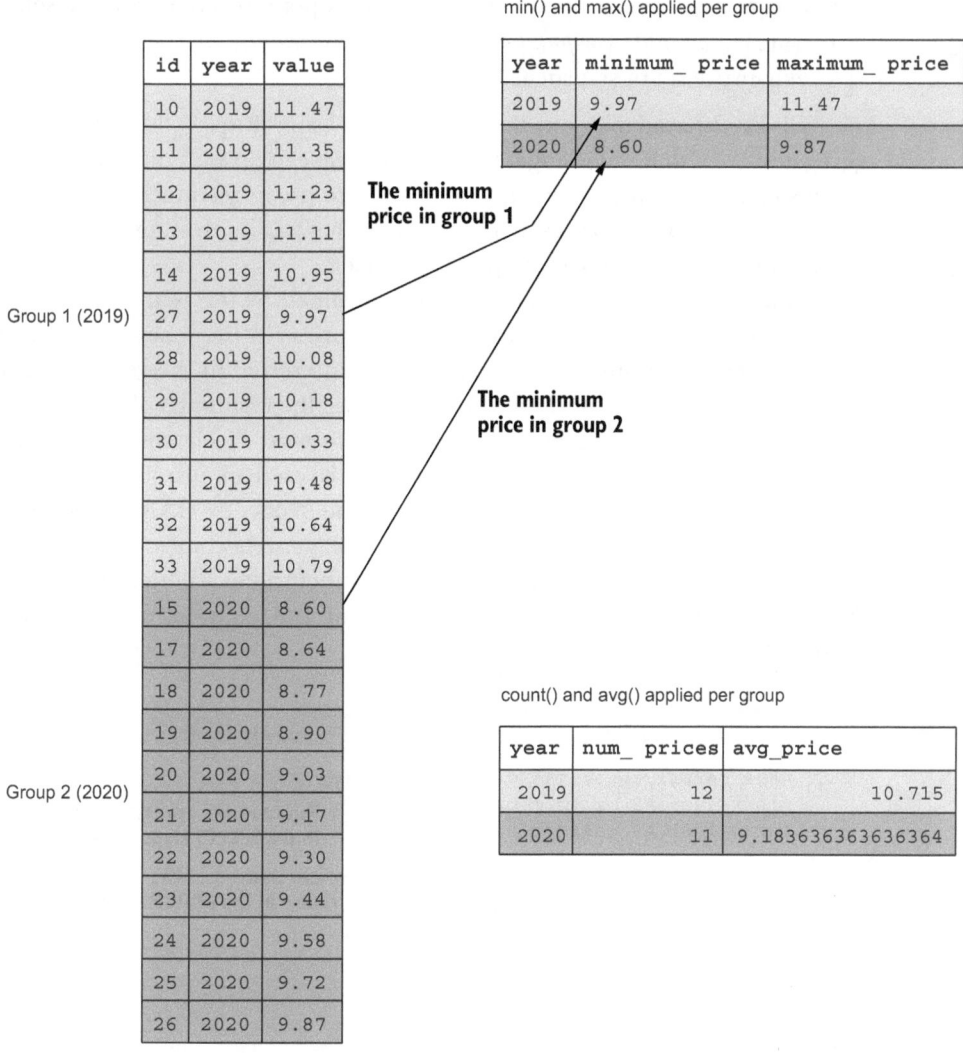

Figure 3.2   Grouping a dataset by year

There are many aggregate functions to choose from. In addition to those previously covered, which are relatively standard, here are some that we think are often helpful:

- `list`—Aggregates all values of each group into a list structure
- `any_value`—Picks any value from a nongrouping column
- `first` *or* `last`—Picks the first or the last value from a nongrouping column if the result is ordered
- `arg_max` *and* `arg_min`—Solves the common task of finding the value of an expression in the row having a maximum or minimum value

- `bit_and`, `bit_or`, `bit_xor`, *and others*—Bit operations that work on sets
- `median`, *quantile computation, computing covariance, and general regressions*—An exhaustive set of statistical aggregates

The full list is available on the DuckDB website: https://duckdb.org/docs/sql/aggregates. With that knowledge, let's see what we can do with our dataset.

Let's pick up the prices example we started to use in section 3.4.4. First, we added the `WHERE` clause to find prices in a year. While that was interesting, how about finding out the minimum and maximum prices per year?

We will use the `min` and `max` aggregates grouped by the year in which the prices have been valid to find the highest and lowest prices in the years from 2019 to 2020. The `valid_from` column is a date; we are only interested in the year. The `date_part` function can extract that. If used without an alias, the resulting column will be named `date_part('year', valid_from)`. This does not read nicely, and it is also cumbersome to refer to. Therefore, the `AS` keyword is used to introduce the alias `year`. DuckDB allows us to refer to such an alias in the `GROUP BY` clause, which is different from the SQL standard and is very helpful. The `year` becomes the grouping key by specifying it in the `GROUP BY` clause, and its distinct values will define the buckets for which the minimum and maximum values of the column we chose should be computed.

Listing 3.11   Grouped aggregates

```
SELECT date_part('year', valid_from) AS year,
       min(value) AS minimum_price,          ◁──┐  You can have as many aggregate functions
       max(value) AS maximum_price              │  in the SELECT clause as you want.
FROM prices
WHERE year BETWEEN 2019 AND 2020       │ Note how we can reuse the alias we gave in
GROUP BY year                          ◁─┘ the SELECT clause in the GROUP BY clause.
ORDER BY year;
```

The result of this query is as follows:

year int64	minimum_price decimal(5,2)	maximum_price decimal(5,2)
2019	9.97	11.47
2020	8.60	9.87

TIP DuckDB offers choices when dealing with date parts. You can use the generic `date_part` function like we did and specify the part as a parameter. There are identifiers for all relevant parts, such as `'day'`, `'hour'`,`'minute'`, and many others. All of them exist also as dedicated functions, so in listing 3.11, we could have used `year(valid_from)` too. The generic function is helpful when the part is derived from other expressions in the statement or when you try to write portable SQL. The dedicated functions are easier to read.

THE VALUES CLAUSE

The VALUES clause is used to specify a fixed number of rows. We have seen it already while inserting data, which is a quite common use case. It is, however, much more versatile in DuckDB than in some other databases, as it can be used both as a standalone statement and as part of the FROM clause, with any number of rows and columns. There are a couple of scenarios in which this is handy: for example, providing seed data for conditions.

Here's how to define a single row with two columns—for example, a simple VALUES (1,2);:

```
┌───────┬───────┐
│ col0  │ col1  │
│ int32 │ int32 │
├───────┼───────┤
│     1 │     2 │
└───────┴───────┘
```

Take note that multiple rows can be generated by simply enumerating multiple tuples: VALUES (1,2), (3,4);. You don't need to wrap them in additional parentheses:

```
┌───────┬───────┐
│ col0  │ col1  │
│ int32 │ int32 │
├───────┼───────┤
│     1 │     2 │
│     3 │     4 │
└───────┴───────┘
```

If you do, however, as in VALUES ((1,2), (3,4));, you will create a single row with two columns, each containing a structured type:

```
┌──────────────────────────────┬──────────────────────────────┐
│             col0             │             col1             │
│ struct(v1 integer, v2 integer) │ struct(v1 integer, v2 integer) │
├──────────────────────────────┼──────────────────────────────┤
│ {'v1': 1, 'v2': 2}           │ {'v1': 3, 'v2': 4}           │
└──────────────────────────────┴──────────────────────────────┘
```

When used in a FROM clause, the resulting types can be named, together with their columns. We will make use of that in the next section while discussing joining logic. The following snippet defines two rows with three columns within the VALUES clause and creates an inline named table that holds the column names. The name of that table is arbitrary; we just picked t:

```
SELECT *
FROM (VALUES
    (1, 'Row 1', now()),
```

```
    (2, 'Row 2', now())
) t(id, name, arbitrary_column_name);
```

The resulting virtual table looks like this:

id	name	arbitrary_column_name
int32	varchar	timestamp with time zone
1	Row 1	2023-06-02 13:44:30.309+02
2	Row 2	2023-06-02 13:44:30.309+02

THE JOIN CLAUSE

While you can get away with not using a JOIN clause when analyzing single Parquet or
CSV files, you should not skip this section: *joins* are a fundamental relational operation used to connect two tables or relations. The relations are referred to as the *left*
and *right sides* of the join, with the left side of the join being the table listed first. This
connection represents a new relation combining previously unconnected information, thus providing new insights.

In essence, a join creates matching pairs of rows from both sides of the join. The
matching is usually based on a key column in the left table being equal to a column in
the right table. Foreign key constraints are not required for joining tables together.
We prefer the SQL standard definition of joins based on the JOIN .. USING over JOIN
.. ON clauses, as you'll see in the following examples and throughout the rest of the
book. Nevertheless, joins can be expressed by simply enumerating the tables in the
FROM clause and comparing the key columns in the WHERE clause.

> **NOTE** We are not using Venn diagrams for explaining joins because join
> operations are not pure set operations, for which Venn diagrams would be a
> great choice. SQL does know set operations, such as UNION, INTERSECT, and
> EXCEPT—and DuckDB supports all of them. Joins, on the other hand, are all
> based on a Cartesian product in relational algebra, or in simple terms, they
> are all based on joining everything with everything else and then filtering
> things out. Essentially, all different joins can be derived from the CROSS JOIN.
> The inner join then filters on some condition, and a left or right outer join
> adds a union to it, but that's all there is to set-based operations in joins.

In the following examples, we will use the VALUES clause to define virtual tables with a
fixed number of rows with a given set of values. These sets are helpful to understanding the joining logic, as you will see both the sources and the resulting rows in the
example. Usually, you will find yourself joining different tables together, such as the
power readings and the prices in our example.

The simplest way of joining is via an INNER JOIN (figure 3.3), which also happens
to be the default. An inner join matches all rows from the left-hand side to rows from
the right-hand side that have a column with the same value.

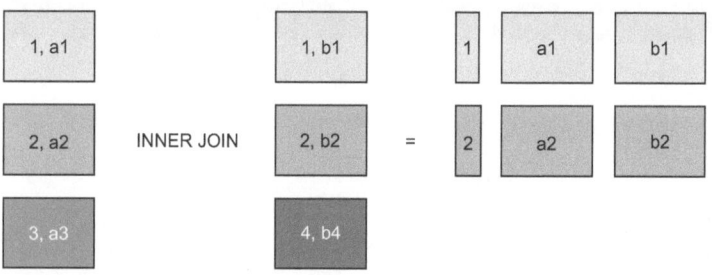

Figure 3.3 The inner join only matching pairs with equal keys

If both relations have a column with the same name, the USING clause can be used to specify that. The USING clause will look up the specified columns in both relations and work the same way as specifying them yourself via the ON clause (ON tab1.col = tab2.col).

Listing 3.12 Using an inner join

```
SELECT *
FROM
    (VALUES (1, 'a1'),
            (2, 'a2'),
            (3, 'a3')) l(id, nameA)
JOIN
    (VALUES (1, 'b1'),
            (2, 'b2'),
            (4, 'b4')) r(id, nameB)       This is equivalent
USING (id);                               to ON r1.id = r2.id.
```

The result will look like this:

```
| id    | nameA   | nameB   |
| int32 | varchar | varchar |
|-------|---------|---------|
|     1 | a1      | b1      |
|     2 | a2      | b2      |
```

An outer join, on the other hand, supplements NULL values for rows on the specified side of the relation that have no matching entry on the other. Think of several power-producing systems in your database: for some, you might have stored additional vendor information in another table, and for some, you don't. You would use an outer join when tasked to give a list of all systems with the optional vendor or an empty column if there's no such vendor. The following listing uses a LEFT OUTER JOIN so that all rows of the left relations are included and supplemented with NULL values for rows that don't have a match.

Listing 3.13   Using a left outer join

```
SELECT *
FROM
    (VALUES (1, 'a1'),
            (2, 'a2'),
            (3, 'a3')) l(id, nameA)
LEFT OUTER JOIN
    (VALUES (1, 'b1'),
            (2, 'b2'),
            (4, 'b4')) r(id, nameB)
USING (id)
ORDER BY id;
```

Joining the virtual tables from listing 3.13 with a LEFT OUTER JOIN results in the following:

id int32	nameA varchar	nameB varchar
1	a1	b1
2	a2	b2
3	a3	

All rows from the left-hand side have been included, and for a3, a NULL value has been joined. Try changing the outer join from LEFT to RIGHT, and observe which values are now included. Both the LEFT and RIGHT outer join will return three rows in total. To get back four rows, you must use a full outer join, as shown in the following listing.

Listing 3.14   Using a full outer join

```
SELECT *
FROM
    (VALUES (1, 'a1'),
            (2, 'a2'),
            (3, 'a3')) l(id, nameA)
FULL OUTER JOIN
    (VALUES (1, 'b1'),
            (2, 'b2'),
            (4, 'b4')) r(id, nameB)
USING (id)
ORDER BY id;
```

Four rows will be returned, with two NULL values, one for nameA and one for nameB:

id int32	nameA varchar	nameB varchar
1	a1	b1
2	a2	b2
3	a3	
4		b4

Figure 3.4 depicts the left outer join; the full outer join, we had in code previously, and the right outer join for comparison. While an outer join always gives you the rows an inner join would give, it would be wrong to suggest always using outer joins. An inner join will filter out rows that have no matching data in the other table, which is often a requirement. An outer join will usually be appropriate when you want to enrich required data with optional data.

Figure 3.4 Types of outer joins

The preceding example applies the USING clause for the join conditions, as both tables have an id column. In our example, we defined an id column in the systems table and the foreign key column in readings as system_id. We, therefore, must use the ON clause. When joined on that column, the join will always produce a matching row, as the join column (id) is the column referenced by the foreign key we defined on system_id. That means there can't be any row in the readings table without a matching entry in the systems table:

```
SELECT name, count(*) as number_of_readings
FROM readings JOIN systems ON id = system_id
GROUP BY name;
```

NOTE A *Cartesian product* is a mathematical term describing the list of all ordered pairs that you can produce from two sets of elements by combining each element from the first set with each element of the second set. The size of a Cartesian product is equal to the product of the sizes of each set.

There are more join types, such as the CROSS JOIN, which creates a Cartesian product of all tuples, and the ASOF (*as of*), which will come in handy when dealing with the prices with a restricted validity. For example, the ASOF join allows you to match rows from one table with rows from another table based on temporal validity (or, as a matter of fact, with anything that has an inequality condition—<=, <, > or >=). You will read about the ASOF join in detail in section 4.8.

The COPY TO command

You are building data pipelines around CSV files and often have data split across several files with one common column per file. What if you wanted to reduce these files to exactly one file without duplicating the common column? That's easy to achieve with an inner join and the COPY TO command. The latter takes any relation and copies it to a file using the specified format:

```
duckdb -c "COPY (SELECT * FROM 'production.csv' JOIN 'consumption.csv'
USING (ts) JOIN 'export.csv' USING (ts) JOIN 'import.csv' USING (ts) )
TO '/dev/stdout' (HEADER)"
```

This command will join four CSV files on a shared column ts, keep only one copy of the shared column in the SELECT * statement, and copy the result to standard out.

We'd like to end this section with something akin to a warning. In our examples, for inner and outer joins, we only discussed what happens when a value of a key column is not found in one of the other tables. But what happens when one of the join columns contains the same value multiple times, either in one of the join tables or in both? Let's find out in the next listing. The value 2 for the id column appears twice in the left table, and the value 3 appears twice in the right table.

Listing 3.15 **An inner join between tables with duplicate key columns**

```
SELECT *
FROM
    (VALUES (1, 'a1'),
            (2, 'a2'),
            (2, 'a2'),
            (3, 'a3')) l(id, nameA)
JOIN
    (VALUES (1, 'b1'),
            (2, 'b2'),
            (3, 'b3'),
            (3, 'b3')) r(id, nameB)
USING (id)
ORDER BY id;
```

The result of this statement won't be four rows, as before, but six:

id int32	nameA varchar	nameB varchar
1	a1	b1
2	a2	b2
2	a2	b2
3	a3	b3
3	a3	b3

This is something you can prepare for when defining your schema. Typically, joins will happen on columns that are known up front. In our example, that would be the `id` pair of the `systems` table referred to as `system_id` in the `readings` table. In the `systems` table, that column is defined as the primary key, and as such, it will always be a unique value; hence, it can only appear once in that table. On the `readings` table, it is defined as the foreign key, meaning it must exist in the other one. The foreign key usually creates a so-called index in the database, which allows quick lookups, without going through all rows, making the join perform well. The foreign key is not unique and does not need to be in most models. In our example, the system appearing multiple times in the `readings` table (the right-hand side) is expected, unless you want your system to produce power only once.

THE WITH CLAUSE

The `WITH` clause is also known as a *common table expression* (CTE). CTEs are essentially views that are limited in scope to a particular query. Like a view, you might want to use them to encapsulate parts of the logic of your query into a standalone statement, or at least into an isolated part of a bigger query. While it would be perfectly fine to create a view, you might not want that because you would only need its result in the specific context of the bigger query. In addition, CTEs have one special trait that views don't: views can reference other views, but they cannot be nested. A CTE can reference other CTEs defined in the same `WITH` clause. With that, you can build your query logic in an incremental fashion.

   `WITH` clauses prevent the anti-pattern of having subqueries defined in the `FROM` clause. A subquery as a source relation in a `FROM` clause is syntactically and semantically valid, as its result is a relation on its own, but it is often hard to read. In addition, nested subqueries are not allowed to reference themselves.

   Finding the row containing the maximum value of a specific column within that row is often computed using a subquery in the `FROM` clause like this:

```
SELECT max_power.v, read_on
FROM (
  SELECT max(power) AS v FROM readings
)  max_power
JOIN readings ON power = max_power.v;
```

As shown in listing 3.16, the subquery is relatively simple, and rewriting it as a CTE doesn't seem to make a big difference at first glance. We take the same query, move it out of the `FROM` clause, and add a name within the `WITH` clause. The `JOIN` statement stays the same.

Listing 3.16   Replacing a subquery with a CTE

```
WITH max_power AS (
  SELECT max(power) AS v FROM readings
)
SELECT max_power.v, read_on
FROM max_power
JOIN readings ON power = max_power.v;
```

For single and rather basic queries like this, it does not make much of a difference whether we use a subquery or a CTE. But what if we ask for something like the maximum average production of power per system and hour? Aggregate functions, like `max` and `avg`, cannot be nested (i.e., you cannot do `avg(max(v))`), so you need to use individual aggregates.

The question of which row contains the minimum or maximum value of a column is such a common task that DuckDB has two built-in functions to perform it: `arg_max` and `arg_min`. These functions compute an expression defined by their first parameter on the columns in the row for which the minimum or maximum value of the second parameter occurs the first time. The following query will produce one row from the dataset at which the highest amount of power was generated (not the five times that the query in listing 3.16 will return). This is because `arg_max` stops at the first value it finds that matches the maximum value, while the join will include all rows:

```
SELECT max(power), arg_max(read_on, power) AS read_on
FROM readings;
```

The next query, shown in listing 3.17, makes use of the `arg_max` aggregate. It first encapsulates the complex logic of grouping the readings into average production by system and hour—creating the first aggregate—in a CTE that we name `per_hour`, and then it takes that CTE and computes a second aggregate over it.

Listing 3.17   Creating multiple groups

```
WITH per_hour AS (                          ◁──────────────────  Using a proper
    SELECT system_id,                                            name for the CTE
           date_trunc('hour', read_on) AS read_on,
           avg(power) / 1000 AS kWh    ◁──   The average value per hour and day is the
    FROM readings                            first aggregate we need; GROUP BY ALL is
    GROUP BY ALL                             a DuckDB extension creating a group from
)                                            all columns not part of an aggregate.
SELECT name,              ┌── The nested aggregate
       max(kWh),     ◁──┘   we look for
       arg_max(read_on, kWh) AS 'Read on'     Using the CTE as the driving
FROM per_hour                  ◁───────────   table in the FROM clause
   JOIN systems s ON s.id = per_hour.system_id
WHERE system_id = 34
GROUP by s.name;
```

The result shows the that the Andre Agassi Preparatory Academy has the system with the highest production in our dataset:

name varchar	max(kWh) double	Read on timestamp
[34] Andre Agassi Preparatory Academy	123.75	2020-04-09 11:00:00

NOTE We looked this building up, and the readings and values add up. According to a fact sheet covering the installation, "Between April 2010 and July 2011, Bombard installed 2,249 Sharp 240-watt solar modules on the roofs of five buildings and three solar support structures at the Agassi Academy in Las Vegas" (https://mng.bz/jXKp).

CTEs can do one more cool thing views and subqueries cannot. The WITH clause features the additional keyword RECURSIVE, which makes it possible to reference a CTE not only from other succeeding CTEs and the FROM clause but from within itself. Such a recursive CTE essentially will follow this pattern (shown in listing 3.18). To make this work, we need to have some kind of initial seed for the recursion. This is easy for a tree structure: we take the row that has no parent row and use this as one leaf of a UNION clause.

Listing 3.18 Selecting a graph-shaped structure with recursive SQL

```
CREATE TABLE IF NOT EXISTS src (
    id INT PRIMARY KEY,
    parent_id INT, name VARCHAR(8)
);

INSERT INTO src (VALUES
    (1, null, 'root1'),
    (2,    1, 'ch1a'),
    (3,    1, 'ch2a'),
    (4,    3, 'ch3a'),
    (5, null, 'root2'),
    (6,    5, 'ch1b')
);

WITH RECURSIVE tree AS (
    SELECT id,
           id AS root_id,          ┐ Initialize a new list
           [name] AS path      ◄──┘ with a list literal.
    FROM src WHERE parent_id IS NULL   ◄─┐ This is the recursive
    UNION ALL                            │ initial seed.
    SELECT src.id,
           root_id,
           list_append(tree.path, src.name) AS path
    FROM src
      JOIN tree ON (src.parent_id = tree.id)   ◄─┐ Recursive join until there are
)                                               │ no more entries from the src
SELECT path FROM tree;                          │ table with the given parent id.
```

The results are several paths, all starting at the root, making up their way to the corresponding leaves:

```
┌─────────────────────────────┐
│           path              │
│         varchar[]           │
├─────────────────────────────┤
│ [root1]                     │
│ [root2]                     │
│ [root1, ch1a]               │
│ [root1, ch2a]               │
│ [root2, ch1b]               │
│ [root1, ch2a, ch3a]         │
└─────────────────────────────┘
```

The example aggregates names into a path from the root of a tree to the leaf by using
list_append. You could use list_prepend and inverse the parameter to build up
paths from the leaves to the root nodes.

As an exercise, you can try to compute the longest path in the tree. The recursive
CTE will stay the same, but you will want to apply the arg_max function you learned
about in the SELECT statement together with the length aggregate on a list.

3.5 *DuckDB-specific SQL extensions*

One of the goals of the authors of DuckDB is to make SQL more accessible and user-
friendly. One way they've done this is by adding additions to their implementation of
SQL that make it easy to do common tasks. In this section, we'll introduce those
additions.

3.5.1 *Dealing with SELECT*

SELECT * is a two-edged sword: it is easy to write down, and the resulting tuples most
likely will contain what you actually need. Some problems associated with selecting all
columns of a relation include the following:

- Instability of the resulting tuples, as a table definition might change (adding or
  removing columns).
- Putting more memory pressure on the database server or process.
- While DuckDB is an embedded database and won't involve network traffic,
  select-stars will cause more traffic on nonembedded databases.
- A select-star might prevent an index-only scan. An index-only scan will occur
  when your query can use an index, and you only return columns from that
  index so that any other IO can be avoided. An index-only scan is a desired
  behaviour in most cases.

While it's best to avoid doing too many SELECT * queries, sometimes they are neces-
sary, and DuckDB actually makes them safer to use with the addition of two keywords:
EXCLUDE and REPLACE. If you are certain you really want all columns, DuckDB offers a
simplified version of the SELECT statement, omitting the SELECT clause altogether.
Instead, it starts with the FROM clause so that, for example, a FROM prices is possible.
We will present another example in listing 3.22.

EXCLUDING SOME COLUMNS WITH **EXCLUDE**

EXCLUDE excludes one or more columns from a star query. This is helpful when you have a table or relation with many columns, of which nearly all are necessary, excluding the few that are irrelevant to your use case. Normally, you would have to enumerate all the columns you are interested in and exclude the ones you don't care about. For example, you want only the relevant data from prices:

```
SELECT value, valid_from, valid_until FROM prices;
```

This becomes tedious and error-prone very quickly, especially with more than a handful of columns. With the EXCLUDE clause, you only have to enumerate the columns you are not interested in:

```
SELECT * EXCLUDE (id)
FROM prices;
```

You can exclude as many columns as you want. You will achieve most of the flexibility of a pure SELECT *, keep the readability of the star, and ensure you don't access something you don't need.

RESHAPING RESULTS WITH **REPLACE**

Think about the view v_power_per_day. It computes the kWh in fractions. Some users may only want to return the integer values. Instead of rewriting the whole view, you can just replace the single column kWh with its rounded value while selecting the remaining columns:

```
SELECT * REPLACE (round(kWh)::int AS kWh)
FROM v_power_per_day;
```

The REPLACE clause takes in one or more pairs of x AS y constructs, with x being an expression that can refer to columns of the original select list, applying functions and other transformations to them, and y being a name that has been used in the original select list.

The structure of the result is the same, but the kWh column is now an integer column:

system_id int32	day date	kWh int32
1200	2019-08-29	289
.	.	.
.	.	.
.	.	.
10	2020-03-19	0
1587 rows (2 shown)	3 columns	

DYNAMICALLY PROJECTING AND FILTERING ON COLUMNS

Let's recap the `prices` table. It has two columns containing information about the validity of a price:

column_name varchar	column_type varchar	null varchar	...	default varchar	extra int32
id	INTEGER	NO	...	nextval('prices_id')	
value	DECIMAL(5,2)	NO	...		
valid_from	DATE	NO	...		
valid_until	DATE	YES	...		
4 rows				6 columns (5 shown)	

The COLUMNS expression can be used to project, filter, and aggregate one or more columns based on a regular expression. To select only columns that contain information about validity, you can query the table like this:

```
SELECT COLUMNS('valid.*') FROM prices LIMIT 3;
```

This returns all the relevant columns:

valid_from date	valid_until date
2018-12-01	2019-01-01
2019-01-01	2019-02-01
2019-02-01	2019-03-01

You will benefit from using this technique if you have a table with lots of columns with similar names. Such a table could, for example, take the form of a readings or measurement table. More specifically, think of an IoT sensor that produces many different readings per measurement. In that use case, there is another interesting feature: you can apply any function over a dynamic selection of columns that will produce as many computed columns. Here, we compute several maximum values at once for all columns in the `price` table that contain the word `valid`:

```
SELECT max(COLUMNS('valid.*')) FROM prices;
```

This results in the maximum values for `valid_from` and `valid_until`:

max(prices.valid_from) date	max(prices.valid_until) date
2023-01-01	2024-02-01

If you find yourself writing long conditions in the WHERE clause, combining many predicates with AND, you can simplify that with the COLUMNS expression as well. To find all the prices that have been valid in 2020 alone, you would want every row for which both the valid_from and valid_until columns are between January 1, 2020 and 2021, which is just what the following query expresses:

```
FROM prices WHERE COLUMNS('valid.*') BETWEEN '2020-01-01' AND '2021-01-01';
```

You might have noticed that the regular expression .* sticks out a bit. Many people are more familiar with the % and _ wildcards used with the LIKE operator. The % character represents zero, one, or multiple characters, while the underscore sign represents only one character. Luckily, COLUMNS supports lambda functions.

> **TIP** A *lambda function* is a self-contained block of functionality that can be passed around and used in your code. Lambda functions have different names in different programming languages, such as lambda expressions in Java, Kotlin, and Python; closures in Swift; and blocks in C.

The preceding query selecting a range of prices can also be written like this:

```
FROM prices
WHERE COLUMNS(col -> col LIKE 'valid%')
BETWEEN '2020-01-01' AND '2021-01-01';
```
The expression inside the **COLUMNS** expression is a Lambda function evaluating to true when the column name is like the given text.

Last but not least, you can combine the COLUMNS expression with the REPLACE or EXCLUDE conditions too. Let's say you want to compute the maximum value over all the columns in the prices table, except the generated id value. You can get them like this:

```
SELECT max(COLUMNS(* EXCLUDE id)) FROM prices;
```

3.5.2 *Inserting by name*

Do you remember listing 3.6? In that listing, we used a statement in the form of INSERT INTO target(col1, col2) SELECT a, b FROM src to populate our systems table. This works but can be fragile to maintain, as the INSERT statement requires either the selected columns to be in the same order as they are defined by the target table or to repeat the column names—once in the INTO clause, once in the select list.

DuckDB offers a BY NAME clause to solve that problem, and listing 3.19 can be rewritten as follows, keeping the mapping from the column names in the source to the column names for the target together in one place. The BY NAME keyword in the listing indicates that the columns in the select clause that follows shall be matched by name onto columns of the target table.

Listing 3.19   Insertion by name

```
INSERT INTO systems BY NAME
SELECT DISTINCT
```

```
        system_id AS id,
        system_public_name AS NAME
FROM 'https://oedi-data-lake.s3.amazonaws.com/pvdaq/csv/systems.csv'
ON CONFLICT DO NOTHING;
```

Whether you add new columns or remove columns from the insertion, you now only need to change the query in one place. Any constraints, however, such as non-null columns, must still be fulfilled.

3.5.3   *Accessing aliases everywhere*

You probably haven't noticed it, but several of our examples benefit from something that should be the standard—but isn't. The moment you introduce an alias to a column, you can access them in succeeding clauses. In listing 3.20, we access the nonaggregate alias `is_not_system10`—as defined in the select list—in the WHERE and GROUP BY clauses without repeating the column definition. The latter is not possible in many other relational databases. The same applies to the alias `power_per_month` we gave to the `sum` aggregate; we can access it in the HAVING clause too.

> **Listing 3.20   Accessing aliases in WHERE, GROUP BY, and HAVING clauses**

```
SELECT system_id > 10 AS is_not_system10,
       date_trunc('month', read_on) AS month,
       sum(power) / 1000 / 1000 AS power_per_month
FROM readings                                          Accessing an alias that
WHERE is_not_system10 = TRUE          ◁───────────     refers to a nonaggregate
GROUP BY is_not_system10, month
HAVING power_per_month > 100;         ◁──┐  Accessing an alias that
                                         │  refers to an aggregate
```

3.5.4   *Grouping and ordering by all relevant columns*

As discussed in the section covering the GROUP BY clause, all nonaggregate columns need to be enumerated in a GROUP BY clause. If you have many nonaggregate columns, this can be a painful experience and one that DuckDB alleviates by allowing you to use GROUP BY ALL. We can rewrite `v_power_per_day` as shown in the following listing.

> **Listing 3.21   Creating grouping sets by grouping by all nonaggregate values**

```
CREATE OR REPLACE VIEW v_power_per_day AS
SELECT system_id,
       date_trunc('day', read_on)        AS day,
       round(sum(power)  / 4 / 1000, 2)  AS kWh,
FROM readings
GROUP BY ALL;
```

A similar concept exists for ordering. An ORDER BY ALL will sort the result by the included columns, from left to right. Querying the freshly created view with

```
SELECT system_id, day FROM v_power_per_day ORDER BY ALL
```

will sort the result first by `system_id` and then by `day`. In the case of a select-star, the order of the columns is defined by the table or view definition, of course. The following statement is valid SQL in DuckDB, and it returns the power produced in kWH per day, sorted first by systems, by days, and then by kWH.

Listing 3.22 Omitting the `SELECT` clause and simplifying ordering

```
FROM v_power_per_day ORDER BY ALL;
```

3.5.5 Sampling data

When working with large datasets, we often want to get a sample of the data rather than look through everything. Assuming you have imported the readings for at least system 34, you will have more than 50,000 records in your database. This can be confirmed with a `SELECT count(*) FROM readings`. We can get an overview of the nonzero power readings by asking for a sample of *n* percent or *n* number of rows, as shown in the following listing.

Listing 3.23 Sampling a relation

```
SELECT power
FROM readings
WHERE power <> 0
USING SAMPLE 10%          ◁──  Retrieves a sample of roughly
  (bernoulli);                  10% the size of the data
                          ◁──  Specifies the sampling
                               method to use
```

This is much easier and more flexible than dealing with arbitrary limits, as it provides a better and more reliable overview. The sampling itself uses probabilistic sampling methods, however, unless a seed is specified with the additional `REPEATABLE` clause. The sampling rate in percent is not meant to be an exact hit. In our example, it varies by about 2,000 rows from the approximately 20,000 with a `power` column not equal to zero.

If you instruct DuckDB to use a specific rate for sampling, it applies `system` sampling, including each vector by an equal chance. Sampling on vectors instead of working on tuples (which is done by the alternative `bernoulli` method) is very effective and has no extra overhead. As one vector is roughly about 2,048 tuples in size (see https://duckdb.org/docs/api/c/data_chunk), it is not suited for smaller datasets, as all data will be included or filtered out. Even for the ~100,000 readings that have a power value greater than zero, we recommend `bernoulli` for a more evenly distributed sampling.

For a fixed sampling size, a method called `reservoir` is used. The reservoir is filled up first with as many elements as requested and then streams the rest, randomly swapping elements in the reservoir. You can learn more about this interesting technique in the samples documentation (https://duckdb.org/docs/sql/samples).

3.5.6   *Functions with optional parameters*

A couple of functions in DuckDB (e.g., `read_json_auto`) have required parameters and one or more parameters with sensible defaults that are optional. The aforementioned example has 17 parameters; you can get a list of them with the following code:

```
SELECT DISTINCT unnest(parameters)
FROM duckdb_functions()
WHERE function_name = 'read_json_auto';
```

We are using a distinct here because there are a couple of overloads with different types. Luckily, DuckDB supports named optional arguments. Assume you want to specify the `dateformat` only; in that case, you would use the `name=value` syntax, as shown in the following listing.

> **Listing 3.24   Using named parameters**

```
echo '{"foo": "21.9.1979"}' > 'my.json'
duckdb -s \
"SELECT * FROM read_json_auto(
  'my.json',
  dateformat='%d.%M.%Y'     ◁──┐ This is using the named
)"                                 parameter dateformat.
```

DuckDB is able to parse the non-iso-formatted string into a proper date since we used the `dateformat` parameter:

```
┌────────────┐
│    foo     │
│   date     │
├────────────┤
│ 1979-01-21 │
└────────────┘
```

Summary

- SQL queries are composed of several statements, which are, in turn, composed of clauses. Queries are categorized as data definition language (DDL) or data manipulation language (DML).
- DML queries cover creating, reading, updating, and deleting rows.
- Manipulation of data is not only about changing persistent state but also about transforming existing relations into new ones; therefore, reading data also falls under DML.
- DDL queries, such as CREATE TABLE and CREATE VIEW, are used in DuckDB to create a persistent schema. This is inline with any other relational database and is independent, regardless of whether DuckDB is started with the database stored on disk or in memory.

- A rigid schema makes data inconsistencies more visible—blindly ingesting data with inconsistencies will fail, due to constraint errors.
- Constraint errors can be mitigated with appropriate actions defined ON CONFLICT when creating or updating rows.
- DuckDB makes SQL even easier to write, with innovations like SELECT * EXCLUDE() and SELECT * REPLACE() and more intuitive alias usage.

Advanced aggregation
and analysis of data

4

This chapter covers

- Preparing, cleaning and aggregating data while ingesting
- Using window functions to create new aggregates over different partitions of any dataset
- Understanding the different types of subqueries
- Using common table expressions
- Applying filters to any aggregate

The goal of this chapter is to give you some ideas on how an analytical database, such as DuckDB, can be used to provide reports that would take a considerably larger amount of code written in an imperative programming language. While we will build upon the foundation laid in chapter 3, we will leave a simple `SELECT xzy FROM abc` behind quickly. Investing your time in learning modern SQL won't be wasted. The constructs presented here can be used everywhere DuckDB can be run or embedded and, therefore, enrich your application.

4.1   Pre-aggregating data while ingesting

Let's move forward with our example scenario. In section 3.4.1, we worked with the data for a photovoltaic grid that—while having some consistency problems—was a good fit for our schema and idea. Remember, the goal is to store measurements in intervals of 15 minutes. If you look at the other datasets you downloaded throughout section 3.2.1, you will notice that some come in intervals of other than 15 minutes. One quick way to peek into the files is the `tail` command, returning the last *n* lines of a file (`head` would work as well). Using it on `2020_10.csv` shows that this file contains measurements in 1-minute intervals:

```
> duckdb -s ".maxwidth 40" -s "FROM read_csv_auto('2020_10.csv') LIMIT 3"
```

| SiteID | Date-Time | ... | module_temp_3 | poa_irradiance |
int64	timestamp			double	double
10	2020-01-23 11:20:00	...	14.971	748.36
10	2020-01-23 11:21:00	...	14.921	638.23
10	2020-01-23 11:22:00	...	14.895	467.67
3 rows			16 columns	(4 shown)

And, of course, `2020_1200.csv` has another interval—this time, 5 minutes—but the overall structure also looks different:

```
> duckdb -s ".maxwidth 40" -s "FROM read_csv_auto('2020_1200.csv') LIMIT 3"
```

| SiteID | Date-Time | ... | ac_power_metered | power_factor |
int64	timestamp			int64	double
1200	2020-01-01 00:00:00	...	20	0.029
1200	2020-01-01 00:05:00	...	20	0.029
1200	2020-01-01 00:10:00	...	20	0.029
3 rows			6 columns	(4 shown)

Remember, those are data files from the same pool. Even those are inconsistent between different sources. Data analytics is quite often about dealing with those exact same problems. Let's use one of the many functions DuckDB offers to deal with dates, times, and timestamps—in this case, `time_bucket()`. `time_bucket()` truncates timestamps to a given interval and aligns them to an optional offset, creating a *time bucket*. Time buckets are a powerful mechanism for aggregating sensor readings and friends. Together with `GROUP BY` and `avg` as aggregate functions, we can prepare and eventually ingest the data according to our requirements. We create time buckets in a 15-minute interval and compute the average power produced of all readings that fall into a specific bucket.

NOTE The following examples will only work if you followed along with our examples in chapter 3, populating the `systems` table.

When you look at the query, you'll notice a CASE WHEN THEN ELSE END construct, a CASE statement, which works like an `if/else` construct. What it does here is turn readings with a value lower than zero, or with no value at all, into zero before computing the average. That's one of the oddities of this dataset: maybe the sensor, or perhaps the network, malfunctioned. You'll never know, but you have to deal with the data. Here, we decided it is OK to treat NULL values like negative values and cap them to zero. In cases that throw off your calculation, you might consider a FILTER for the aggregate. We will discuss this in section 4.6.3.

Listing 4.1 Cleaning and transforming data during ingestion

> This picks any value of the column SiteId from the CSV file. The files are per system, which means that this column is the same in each row, so picking any one of them is correct. Applying any_value() is necessary, as we compute an aggregate (avg).

```
INSERT INTO readings(system_id, read_on, power)
SELECT any_value(SiteId),          ◄
       time_bucket(
           INTERVAL '15 Minutes',
           CAST("Date-Time" AS timestamp)
       ) AS read_on,                ◄
       avg(
           CASE
               WHEN ac_power < 0 OR ac_power IS NULL THEN 0
               ELSE ac_power END)   ◄
FROM
    read_csv_auto(
        'https://developer.nrel.gov/api/pvdaq/v3/' ||
        'data_file?api_key=DEMO_KEY&system_id=10&year=2019'
    )
GROUP BY read_on
ORDER BY read_on;
```

> This truncates the timestamp to a quarter-hour. Notice how we explicitly cast the column to a timestamp with standard SQL syntax; in addition, the transformed value gets an alias (read_on).

> Here, avg computes the average of all readings in the bucket created previously because we group the result by this bucket.

The imports for the remaining dataset are identical. You will want to change the file-name in the FROM clause accordingly.

NOTE There are many more date- and time-based functions in DuckDB. When in doubt, have a look at the reference documentation: https://duckdb.org/docs/sql/functions/timestamp. You will be able to parse nearly any string into a proper date or timestamp.

Your decision on whether to avoid ingesting altogether and do all kinds of analytics in-memory based on external files; aggregate, to some extent, during ingestion; or only aggregate during analysis usually comes down to a tradeoff between, among other things, the size of your dataset, your goals for long-term storage, and your further processing needs. Trying to make a generally applicable solution here is, therefore, bound to fail. In the scenario here, we decided to both ingest and aggregate for educational purposes and keep the dataset small enough to be shareable.

4.2 Summarizing data

You usually want to know some characteristics of a new dataset before going into an in-depth analysis of it, such as the number of values (in our example, how many readings), the distribution and magnitude of numerical values (without knowing if we are dealing in watts or kilowatts, our reports would be blatantly wrong), and the interval size of time series. DuckDB has the unique SUMMARIZE command, which quickly gives you this information about any dataset. Run SUMMARIZE readings; in your database. Your results should be similar to this:

column_name varchar	column_type varchar	max varchar	...	q75 varchar	count int64
system_id	INTEGER	1200	...	1200	151879
read_on	TIMESTAMP	2020-06-26 11:00:00	...		151879
power	DECIMAL(10,3)	133900.000	...	5125	151879

There are many more columns, but we abbreviated the list for readability. Switch your CLI to line mode by running .mode line and then summarizing a subset of the readings with

```
SUMMARIZE SELECT read_on, power FROM readings WHERE system_id = 1200;
```

as follows:

```
column_name = read_on
    column_type = TIMESTAMP
            min = 2019-01-01 00:00:00
            max = 2020-06-26 11:00:00
  approx_unique = 50833
            avg =
            std =
            q25 =
            q50 =
            q75 =
          count = 52072
null_percentage = 0.0%

    column_name = power
    column_type = DECIMAL(10,3)
            min = 0.000
            max = 47873.333
  approx_unique = 6438
            avg = 7122.5597121293595
            std = 11760.089219586542
            q25 = 20
            q50 = 27
            q75 = 9532
```

```
        count = 52072
null_percentage = 0.0%
```

SUMMARIZE works directly on tables, but as shown in the preceding code snippet, it works on query results too. You don't even have to ingest data at all before applying SUMMARIZE; it can be run against a CSV or Parquet file as well.

4.3   *On subqueries*

Imagine you want to compute the average of the total power produced by the systems you manage. For that, you would need to apply two aggregate functions: avg and sum. It turns out that you cannot nest them. A naive approach, like

```
SELECT avg(sum(kWh)) FROM v_power_per_day GROUP BY system_id
```

fails with

```
Error: Binder Error: aggregate function calls cannot be nested
```

You need to stage that computation, and a subquery is one way to achieve this, as shown in the following listing.

Listing 4.2   A subquery being used to compute nested aggregates

```
SELECT avg(sum_per_system)
FROM (
    SELECT sum(kWh) AS sum_per_system
    FROM v_power_per_day
    GROUP BY system_id
);
```

This statement now dutifully returns avg(sum_per_system) = 133908.087. The inner query in this statement has two characteristics:

- It returns several rows.
- It does not depend on values from the outer query.

This query is called an *uncorrelated subquery*. An uncorrelated subquery is just a query nested inside another one, and it operates as if the outer query executed on the results of the inner query.

Now on to the next question you might be faced with: On which day and for which system was the highest amount of power produced? One way to solve this problem is by using a subquery as the right-hand side of a comparison in the WHERE clause, as shown in the following listing.

Listing 4.3   A subquery being used as a right-hand side in a comparison

```
SELECT read_on, power
FROM readings
WHERE power = (SELECT max(power) FROM readings);
```

This subquery is different from the first one in that it only returns a single, scalar value. This is called a *scalar, uncorrelated subquery.*

> **NOTE** arg_min and arg_max are aggregate functions that compute an expression of the row in which the minimum or maximum value appears. If you are interested in only one expression, using these functions as your solution is preferable to any subquery for tasks like the ones we've covered in the preceding text. If you are interested in more than one expression or evaluating other values than minimum or maximum values, you won't get around subqueries in conditions.

The result essentially reads as follows: *the maximum output of 133,900 W has been produced at five different times.* The following snippet shows the full result:

```
| read_on              | power          |
| timestamp            | decimal(10,3)  |
|----------------------|----------------|
| 2019-05-08 12:15:00  |   133900.000   |
| 2019-05-23 10:00:00  |   133900.000   |
| 2019-05-23 11:30:00  |   133900.000   |
| 2019-05-28 11:45:00  |   133900.000   |
| 2020-04-02 11:30:00  |   133900.000   |
```

What if you wanted to determine the maximum power and reading time on a per-system basis? This would be tricky to do with the original subquery because that only shows us the values for the overall max-power production. Therefore, we would need the subquery to return different values for different rows; to achieve this, we can use a correlated subquery, which uses the fields from the outer query inside the inner one, as shown in the following listing.

Listing 4.4 Using correlated, scalar subqueries

```
SELECT system_id, read_on, power
FROM readings r1
WHERE power = (
    SELECT max(power)
    FROM readings r2
    WHERE r2.system_id = r1.system_id
)
ORDER BY ALL;
```

This is the condition that correlates the subquery to the outer query, not the comparison of the power value.

This subquery is a *scalar, correlated subquery.* The inner query is related to the outer query in the way the database must evaluate it for every row of the outer query. In the result, we again see the five days for the highest overall value, and now we also see the highest values produced for systems 10 and 1,200:

system_id int32	read_on timestamp	power decimal(10,3)
10	2019-02-23 12:45:00	1109.293
34	2019-05-08 12:15:00	133900.000
34	2019-05-23 10:00:00	133900.000
34	2019-05-23 11:30:00	133900.000
34	2019-05-28 11:45:00	133900.000
34	2020-04-02 11:30:00	133900.000
1200	2020-04-16 12:15:00	47873.333

When used as expressions, subqueries may be rewritten as joins—with the computation of nested aggregates being the exception. For the last example, it would look like the code in the following listing.

Listing 4.5 An uncorrelated subquery join with the outer table

```
SELECT r1.system_id, read_on, power
FROM readings r1
JOIN (
    SELECT r2.system_id, max(power) AS value
    FROM readings r2
    GROUP BY ALL
) AS max_power ON (
    max_power.system_id = r1.system_id AND
    max_power.value = r1.power
  )
ORDER BY ALL;
```

It's up to the reader to judge whether this adds to readability or not. In other relational databases, people often do this, as the evaluation of a correlated subquery for every row in a large table might be slow. DuckDB, on the other hand, uses a subquery decorrelation optimizer that always makes subqueries independent of outer queries, thus allowing users to freely use subqueries to create expressive queries without having to worry about manually rewriting subqueries into joins. It is not always possible to manually decorrelate certain subqueries by rewriting the SQL. Internally, DuckDB uses special types of joins that will decorrelate all subqueries. In fact, DuckDB does not have support for executing subqueries that are not decorrelated.

This is a positive for you because it allows you to focus on the readability and expressiveness of your queries and the business problem you are trying to solve. Indeed, DuckDB allows you to spend all your time focusing on the bigger picture—you don't need to worry about what type of subquery you use at all.

4.3.1 Subqueries as expressions

All forms of subqueries, both correlated and uncorrelated, that are not used as a relation in a JOIN are expressions. As such, many other operators can be used with them.

The = operator and the inequality operators <, <=, >=, and > require the subquery to be scalar, returning exactly one row. When working with both scalar and nonscalar subqueries, additional operators are available—IN, EXISTS, ANY, and ALL—all of which work via set comparisons.

Subqueries can also be used in set comparisons, completing tasks like this one: *identify all the rows that compare successfully to all or any of the rows returned by another query.* The artificial examples in this section will all return v = 7.

EXISTS

You might want to select all the rows of a table that have a value that might exist inside one row of another table. For this, you can use the EXISTS expression, shown in the following listing.

Listing 4.6 A subquery used with the EXISTS expression

```
.mode line
SELECT * FROM VALUES (7), (11) s(v)
WHERE EXISTS (SELECT * FROM range(10) WHERE range = v);
```

Defines an inline table named s with one column named v

IN

EXISTS can usually be rewritten as an uncorrelated subquery using the IN operator, as shown in the following listing. When the outer value is contained at least once in the results of the subquery, this operator evaluates to true.

Listing 4.7 A subquery used with the IN expression

```
.mode line
SELECT * FROM VALUES (7), (11) s(v)
WHERE v IN (SELECT * FROM range(10));
```

This is useful to know when you work with relational databases other than DuckDB that might not do all kinds of optimizations on subqueries.

ANY

The IN operator works with an equal comparison of each value. You might find yourself in a situation in which you want to answer whether any value does satisfy an inequality condition. Here, you need to use the ANY operator together with the desired comparison, as shown in the following listing. When the comparison of the outer value with any of the inner values evaluates to true, the whole expression evaluates to true.

Listing 4.8 A subquery used with the ANY expression

```
.mode line
SELECT * FROM VALUES (7), (11) s(v)
WHERE v <= ANY (SELECT * FROM range(10));
```

Please take note of the additional comparison prior to ANY.

ALL

Last but not least, we cover the ALL operator, which evaluates to true when the comparison of the outer value with all of the inner values evaluates to true. It helps you find rows in which a value satisfies a comparison between all values of a subquery, as shown in the following listing. While you can replace = ANY() with IN(), there is no such simplification for the ALL operator.

Listing 4.9   A subquery used with the ALL expression

```
.mode line
SELECT * FROM VALUES (7), (11) s(v)
WHERE v = ALL (SELECT 7);
```

4.4   Grouping sets

In listing 3.2, we created a table named readings, which contains the date, time, and actual value of power produced at that time. We also suggested several example datasets from the National Renewable Energy Laboratory to import. When looking at such a dataset, it is always helpful to get an overview of the minimum and maximum values of an attribute, or maybe the average. Sometimes, you may have outliers in there that you want to delete, or you may have made a mistake with the units. The easiest way to compute that is by using them in one query, without any GROUP BY clause, as shown in the following listing, so that the aggregation happens in one bucket: the whole table.

Listing 4.10   Using various aggregates to check if the imports make sense

```
SELECT count(*),
       min(power) AS min_W, max(power) AS max_W,
       round(sum(power) / 4 / 1000, 2) AS kWh          ◁────────────────
FROM readings;
```
> When finding the amount of power produced, we express the conversion from units of W per 15 minutes to units of kW per hour (kWh) by summing the values, dividing them by 4, which gives us a result in W per hour (Wh), and then dividing them by 1,000, achieving a result in kWh.

If you followed the suggestion, your readings table should have key figures like the following, which is the result of the preceding query:

count_star()	min_W	max_W	kWh
151879	0.000	133900.000	401723.22

The readings seem to be reasonable, even the minimum value of zero—there is just no production during nighttime. As we already learned about the GROUP BY clause in figure 3.2, we could go further and have a look at the production of kWh and system. We will also select the number of readings per system. We imported several years, truncating the readings to 15-minute intervals, so we should find roughly 35,040 readings per year. A GROUP BY system_id, year confirms this assumption, as shown in the next listing.

Listing 4.11 A plain GROUP BY **with essentially one set of grouping keys ()**

```
SELECT year(read_on) AS year,
       system_id,
       count(*),
       round(sum(power) / 4 / 1000, 2) AS kWh
FROM readings
GROUP BY year, system_id
ORDER BY year, system_id;
```

The result adds up. We did have a bunch of invalid values, and the second year ends halfway through 2020:

year	system_id	count_star()	kWh
2019	10	33544	1549.34
2019	34	35040	205741.9
2019	1200	35037	62012.15
2020	10	14206	677.14
2020	34	17017	101033.35
2020	1200	17035	30709.34

Now what about the totals (i.e., the total number of readings as well as the total power production per year, per year and system, and overall)? In other words, can we create a drill-down report, showing different levels of detail per group? While we could now enter the numbers into a calculator one by one and sum them manually or write an additional count query without a grouping key like the initial one, there's a better option, as shown in the following listing: *grouping sets*.

Listing 4.12 Explicitly using GROUPING SETS

```
SELECT year(read_on) AS year,
       system_id,
       count(*),
       round(sum(power) / 4 / 1000, 2) AS kWh
FROM readings
GROUP BY GROUPING SETS ((year, system_id), year, ())
ORDER BY year NULLS FIRST, system_id NULLS FIRST;
```

Before we dissect

```
GROUP BY GROUPING SETS ((system_id, year), year, ())
```

let's have a look at the result:

year	system_id	count_star()	kWh
		151879	401723.22
2019		103621	269303.39
2019	10	33544	1549.34
2019	34	35040	205741.9
2019	1200	35037	62012.15
2020		48258	132419.83
2020	10	14206	677.14
2020	34	17017	101033.35
2020	1200	17035	30709.34

The grouping sets created several buckets to compute the aggregates as follows:

- Over a bucket defined by the combined values of `system_id` and `year` (six different combinations in our example, thus leading to six rows)
- Over a bucket defined by the `year` alone. For keys not included in this but in other sets, `NULL` values are provided (here for the `system_id`).
- The last one (`()`) can be described as the empty bucket or group—`NULL` values are provided for all other keys.

The result contains everything listing 4.11 returned plus the number of readings per year (grouping by `year` alone) plus the overall count (grouping by nothing).

The same result can be achieved by using the shorthand clause `ROLLUP`. As shown in the following listing, the `ROLLUP` clause automatically produces the previously discussed sets as $n + 1$ grouping sets, where n is the number of terms in the `ROLLUP` clause.

Listing 4.13 Using `GROUP BY ROLLUP`

```
SELECT year(read_on) AS year,
       system_id,
       count(*),
       round(sum(power) / 4 / 1000, 2) AS kWh
FROM readings
GROUP BY ROLLUP (year, system_id)
ORDER BY year NULLS FIRST, system_id NULLS FIRST;
```

If we want to see the totals by system in all years, this is quite possible too. Instead of falling back from `ROLLUP` to `GROUP BY GROUPING SETS` and manually adding, you can use `GROUP BY CUBE`. `GROUP BY CUBE` will not produce subgroups but actual combinations (2^n grouping sets). In our example, it produces (`year, system_id`), (`year`), (`system`), and ().

Listing 4.14 Using GROUP BY CUBE

```
SELECT year(read_on) AS year,
       system_id,
       count(*),
       round(sum(power) / 4 / 1000, 2) AS kWh
FROM readings
GROUP BY CUBE (year, system_id)
ORDER BY year NULLS FIRST, system_id NULLS FIRST;
```

This produces the following:

year	system_id	count_star()	kWh
		151879	401723.22
	10	47750	2226.48
	34	52057	306775.25
	1200	52072	92721.48
2019		103621	269303.39
2019	10	33544	1549.34
2019	34	35040	205741.9
2019	1200	35037	62012.15
2020		48258	132419.83
2020	10	14206	677.14
2020	34	17017	101033.35
2020	1200	17035	30709.34

We now have a complete overview of our power production readings in a single compact query, instead of several queries. All the drill downs we added on the way can be expressed with grouping sets. The minimum and maximum values have only been omitted to keep the listing readable.

4.5   *Window functions*

Windows and functions applied over windows are an essential part of modern SQL and analytics. *Window functions*, in general, let you look at other rows. Normally, an SQL function can only see the current row at a time, unless you're aggregating. In that case, however, you reduce the number of rows.

Unlike a regular aggregate function, the use of a window function does not cause rows to become grouped into a single output row—the rows retain their separate identities. If you wanted to peek at other rows, you would use a window function. A window is introduced by the OVER() clause, following the function you want to apply to the data inside that window. The window itself is the definition of the rows that are worked on, and you can think of it as a window that moves along a defined order with a defined size of rows over your dataset. Windowing works by breaking a relation up into independent partitions, optionally ordering those partitions, and then computing a new column for each row as a function of the nearby values.

For looking at all rows, you can use an empty window OVER (). If you want to look at all rows that have the same value matching another field, use a partition for that field. And last but not least, if you want to look at nearby rows, you can use a frame.

The size of a window is not equal to the size of a partition; both can be defined independently. Eventually, the contents of a window are fed to a function to compute new values. While there are a couple of dedicated functions that work only in the context of windows, all regular aggregate functions can be used as window functions.

This allows use cases such as

- Ranking
- Computing independent aggregates per window
- Computing running totals per window
- Computing changes by accessing preceding or following rows via lag or lead

Let's have a look at a concrete example. Suppose you want to retrieve the system as well as the top three times (by quarter-hour) at which the most power was produced. One naive approach would be ordering the results by amount of power produced and limiting to 3, as follows:

```
SELECT * FROM readings ORDER BY power DESC LIMIT 3;
```

This approach yields the following results:

system_id int32	read_on timestamp	power decimal(10,3)
34	2019-05-08 12:15:00	133900.000
34	2019-05-23 10:00:00	133900.000
34	2019-05-23 11:30:00	133900.000

While these results present readings for system 34 at different dates, you should notice that they have the same value in the power column. This might be good enough, but it is not necessarily what we have been asked for. For the raw value of power produced, we only get the time at which the very most power was produced (i.e., top 1), not readings for each of the top three power values. To compute a proper top three, we will use the window function dense_rank(). This function computes the rank for a row without skipping ranks for equal rankings. dense_rank, shown in listing 4.15, returns the rank of the current row without gaps. That means, for example, that if five rows are ranked 1 in power production, the row producing the next highest amount of power will still be ranked 2, as opposed to 6. If you need gaps to be included (i.e., the next row to be ranked 6, as opposed to 2), use rank instead.

Listing 4.15 A proper top-*n* query

```
WITH ranked_readings AS (
    SELECT *,
```

```
        dense_rank()
            OVER (ORDER BY power DESC) AS rnk
    FROM readings
)
SELECT *
FROM ranked_readings
WHERE rnk <= 3;
```

> Here, the window is opened over one row each, ordered by the amount of power, in descending order.

The result looks very different now, with three different decreasing values for `power`, as shown in figure 4.1. We will revisit the preceding statement when we learn about the `QUALIFY` clause in section 4.6.2, avoiding the somewhat odd condition in the `WHERE` clause that filters on the rank.

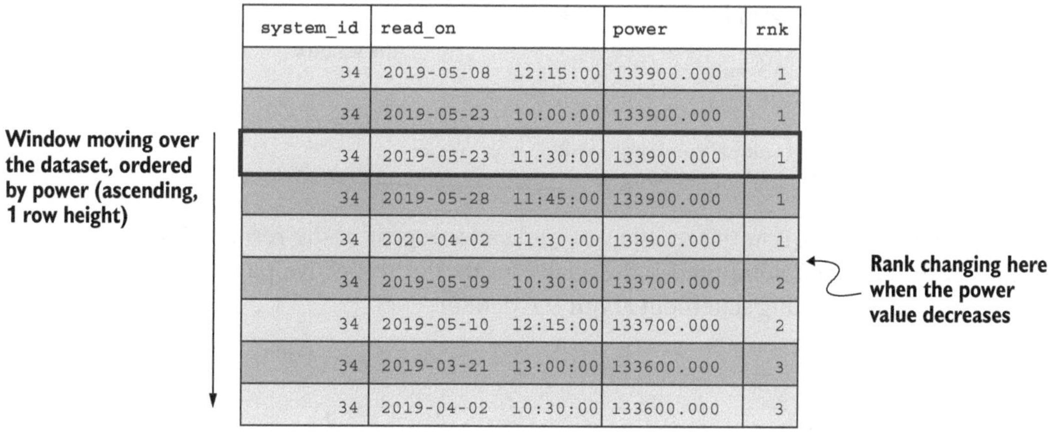

Window moving over the dataset, ordered by power (ascending, 1 row height)

system_id	read_on		power	rnk
34	2019-05-08	12:15:00	133900.000	1
34	2019-05-23	10:00:00	133900.000	1
34	2019-05-23	11:30:00	133900.000	1
34	2019-05-28	11:45:00	133900.000	1
34	2020-04-02	11:30:00	133900.000	1
34	2019-05-09	10:30:00	133700.000	2
34	2019-05-10	12:15:00	133700.000	2
34	2019-03-21	13:00:00	133600.000	3
34	2019-04-02	10:30:00	133600.000	3

Rank changing here when the power value decreases

Figure 4.1 The simplest possible window over the power readings

The `ORDER` clause as part of the window definition inside the `OVER()` clause is optional, and unlike the `ORDER BY` clause at the end of a statement, it does not sort the query result. When used as part of the `OVER()` clause, `ORDER BY` defines the order in which window functions are executed. If `ORDER BY` is omitted, the window function is executed in an arbitrary order. In our preceding example, it would make no sense to omit it, as an unordered, dense rank would always be one. We will see an example in the next section, where we can safely omit `ORDER BY`.

4.5.1 Defining partitions

The preceding ranked power values are better, but they are not yet particularly helpful, as the systems have production values that are orders of magnitudes different. Computing ranks without differentiating the systems might not be what you are after. What you actually need in this case is the top three readings per system, with each system making up its own partition of the data. Partitioning breaks the relation up into independent, unrelated pieces, in which the window function is applied. If we don't define how a partition is made up by using the PARTITION BY clause, the entire relation is treated as a single partition. Window functions cannot access values outside the partition containing the row they are being evaluated at.

Requesting the top *n* measurements per system would be a partitioning task. For the sake of readability of the results, in the following listing, we only request the two highest power-production values per system.

Listing 4.16 Applying a partition to a window

```
WITH ranked_readings AS (
    SELECT *,
            dense_rank()              Starting the definition
              OVER (            ◁──┘  of the moving window
                PARTITION BY system_id    ◁──┐  Defining a partition:
                ORDER BY power DESC             │  the window
              ) AS rnk
        FROM readings
)
SELECT * FROM ranked_readings WHERE rnk <= 2
ORDER BY system_id, rnk ASC;
```

Look closely at how the number of ranks now repeat in the result in figure 4.2. They have now been computed individually inside the respective partitions, which makes quite a contrasting statement about the dataset.

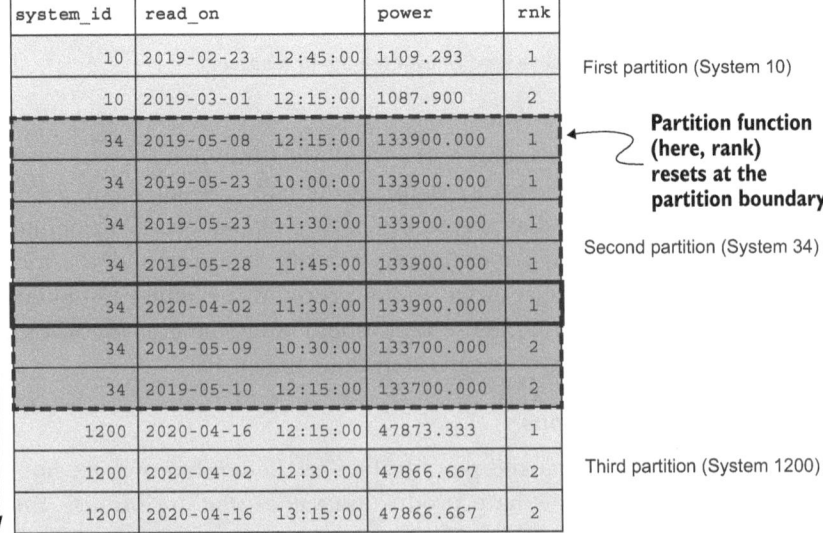

Figure 4.2 Partitioning the data before applying a window

We see ranks 1 and 2 for all systems; system 34 reaches its highest rate of production, 133,900 W, five separate times and its second highest twice. System 1,200 only reaches its top rate of production once and its second highest twice. The window was partitioned by the systems and then ordered by the value of power produced.

Of course, ranking tasks are not the only things that can be applied within partitions. Aggregate functions, like `avg`, `sum`, `max`, and `min`, are other excellent candidates to be used in a windowing context. The difference with using aggregates within a window context is that they don't change the number of rows being produced. Let's say you want to select both the production on each system each day and in an additional column, the average overall production of system. You might consider using `GROUP BY ROLLUP`—and you would not be wrong. That grouping set would, however, be quite large (`GROUP BY ROLLUP (system_id, day, kwh)`) and not produce the average value in an additional column but additional rows instead. The value you would be looking for (the overall production per system) would be found in the rows that have a value for the system and no value for the day.

One way to avoid dealing with additional rows is a *self-join*, in which you select the desired aggregate grouping by a key to join the same table again. While it does produce the results you want, it will be hard to read and most likely will not perform well, as the whole table would be scanned twice. Using `avg` in a partitioned window context is much easier to read and will perform well. The aggregate—in this case, `avg(kWh)`—is computed over the window that follows; it does not change the number of rows and will be present in each row. It will be computed for every system, as defined by the partition:

```
SELECT *,                    │ Computing an aggregate
       avg(kWh)          ◁──┘ over a partition
         OVER (
           PARTITION BY system_id
         ) AS average_per_system
FROM v_power_per_day;
```

And you will find the requested value in an additional column:

system_id int32	day date	kWh double	average_per_system double
10	2019-01-01	2.19	4.444051896207586
10	2019-01-04	5.37	4.444051896207586
.	.	.	.
.	.	.	.
.	.	.	.
1200	2019-07-25	232.37	170.75771639042347
1200	2019-04-29	210.97	170.75771639042347
1587 rows (4 shown)			4 columns

Note that we omitted the ORDER BY inside the window definition, as it is irrelevant for the average value, in which order values are fed to the aggregate. As a rule of the thumb, you should probably use a window function every time you consider writing a self-join like the one previously discussed for adding aggregates to your query without changing the row count.

4.5.2 Framing

Top *n* queries are useful, for example, if you happen to have a streaming service and want to present the top *n* charts. A more interesting question in our example is this: *What is the seven-day moving average of energy produced system wide?* To answer this question, we must do the following:

- Aggregate the readings per 15-minute interval into days (grouping and summing).
- Partition by day and systems.
- Create frames of seven days.

This is where framing comes into play. *Framing* specifies a set of rows relative to each row where the function is evaluated. The distance from the current row is given as an expression either preceding or following the current row. This distance can either be specified as an integral number of rows or as a range delta expression from the value of the ordering expression.

For readability and to keep the following examples focused on the window definitions, we will use the view v_power_per_day defined in chapter 3, which returns the amount of energy produced in kWh per system and day. We could just as easily express v_power_per_day as a CTE.

The following statement computes the average power over a window per system that moves along the days and is seven days wide (three days before, the actual day, and three days ahead). The statement utilizes all options for defining a window.

Listing 4.17   Using a range partition for applying a window function

```
SELECT system_id,
       day,
       kWh,
       avg(kWh) OVER (                            The window should move over
           PARTITION BY system_id        ◄──      partitions defined by the system id.
           ORDER BY day ASC
           RANGE BETWEEN INTERVAL 3 Days PRECEDING    ◄──   With a size of seven
                     AND INTERVAL 3 Days FOLLOWING          days in total
       ) AS "kWh 7-day moving average"
FROM v_power_per_day
ORDER BY system_id, day;
```

Ordered by day (annotation pointing to ORDER BY day ASC)

The result will have as many rows as there are full days in the source readings, so we can only show a subset as an example. Figure 4.3 demonstrates the size of the window and how rows are included.

system_id	day	kWh	kWh 7-day moving average
10	2019-01-01	2.19	4.7075000000000005
10	2019-01-02	5.55	4.69
10	2019-01-03	5.72	4.5523333333333334
10	2019-01-04	5.37	4.707142857142857
10	2019-01-05	4.62	5.154285714285714
10	2019-01-06	3.69	4.864285714285715
10	2019-01-07	5.81	4.541428571428571
10	2019-01-08	5.32	3.8142857142857145
10	2019-01-09	3.52	3.3800000000000003
10	2019-01-10	3.46	3.6957142857142853
10	2019-01-11	0.28	3.7542857142857144
10	2019-01-12	1.58	3.7214285714285715
10	2019-01-13	5.9	3.7814285714285716
10	2019-01-14	6.22	4.064285714285715
10	2019-01-15	5.09	4.042857142857143
1200	2019-01-01	46.81	42.7875
1200	2019-01-02	24.78	40.444
1200	2019-01-03	53.1	59.89833333333333
1200	2019-01-04	46.46	55.87142857142857
1200	2019-01-05	31.07	56.79857142857143
1200	2019-01-06	157.17	62.63857142857142
1200	2019-01-07	31.71	82.05142857142857
1200	2019-01-08	53.3	102.12428571428572
1200	2019-01-09	65.66	105.99714285714286
1200	2019-01-10	188.99	83.61285714285714
1200	2019-01-11	186.97	79.31999999999998
1200	2019-01-12	58.18	72.66000000000001
1200	2019-01-13	0.48	64.62857142857145
1200	2019-01-14	1.66	39.99571428571429

Moving direction

Fourth window inside partition 1, applying the average function to the current row and 3 preceding and following rows

First partition

First window inside partition 2, applying the average function to the current row and 3 following rows

Second partition

Figure 4.3   The result of framing a window

4.5.3 *Named windows*

Window definitions can be pretty complex, as we just learned while discussing windows with ranges. They can include the definition of the partition, the order, and the actual range of a window. Sometimes, you are interested in more than just one aggregate over a given window. Repeating the window definition over and over again would be a tedious task.

For our domain—measuring power production from photovoltaic systems—we could use quantiles to create a report that essentially takes in both the seasons and the weather by computing the quantiles over a seven-day window per month. Sometimes, a broad monthly average will be enough, but a chart would represent only a relatively smooth curve, changing with the months. The fluctuation of the amount of power produced is higher throughout the changing weather in a week. Outliers and runaway values would be better caught and represented by quantiles. The result can easily be used to create a moving box-and-whisker plot, for example.

We need three aggregates (`min`, `max`, and `quantiles`) for caching outliers and computing the quantiles, and we don't want to define the window each time. We basically take the definition from listing 4.17 and add the month of the reading to the partition, as shown in the following listing. Otherwise, the window definition is the same. We move the definition after the FROM clause and name it seven_days. It can be referenced from as many aggregates as necessary.

Listing 4.18 Using a named window with a complex order and partition

```
SELECT system_id,
       day,
       min(kWh) OVER seven_days AS "7-day min",          ⟵  Referencing the window
                                                              defined after the FROM clause
       quantile(kWh, [0.25, 0.5, 0.75])           ⟵
          OVER seven_days AS "kWh 7-day quartile",       The quantile function takes in
       max(kWh) OVER seven_days AS "7-day max",          the value for which the quantiles
                                                          should be computed and a list of
FROM v_power_per_day                                      the desired quantiles.
WINDOW                  ⟵
    seven_days AS (
        PARTITION BY system_id, month(day)               The window clause must be
        ORDER BY day ASC                                 specified after the FROM clause,
        RANGE BETWEEN INTERVAL 3 Days PRECEDING          and the definition of window
                      AND INTERVAL 3 Days FOLLOWING      itself follows inline windows.
    )
ORDER BY system_id, day;
```

The result now showcases a structured column type—kWh 7-day quartile:

| system_id | day | 7-day min | kWh 7-day quartile | 7-day max |
int32	date	double	double[]	double
10	2019-01-01	2.19	[2.19, 5.37, 5.55]	5.72
10	2019-01-02	2.19	[4.62, 5.37, 5.55]	5.72
10	2019-01-03	2.19	[3.69, 4.62, 5.55]	5.72
10	2019-01-04	2.19	[3.69, 5.37, 5.72]	5.81
10	2019-01-05	3.69	[4.62, 5.37, 5.72]	5.81
.	.	.	.	.
.	.	.	.	.
.	.	.	.	.
1200	2020-06-22	107.68	[149.11, 191.61, 214.68]	279.8
1200	2020-06-23	0.0	[107.68, 191.61, 214.68]	279.8
1200	2020-06-24	0.0	[190.91, 191.61, 214.68]	279.8
1200	2020-06-25	0.0	[191.61, 203.06, 214.68]	279.8
1200	2020-06-26	0.0	[0.0, 203.06, 214.68]	279.8

| 1587 rows (10 shown) | | | | 5 columns |

All aggregates can be used as windowing functions, as we already learned. That includes complex statistical functions, such as computing the exact quantiles in a group (`quantile` and `quantile_disc`) or the interpolated ones (`quantile_cont`), as previously shown. The implementations of these functions have been optimized for windowing, and we can use them without worrying about performance. Use a named window when you're querying for several aggregates.

4.5.4 *Accessing preceding or following rows in a partition*

We already discussed ranking and will see an example of computing running totals in section 4.8, but we haven't used the ability to jump back and forth between rows inside a partition. So let's explore computing changes and what might be a better example than prices these days.

In chapter 3, we created a table named `prices`, which contained the sales prices (in ct/kWH) for feeding energy back to the grid in Germany. Suppose those sales prices have since decreased as a reaction to a decrease in policy incentives promoting renewable energy. You now want to know by how much the compensation for renewable energy has changed over time. To compute a difference, you need the price value of row n, and then you need to compare it with the value in row n-1. This is not possible without windows, as the rows of a table are processed in isolation, essentially row by row. If you, however, span a window over any orderable column, you can use `lag()` and `lead()` to access rows outside the current window. This allows you to pick the price from yesterday that you want to compare with today's price.

The `lag` function will give you the value of the expression in the row preceding the current one within the partition or NULL if there is none. This is the case for the first row in a partition. `lead` behaves in the opposite manner (i.e., it returns NULL for the last row in a partition). Both functions have several overloads in DuckDB that allow you to specify not only by how many rows to lag or lead but also a default window. Otherwise, working with `coalesce` would be an option when NULL values are not practicable.

NOTE The `coalesce` function will return its first non-NULL argument.

Using `lag()`, the following query computes the difference between the original prices (i.e., those in the `prices` table in chapter 3) and the current prices (i.e., which have increased in response to new regulations).

Listing 4.19 Computing lagging and leading values of windows

```
SELECT valid_from,
       value,
       lag(value)                              Jumps back a row and picks
         OVER validity AS "Previous value",    out the value column
       value - lag(value, 1, value)
         OVER validity AS Change
```

The change is computed as the difference of the price in the current row and the price in the row before that, or the same value if there is no row before.

```
FROM prices
WHERE date_part('year', valid_from) = 2019
WINDOW validity AS (ORDER BY valid_from)
ORDER BY valid_from;
```

As you can see, in each successive period, the price decreased considerably in 2019:

valid_from date	value decimal(5,2)	Previous value decimal(5,2)	Change decimal(6,2)
2019-01-01	11.47		0.00
2019-02-01	11.35	11.47	-0.12
2019-03-01	11.23	11.35	-0.12
2019-04-01	11.11	11.23	-0.12
.	.	.	.
.	.	.	.
.	.	.	.
2019-09-01	10.33	10.48	-0.15
2019-10-01	10.18	10.33	-0.15
2019-11-01	10.08	10.18	-0.10
2019-12-01	9.97	10.08	-0.11
12 rows (8 shown)			4 columns

If we are interested in computing the total change in prices in 2019, we must use a CTE, as we cannot nest window function calls inside aggregate functions. A solution is shown in the following listing.

Listing 4.20   Computing the aggregate over a window

```
WITH changes AS (
    SELECT value - lag(value, 1, value) OVER (ORDER BY valid_from) AS v
    FROM prices
    WHERE date_part('year', valid_from) = 2019
    ORDER BY valid_from
)
SELECT sum(changes.v) AS total_change
FROM changes;
```

The result of this computation gives us the price difference for Germany in 2019 that we've been looking for. For privately produced renewable energy, we find that the compensation has been cut by 1.50 ct/kWh.

4.6 *Conditions and filtering outside the WHERE clause*

Neither computed aggregates nor the result of a window function can be filtered via the standard WHERE clause. Such filtering is necessary to answer questions like the following:

- *Selection of groups that have an aggregated value that exceeds value* x—For this, you would have to use the HAVING clause.

- *Selection of data that exceeds a certain value in a range of days*—Here, the QUALIFY clause must be used.

In addition, you might need to filter out values to keep them from entering an aggregate function at all, using the FILTER clause. Table 4.1 summarizes the options for filtering the values that go into aggregates or filtering the results of those aggregates.

Table 4.1   Filtering clauses and where to use them

	Where to use it	Effect
HAVING	After GROUP BY	Filters rows based on aggregates computed for a group
QUALIFY	After the FROM clause referring to any window expression	Filters rows based on anything computed in that window
FILTER	After any aggregate function	Filters the values passed to the aggregate

4.6.1   Using the HAVING clause

Please give me all the days with production exceeding 900 kWh! In chapter 3, you learned about both the WHERE clause and how GROUP BY works. You can attempt to combine them like this:

```
SELECT system_id,
       date_trunc('day', read_on)      AS day,
       round(sum(power)  / 4 / 1000, 2)  AS kWh,
FROM readings
WHERE kWh >= 900
GROUP BY ALL;
```

Prior to DuckDB 0.10, the query gave you an error like this: *Error: Binder Error: Referenced column "kWh" not found in FROM clause!* Recent versions have improved the wording of this error, now telling you that a WHERE clause cannot contain aggregates. What that means is this: the computed column kWh is not yet known when the WHERE clause will be applied, and it can't be known at that point (in contrast to day, which is a computed column as well). Selecting rows in the WHERE clause, or filtering rows, in other words, modifies what rows get aggregated in the first place. Therefore, you need another clause that gets applied after aggregation: the HAVING clause. It is used after the GROUP BY clause to provide filter criteria after the aggregation of all selected rows has been completed.

Returning to the initial task, all you need to do is move the condition out of the WHERE clause into the HAVING clause that follows GROUP BY, as shown in the following listing.

Listing 4.21   Using the HAVING clause to filter rows based on aggregated values

```
SELECT system_id,
       date_trunc('day', read_on)      AS day,
       round(sum(power)  / 4 / 1000, 2)  AS kWh,
```

```
FROM readings
GROUP BY ALL
HAVING kWh >= 900
ORDER BY kWh DESC;
```

The results are now filtered after they have been grouped together by the sum aggregate:

```
| system_id |    day     |  kWh   |
|   int32   |    date    | double |
|-----------+------------+--------|
|        34 | 2020-05-12 | 960.03 |
|        34 | 2020-06-08 | 935.33 |
|        34 | 2020-05-23 | 924.08 |
|        34 | 2019-06-09 |  915.4 |
|        34 | 2020-06-06 | 914.98 |
|        34 | 2020-05-20 | 912.65 |
|        34 | 2019-05-01 |  912.6 |
|        34 | 2020-06-16 | 911.93 |
|        34 | 2020-06-07 | 911.73 |
|        34 | 2020-05-18 | 907.98 |
|        34 | 2019-04-10 | 907.63 |
|        34 | 2019-06-22 | 906.78 |
|        34 | 2020-05-19 |  906.4 |
```

4.6.2 *Using the QUALIFY clause*

Let's say you want to only return rows where the result of a window function matches some filter. You can't add that filter in the WHERE clause because that would filter out rows that get included in the window, and you need to use the results of the window function. However, you also can't use HAVING because window functions get evaluated before an aggregation. So QUALIFY lets you filter on the results of a window function.

When we introduced window functions, we had to use a CTE to filter the results. We can rewrite the query much more simply and clearly by using QUALIFY, still getting the three highest-ranked values.

> **Listing 4.22 Filter aggregated values in a window with the QUALIFY clause**

```
SELECT dense_rank() OVER (ORDER BY power DESC) AS rnk, *
FROM readings
QUALIFY rnk <= 3;
```

Let's return to our example using a seven-day moving window (see listing 4.17). The seven-day average production value is a good indicator of the efficiency of a photovoltaic grid, and we might ask for the days at which a certain threshold was reached. We only want results for which the average in a seven-day window was higher than 875 kWh, as shown in the following listing, so it goes into the QUALIFY clause. The QUALIFIY clause can refer to the window function by name.

Listing 4.23 Using the `QUALIFY` clause on windows spawning more than one row

```
SELECT system_id,
       day,
       avg(kWh) OVER (
              PARTITION BY system_id
              ORDER BY day ASC
              RANGE BETWEEN INTERVAL 3 Days PRECEDING
                        AND INTERVAL 3 Days FOLLOWING
       ) AS "kWh 7-day moving average"
FROM v_power_per_day
QUALIFY "kWh 7-day moving average" > 875        ⟵─┐ Here's where we
ORDER BY system_id, day;                           │ set the threshold.
```

With the example data, we find three dates that represent a typical "good day" of photovoltaic power production in the western hemisphere:

system_id int32	day date	kWh 7-day moving average double
34	2020-05-21	887.4628571428572
34	2020-05-22	884.7342857142858
34	2020-06-09	882.4628571428572

4.6.3 Using the FILTER clause

Sometimes, you want to compute an aggregate, an average, or a count of values, and you realize there are some rows you don't want to include. You could add to the `FILTER` clause, but in a complex query, you might need to keep those rows to compute other fields. For example, let's say you sometimes get bad readings, which show up as negative values. You want to compute the total number of readings and the average reading of the sensor. If you were to filter out the bad readings in the `WHERE` clause, you wouldn't be able to compute the total number of readings. But if you were to simply average all the readings, you would be including some of the bad, negative values. To solve this type of problem, you can use `FILTER` expressions as part of the aggregation.

Returning to section 4.1, in which we had to deal with inconsistent sensor readings, we are actually presented with the very problem of pulling `NULL` values into the average, which is most likely not what we want. Instead of capping `NULL` values at zero, we can filter them out of the average value altogether like this.

Listing 4.24 Keeping nonsensical data out of the aggregates

```
INSERT INTO readings(system_id, read_on, power)
SELECT any_value(SiteId),
       time_bucket(
           INTERVAL '15 Minutes',
           CAST("Date-Time" AS timestamp)
       ) AS read_on,
```

```
    coalesce(avg(ac_power)
      FILTER (
        ac_power IS NOT NULL AND
        ac_power >= 0
      ),0 )
FROM
    read_csv_auto(
        'https://developer.nrel.gov/api/pvdaq/v3/' ||
        'data_file?api_key=DEMO_KEY&system_id=10&year=2019'
    )
GROUP BY read_on
ORDER BY read_on
ON CONFLICT DO NOTHING;
```

> **Values that are NULL or less than zero are not included in the average anymore.**

> **We use the ON CONFLICT clause to avoid failures if you run this statement on a database that is already populated.**

You might wonder why we use the coalesce function; if all data is filtered out, nothing goes into the aggregate, and the whole expression turns to NULL. That means that if you filter out all the input from the aggregate, the value turns to NULL, which would violate the constraint on our reading table. As usual, there is no one correct approach here—it's OK to prefer the solution in either listing 4.1 or 4.24. In this case, using the FILTER-based solution combined with coalesce is a slightly better option because its intention is slightly clearer.

4.7 *The PIVOT statement*

You can have many aggregates in one query, and all of them can be filtered individually. This may help you answer a task like this: *I want a report of the energy production per system and year, and the years should be columns!* Aggregating the production per system is easy, and so is aggregating the production per year. Grouping by both keys isn't difficult either—a statement like

```
SELECT system_id, year(day), sum(kWh) FROM v_power_per_day GROUP BY ALL ORDER
    BY system_id;
```

will do just fine and returns the following:

system_id int32	year("day") int64	sum(kWh) double
10	2019	1549.280000000001
10	2020	677.1900000000003
34	2019	205742.59999999992
34	2020	101033.75000000001
1200	2019	62012.109999999986
1200	2020	30709.329999999998

While we did group the data by system and year, the years per system appear in rows, not columns. We want three rows with two columns, 2019 and 2020, containing the values, pretty much as you would find the preceding data in a spreadsheet program. The process of reorganizing such a table is called *pivoting*, and DuckDB offers a few ways to achieve this—one of which is the use of multiple filtered aggregates. Instead of having only one `sum` aggregate, we define several and filter out each value we don't want for a specific column. We then end up with the following statement.

Listing 4.25 Statically pivoting a result by applying a filter to all aggregates selected

```
SELECT system_id,
       sum(kWh) FILTER (WHERE year(day) = 2019)
           AS 'kWh in 2019',
       sum(kWh) FILTER (WHERE year(day) = 2020)
           AS 'kWh in 2020'
FROM v_power_per_day
GROUP BY system_id;
```

The values for the sum are equal, but the years are now columns, rather than individual groups. Now your fictitious boss can view that data in the way they are used to in their spreadsheet program:

```
┌───────────┬───────────────────┬───────────────────┐
│ system_id │    kWh in 2019    │    kWh in 2020    │
│   int32   │      double       │      double       │
├───────────┼───────────────────┼───────────────────┤
│        10 │   1549.280000000001 │   677.1900000000003 │
│        34 │ 205742.59999999992 │ 101033.75000000001 │
│      1200 │ 62012.109999999986 │  30709.329999999998 │
└───────────┴───────────────────┴───────────────────┘
```

There's one downside to this approach: the columns are essentially hardcoded, and you need to revisit that query every time a year gets added. If you are sure that your desired set of columns is constant, or you find yourself targeting other databases that might not support any other form of pivoting, the static approach might be the right solution for you.

To solve this problem with DuckDB, use the `PIVOT` clause, shown in the following listing, instead. DuckDB's `PIVOT` clause allows for dynamically pivoting tables on arbitrary expressions.

Listing 4.26 Using DuckDB's `PIVOT` statement

> You can omit the **FROM** if you want to select all
> columns, but we included it to demonstrate
> that this can actually be a full **SELECT**.

```
PIVOT (FROM v_power_per_day) ◀─┘
ON year(day) ◀─────────────
USING sum(kWh); ◀─┐
```
> The aggregate to be
> computed for the columns

> All distinct values from this
> expression are turned into columns.

The preceding statement is visualized in figure 4.4. We see all the steps from listing 4.26: selecting all columns, then using the `ON` clause to turn all distinct years into columns and the `sum` aggregate for computing their value. The steps are numbered in the same order as in the listing.

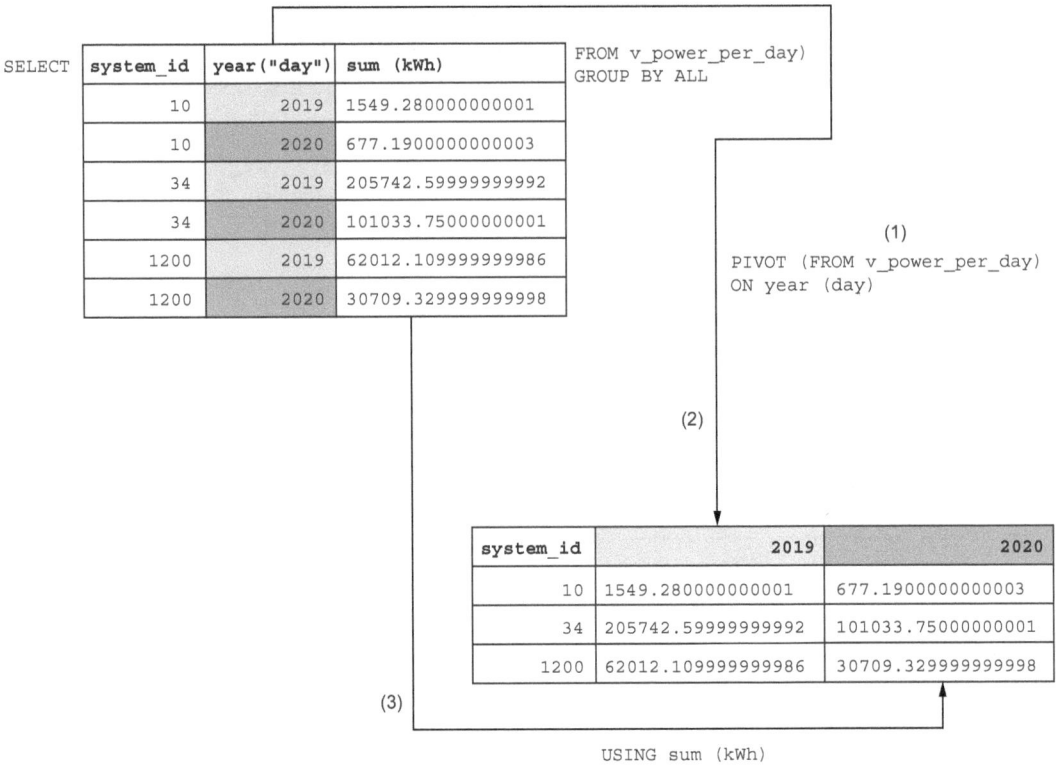

Figure 4.4   Pivoting the power values on the year

The result produced by the simplified, dynamic statement matches exactly what we statically constructed in listing 4.25— years as columns and systems as rows, with the sum of the power produced by a system and year forming the intersection of rows and columns:

```
| system_id |       2019       |       2020       |
| int32     |      double      |      double      |
|        10 |  1549.280000000001 |  677.1900000000003 |
|        34 | 205742.59999999992 | 101033.75000000001 |
|      1200 | 62012.109999999986 | 30709.329999999998 |
```

In case you are using an aggregate for the cell values, all columns that are not part of the ON clause will be used as a grouping key for the aggregate. However, you do not need to use an aggregate. PIVOT v_power_per_day ON day will produce a result of 1,382 rows and 545(!) columns. Why is that? v_power_per_day contains 1,382 distinct values of (system_id, kWh), which make up the rows. The system has been asked to create a column using the day, not year(day), and there are 543 different days recorded. The two additional columns are the system_id and kWh columns. So what's in the cells? There are many, many 0s and just a few 1s. Without the USING clause, DuckDB will fill the cells with 0s for days that didn't have the specific value and 1s for days that did. So if you are actually interested in a tabular view of all days, you might want to use the first aggregate like this in such a case:

```
PIVOT (
    FROM v_power_per_day WHERE day BETWEEN '2020-05-30' AND '2020-06-02'
)
ON DAY USING first(kWh);
```

Note that we deliberately chose to select only a couple of days instead of trying to print several hundred columns. The preceding query pivots this result into a tabular view on the day:

system_id int32	day date	kWh double
1200	2020-05-30	280.4
1200	2020-05-31	282.25
1200	2020-06-01	288.29
1200	2020-06-02	152.83
.	.	.
.	.	.
.	.	.
10	2020-05-30	4.24
10	2020-05-31	3.78
10	2020-06-01	4.47
10	2020-06-02	5.09
12 rows (8 shown)		3 columns

This result would make any spreadsheet artist happy:

system_id int32	2020-05-30 double	2020-05-31 double	2020-06-01 double	2020-06-02 double
10	4.24	3.78	4.47	5.09
34	732.5	790.33	796.55	629.17
1200	280.4	282.25	288.29	152.83

All of the preceding queries use the proprietary DuckDB variant of PIVOT. DuckDB's syntax makes writing pivot statements much easier and less error-prone, as it completely eliminates any static enumeration of the rows on which the table should be pivoted. DuckDB also supports a more standard SQL form of PIVOT. However, the support for the PIVOT clause wildly differs across different databases systems, and it is unlikely other possible target databases will have the exact same flavor of the standard. Therefore, we would rather use the proprietary syntax in this case, which is easier to read than hoping for more portable SQL.

In DuckDB, it is perfectly possible to compute multiple aggregates in the USING clause as well as use multiple columns for pivoting. We could use this to not only compute the total production per year (which is the sum of all days) but also add two more columns that highlight the best day:

```
PIVOT v_power_per_day
ON year(day)
USING round(sum(kWh)) AS total, max(kWh) AS best_day;
```

We've rounded the totals so that the result is more readable:

system_id int32	2019_total double	2019_best_day double	2020_total double	2020_best_day double
10	1549.0	7.47	677.0	6.97
34	205743.0	915.4	101034.0	960.03
1200	62012.0	337.29	30709.0	343.43

4.8   Using the ASOF JOIN

Imagine you are selling a volatile product at arbitrary times of day. You are able to predict prices at an interval, let's say 15 minutes, but that's as precise as you can get. However, people demand your product all the time, which leads to the following fictive situation. The query in listing 4.27 generates two CTEs: a fictive price table with 4 entries for an hour of a random day as well as a sales table with 12 entries. It then joins them together naively, and instead of the prices of 12 sales, you find only 4 results, as shown in the following listing.

Listing 4.27   Using an inner join for timestamps

```
WITH prices AS (
  SELECT range AS valid_at,
         random()*10 AS price
  FROM range(
      '2023-01-01 01:00:00'::timestamp,
      '2023-01-01 02:00:00'::timestamp, INTERVAL '15 minutes')
),
sales AS (
  SELECT range AS sold_at,
         random()*10 AS num
  FROM range(
      '2023-01-01 01:00:00'::timestamp,
      '2023-01-01 02:00:00'::timestamp, INTERVAL '5 minutes')
)
SELECT sold_at, valid_at AS 'with_price_at', round(num * price,2) as price
FROM sales
JOIN prices ON prices.valid_at = sales.sold_at;
```

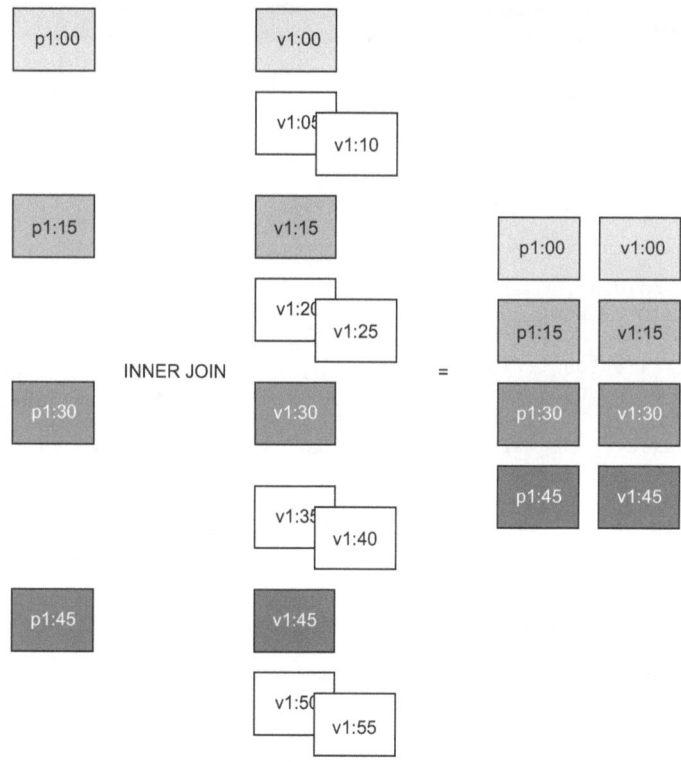

Figure 4.5   The inner join of time-series data gone wrong

Sales are quite poor, as clearly indicated by this result and represented in figure 4.5:

```
|       sold_at        |    with_price_at     |  price  |
|      timestamp       |      timestamp       |  double |
|----------------------|----------------------|---------|
| 2023-01-01 01:00:00  | 2023-01-01 01:00:00  |  21.17  |
| 2023-01-01 01:15:00  | 2023-01-01 01:15:00  |  12.97  |
| 2023-01-01 01:30:00  | 2023-01-01 01:30:00  |  44.61  |
| 2023-01-01 01:45:00  | 2023-01-01 01:45:00  |   9.45  |
```

Enter the ASOF JOIN—the ASOF (pronounced *as of*) JOIN is a JOIN clause that joins on inequality, picking a "good enough" value for the gaps where the JOIN columns are not exactly equal. Returning to listing 4.27, we must change two things: replacing the JOIN keyword with ASOF JOIN and providing an inequality operator. The following

```
prices.valid_at <= sales.sold_at
```

inequality condition indicates that all prices valid at or before the point of sale can be used to compute the total price.

Listing 4.28   Using an `ASOF JOIN` **for timestamps**

```
WITH prices AS (
  SELECT range AS valid_at,
         random()*10 AS price
  FROM range(
      '2023-01-01 01:00:00'::timestamp,
      '2023-01-01 02:00:00'::timestamp, INTERVAL '15 minutes')
),
sales AS (
  SELECT range AS sold_at,
         random()*10 AS num
  FROM range(
      '2023-01-01 01:00:00'::timestamp,
      '2023-01-01 02:00:00'::timestamp, INTERVAL '5 minutes')
)
SELECT sold_at, valid_at AS 'with_price_at', round(num * price,2) as price
FROM sales
ASOF JOIN prices
    ON prices.valid_at <= sales.sold_at;
```

Specify the JOIN as ASOF.

Note the `< =`, in contrast to the `=` in listing 4.27.

Note how DuckDB picks the price closest to that at the time of the sale. Additionally, we now get the 12 expected rows:

sold_at timestamp	with_price_at timestamp	price double
2023-01-01 01:00:00	2023-01-01 01:00:00	1.59
2023-01-01 01:05:00	2023-01-01 01:00:00	3.56
2023-01-01 01:10:00	2023-01-01 01:00:00	2.71
2023-01-01 01:15:00	2023-01-01 01:15:00	29.12
2023-01-01 01:20:00	2023-01-01 01:15:00	14.92
2023-01-01 01:25:00	2023-01-01 01:15:00	4.83
2023-01-01 01:30:00	2023-01-01 01:30:00	2.84
2023-01-01 01:35:00	2023-01-01 01:30:00	3.84
2023-01-01 01:40:00	2023-01-01 01:30:00	4.95
2023-01-01 01:45:00	2023-01-01 01:45:00	23.1
2023-01-01 01:50:00	2023-01-01 01:45:00	30.07
2023-01-01 01:55:00	2023-01-01 01:45:00	11.6
12 rows		3 columns

Figure 4.6 visualizes the algorithm: given four items *p*, each with a timestamp increasing by 15 minutes each, and 12 items *v*, with a timestamp increasing by five minutes. The ASOF JOIN in the figure is defined as p<=v so that each *p* item will be joined together with three *v* items that have the same or higher timestamp.

The ASOF JOIN is often used to work with time series data, such as stock quotes, prices, or IoT sensors. In our example, it can be used to join the changing selling prices with the readings from the systems to compute the prices at any given point in

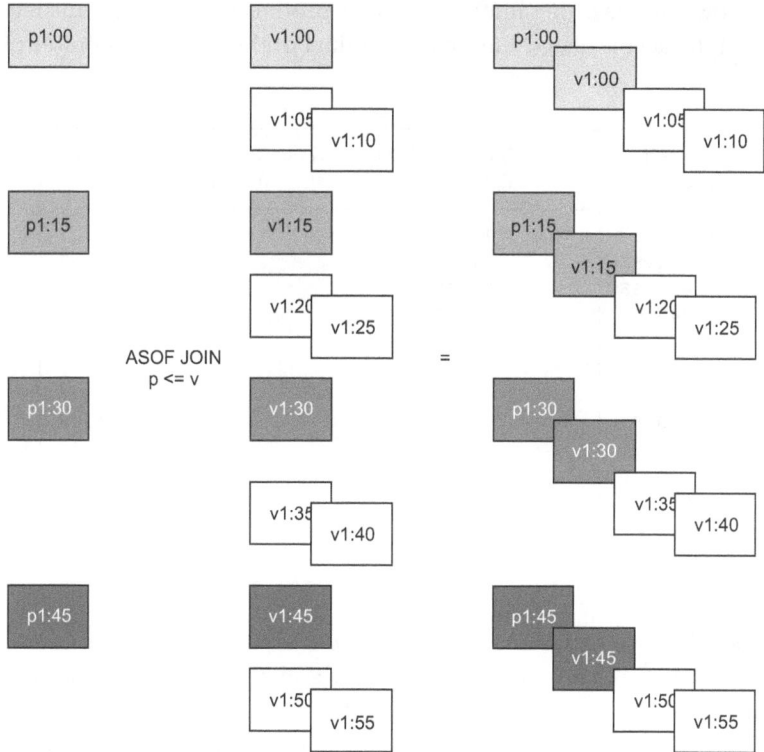

Figure 4.6 Using `ASOF JOIN` to join all timestamps that don't have an exact match

time. The final example, which follows, uses our photovoltaic example data again, applying the same logic to pick a valid price. It then demonstrates that the `ASOF JOIN` can be used with other constructs we learned in this chapter, such as using a window to accumulate the running total earnings in a sales period with different prices, as shown in the following listing.

Listing 4.29 Computing a running total earning using `ASOF JOIN` and a window function

```
SELECT power.day,
       power.kWh,
       prices.value as 'ct/kWh',
       round(sum(prices.value * power.kWh)
          OVER (ORDER BY power.day ASC) / 100, 2)
          AS 'Accumulated earnings in EUR'
FROM v_power_per_day power
    ASOF JOIN prices
    ON prices.valid_from <= power.day
WHERE system_id = 34
ORDER BY day;
```

The result shows the day, the amount of kWH produced, the price on that day (in ct/kWH), and the accumulated sum of the product of the amount of power produced and the price:

day date	kWh double	ct/kWh decimal(5,2)	Accumulated earnings in EUR double
2019-01-01	471.4	11.47	54.07
2019-01-02	458.58	11.47	106.67
2019-01-03	443.65	11.47	157.56
2019-01-04	445.03	11.47	208.6
.	.	.	.
.	.	.	.
.	.	.	.
2020-06-23	798.85	9.17	31371.86
2020-06-24	741.15	9.17	31439.83
2020-06-25	762.6	9.17	31509.76
2020-06-26	11.98	9.17	31510.86
543 rows (8 shown)			4 columns

DuckDB is positioned as an OLAP database with a broad range of use cases. Dealing with time-series data is certainly one of them, and the ASOF JOIN is part of that. Regardless of the domain—which can take the form of anything from the sensor readings in our example to the readings of a patient's heart rate monitor to fluctuations in the stock market—values recorded at a certain time are often enriched by joining them with specific key values that have been valid for a time. Having support for ASOF enables all scenarios in which timestamps are not aligned perfectly well.

4.9   *Using table functions*

Most functions in SQL take parameters and return a single value. *Table functions*, on the other hand, don't just return a single value—they return a collection of rows. As such, they can appear anywhere a table can appear. Depending on their function, they can access external resources, such as files or URLs, and turn them into relations that are part of standard SQL statements. DuckDB is not the only relational database supporting the concept of table-producing functions, but it comes with an impressive set of table functions, catering to many use cases. A list of all table functions in your DuckDB installation can be retrieved via the following statement, which uses a table function named duckdb_functions().

> Listing 4.30   Getting a list of all available table functions

```
SELECT DISTINCT ON(function_name) function_name
FROM duckdb_functions()          ◁──┐  The FROM clause is the most
WHERE function_type = 'table'         common place to call a
ORDER BY function_name;               table-producing function.
```

In this chapter's examples and during the ingestion of data, we have already made extensive use of read_csv*, read_parquet, and others. Additional extensions, such as the spatial extension, can be added to the list of table functions that read external resources and produce relational data.

range(start, stop) and generate_series(start, stop) are a couple of very useful table functions. Both functions create a list of values in the range between start and stop. The start parameter is inclusive. For the range function, the stop parameter is exclusive, while it is inclusive for generate_series. Both functions provide overloads, with an additional third parameter step defining the step size, which defaults to 1. Variants that only take the stop parameter and default at 0 for start exist too. While used as normal functions, they provide useful constructs but are much more powerful when queried like a table.

If you need a list of numbers between 1 and 5 and don't want to hardcode them, you can use SELECT generate_series(1, 5);. Numbers are helpful, but those functions also work with temporal data. When using temporal data, be aware, though, that you need to specify both start and end parameters, as there is no sensible default for either. Let's put this to practical use. The readings in our example data end in the middle of 2020. Reports based on this would end prematurely if they were intended for a whole year, as shown in the following snippet:

```
SELECT strftime(day, '%Y-%m') AS month, avg(kwh)
FROM v_power_per_day WHERE year(day) = 2020
GROUP BY ALL ORDER BY month;
```

The result will look like the following output:

```
┌──────────┬────────────────────┐
│  month   │      avg(kwh)      │
│ varchar  │       double       │
├──────────┼────────────────────┤
│ 2020-01  │ 222.13169014084497 │
│ 2020-02  │ 133.52356321839076 │
│ 2020-03  │ 207.86670454545438 │
│ 2020-04  │ 309.7838888888888  │
│ 2020-05  │ 349.5753763440861  │
│ 2020-06  │ 337.80820512820515 │
└──────────┴────────────────────┘
```

If you are tasked to create a chart, you might find yourself in a situation in which you need to think about how to represent the future months. Here's one way to use the range() function to cover a whole year and indicate missing values with 0s.

Listing 4.31   Using a range of dates as a driving table

```
WITH full_year AS (
    SELECT generate_series AS day          ┌── A range defined from the first up to the last
    FROM generate_series(               ◄──┘    day of the year, in an interval of 1 day
        '2020-01-01'::date,
```

```
                 '2020-12-31'::date, INTERVAL '1 day')
)
SELECT strftime(full_year.day, '%Y-%m') AS month,
       avg(kWh) FILTER (kWh IS NOT NULL) AS actual
FROM full_year
LEFT OUTER JOIN v_power_per_day per_day
  ON per_day.day = full_year.day
GROUP BY ALL ORDER BY month;
```

Use the output of the table function in the FROM clause as a driving table.

OUTER JOIN the values of interest.

The result is now a report for a full year, which, sadly, lacks values after June 2020:

```
| month   |       actual       |
| varchar |       double       |
|---------|--------------------|
| 2020-01 | 222.13169014084508 |
| 2020-02 | 133.52356321839076 |
| 2020-03 | 207.86670454545455 |
| 2020-04 |  309.7838888888888 |
| 2020-05 | 349.57537634408607 |
| 2020-06 | 337.80820512820515 |
| 2020-07 |                    |
| 2020-08 |                    |
| 2020-09 |                    |
| 2020-10 |                    |
| 2020-11 |                    |
| 2020-12 |                    |
|---------|--------------------|
| 12 rows |          2 columns |
```

Taking this idea one step further, you could use the value of the same month in the previous year to forecast the production value. To do that, you would have to join v_power_per_day a second time, using an offset of one year, as shown in the following listing.

> **Listing 4.32   Projecting past data into the future**

```
WITH full_year AS (
    SELECT generate_series AS day
    FROM generate_series(
        '2020-01-01'::date,
        '2020-12-31'::date, INTERVAL '1 day')
)
SELECT strftime(full_year.day, '%Y-%m') AS month,
       round(avg(present.kWh) FILTER (present.kWh IS NOT NULL),3) AS actual,
       round(avg(past.kWh) FILTER (past.kWh IS NOT NULL), 3) AS forecast,
FROM full_year
LEFT OUTER JOIN v_power_per_day present
  ON present.day = full_year.day
LEFT OUTER JOIN v_power_per_day past
  ON past.day = full_year.day - INTERVAL '1 year'
GROUP BY ALL ORDER BY month;
```

Using the generated series as a driving table in the FROM clause

Joining power per day a second time but subtracting a year from the values of the generated series

Note that we also added a call to `round` to both the `actual` and the `forecast` column, avoiding clutter, as fractions with more than three digits don't make much sense for kWh values. Additionally, this change shows that the `FILTER` clause can also appear inside a function call, as it belongs to the `avg` aggregate function, not the whole column. The result is much more pleasant and happens to provide a comparison between this year and last year, essentially for free:

```
| month   | actual  | forecast |
| varchar | double  |  double  |
|---------|---------|----------|
| 2020-01 | 222.132 | 161.593  |
| 2020-02 | 133.524 | 111.073  |
| 2020-03 | 207.867 | 150.652  |
| 2020-04 | 309.784 | 316.178  |
| 2020-05 | 349.575 | 325.369  |
| 2020-06 | 337.808 | 351.607  |
| 2020-07 |         | 334.323  |
| 2020-08 |         | 314.929  |
| 2020-09 |         | 289.605  |
| 2020-10 |         | 253.829  |
| 2020-11 |         | 191.384  |
| 2020-12 |         | 164.886  |
|---------|---------|----------|
| 12 rows |      3 columns     |
```

4.10   Using LATERAL joins

In section 4.3, we learned about correlated and uncorrelated subqueries. Listing 4.5 demonstrated how an uncorrelated subquery can be joined once with the outer query. From a performance perspective, that might be beneficial, as the subquery only needs to be evaluated once and the join is then performed for each row of the other table against the memorized values.

Sometimes, however, you want to evaluate precisely the inner query for each value of an outer query. This is where the `LATERAL JOIN` comes into play. You can think of it as the inner block of a `for` loop with the outer query being the control structure.

Unnesting arrays, fanning out data, and similar tasks can be dealt with using `LATERAL`. Assume you are interested in the intensity of the sun, specifically how much of its energy reaches your place at certain hours of the day, past or future. Open Meteo (https://open-meteo.com) offers a free API that provides a broad range of weather data, including the so-called global horizontal irradiance (GHI)—that is, the total amount of short-wave radiation received from above by a surface horizontal to the ground. This value is of particular interest to photovoltaic installations and is measured in W/m^2. As shown in the following listing, their API generates a JSON object that contains two individual arrays, one with the timestamps and another with the selected values. The latter array is the array of interest; we want to retrieve specific values for some given facts.

> **Listing 4.33   Excerpt of a JSON response from Open Meteo containing GHI data**

```
{
    "latitude": 50.78,
    "longitude": 6.0799994,
    "utc_offset_seconds": 7200,
    "timezone": "Europe/Berlin",
    "timezone_abbreviation": "CEST",
    "elevation": 178.0,
    "hourly_units": {
        "time": "iso8601",
        "shortwave_radiation_instant": "W/m\u00b2"
    },
    "hourly": {
        "time": [
            "2023-08-26T00:00",
            "2023-08-26T01:00",
            "2023-08-26T02:00",
            "2023-08-26T03:00",
            "2023-08-26T04:00",
            "2023-08-26T05:00"
        ],
        "shortwave_radiation_instant": [
            0.0,
            0.0,
            0.0,
            0.0,
            0.0,
            9.1
        ]
    }
}
```

The preceding JSON is in the code repository of the book under ch04/ghi_past_and_future.json. Alternatively, you can access fresh data via Open-Meteo's API: https://mng.bz/WE5w.

At first sight, it might seem like a daunting task to use SQL to pick out the morning hours, noon, and the evening hours from that array. Let's see how LATERAL can solve this task. We already read in chapter 1 that DuckDB is able to process JSON, and we will examine this in greater detail in chapter 5. For now, it is enough to know that you can select from a JSON file like from any other table in the FROM clause. The following query generates a series of seven days and then joins those with the hours 8, 13, and 19 (7 p.m.) to create indexes. Those indexes are the day number multiplied by 24 plus the hour of day at which you desire to find the value in the JSON array. That index is the lateral driver for the subquery:

```
INSTALL json;
LOAD json;

WITH days AS (
  SELECT generate_series AS value FROM generate_series(7)
```

```
), hours AS (
  SELECT unnest([8, 13, 18]) AS value
), indexes AS (
  SELECT days.value * 24 + hours.value AS i
  FROM days, hours
)
SELECT date_trunc('day', now()) - INTERVAL '7 days' +
       INTERVAL (indexes.i || ' hours') AS ts,
     ghi.v AS 'GHI in W/m^2'
FROM indexes,
LATERAL (
  SELECT hourly.shortwave_radiation_instant[i+1]
         AS v
  FROM 'code/ch04/ghi_past_and_future.json'
) AS ghi
ORDER BY ts;
```

Recreates data from the hourly index ← (for the `SELECT date_trunc` line)

Arrays are 1 based in DuckDB (and SQL in general). ← (for the `shortwave_radiation_instant[i+1]` line)

DuckDB automatically detects that this string refers to a JSON file, loads it, and then parses it. ← (for the JSON file string line)

The end of August 2023 did look like this in Aachen; it was not a great month for photovoltaics:

ts timestamp with time zone	GHI in W/m^2 double
2023-08-26 08:00:00+02	36.0
2023-08-26 13:00:00+02	490.7
2023-08-26 18:00:00+02	2.3
2023-08-27 08:00:00+02	243.4
2023-08-27 13:00:00+02	124.3
·	·
·	·
·	·
2023-09-01 13:00:00+02	392.0
2023-09-01 18:00:00+02	0.0
2023-09-02 08:00:00+02	451.0
2023-09-02 13:00:00+02	265.0
2023-09-02 18:00:00+02	0.0
24 rows (10 shown)	2 columns

The subquery can produce zero, one, or a larger number of rows for each row of the driving outer table. In the preceding example, it produced one row for each outer row. If the subquery produces more rows, the values of the outer row will be repeated, in a manner similar to a CROSS JOIN. If the subquery does not produce any value, the join won't produce a value either. We must apply an OUTER JOIN in this case as well. At this point, the LATERAL keyword alone is not enough, and we must use the full JOIN syntax like this. The following query is artificial and of little value, except in demonstrating the syntax. Both queries produce a series of values from 1 to 4, with the outer in a step size of 1 and the inner in a step size of 2. We compare both values in the ON clause:

```
SELECT i, j
FROM generate_series(1, 4) t(i)
```

```
LEFT OUTER JOIN LATERAL (
   SELECT * FROM generate_series(1, 4, 2) t(j)
) sq ON sq.j = i
ORDER BY i;
```
◁─┐ While the condition is now on the outside
   and cannot be formulated otherwise, it is
   still a correlated subquery.

The result of this query looks like this:

i	j
int64	int64
1	1
2	
3	3
4	

The problem with the prices in section 4.8 can be solved with a subquery and LATERAL JOIN too. In essence, the subquery must return a row from the price table that has a validity as close to the date in time of the sale as possible. For that to work, we cannot use a normal JOIN, as the subquery must produce different values for each incoming date. Therefore, the date column that would normally be part of the JOIN must move inside the subquery. Thus, the joined subquery now becomes correlated, or laterally joined to the outer query. The correlation in the following example is the validity of the price compared to the day the power production was recorded.

Listing 4.34 Comparing the ASOF JOIN from listing 4.29 to a LATERAL JOIN

```
SELECT power.day, power.kWh,
       prices.value as 'EUR/kWh'
FROM v_power_per_day power,                    Mark the subquery as lateral,
   LATERAL (                        ◁───┘     allowing correlation.
      SELECT *
      FROM prices                                    Correlate by
      WHERE prices.valid_from <= power.day   ◁───┘  inequality.
      ORDER BY valid_from DESC limit 1   ◁─┐ While the ASOF JOIN would
   ) AS prices                              automatically pick the closest value
WHERE system_id = 34                         for us, we must order the values
ORDER BY day;                                ourselves when using LATERAL.
```

For time-series-related computations with DuckDB, we would most certainly use the ASOF JOIN. LATERAL is attractive when considering portability, and there are probably more databases supporting LATERAL than ASOF JOIN. Use LATERAL in scenarios in which you want to fan out of a dataset to produce more rows.

Summary

- The SQL standard has evolved greatly since its last major revision in 1992 (SQL-92). DuckDB supports a broad range of modern SQLs, including CTEs (SQL:1999), window functions (SQL:2003), list aggregations (SQL:2016), and more.
- Grouping sets allow the computation of aggregates over multiple groups, performing a drill down into different levels of detail; ROLLUP and CUBE can be used to generate subgroups or combinations of grouping keys.
- DuckDB fully supports window functions, including named windows and ranges, enabling use cases such as computing running totals, ranks, and more.
- All aggregate functions, including statistic computations and interpolations, are optimized for usage in a windowed context.
- HAVING and QUALIFY can be used to select aggregates and windows after they have been computed; FILTER prevents unwanted data from going into aggregates.
- DuckDB includes ASOF JOIN, which is necessary in use cases involving time-series data.
- DuckDB also supports LATERAL joins that help fan out data and can emulate loops, to an extent.
- Results can be pivoted, either with a simplified, DuckDB-specific PIVOT statement or a more static, standard SQL approach.

Exploring data without persistence

In this chapter, we're going to learn how to query data without persisting the data in DuckDB, a technique that is quite unusual for a database and seems counterintuitive, but which is useful in the right situations. For example, if we need to transform data from one format to another, we might not necessarily want to create an intermediate storage model while doing this.

This chapter also demonstrates the power of DuckDB's analytical engine, even when your data isn't stored in the native format. We'll show how to query several common data formats, including JSON, CSV, and Parquet, as well as other databases, such as SQLite.

The JSON and CSV sources we are working with in this chapter are located in the ch05 folder of our example repository on GitHub: https://github.com/duckdb-in -action/examples. We assume you have navigated to the root of this repository before invoking the DuckDB CLI for the examples in this chapter.

5.1 Why use a database without persisting any data?

Exploring and analyzing data without persisting makes sense when we are working with data stored in a remote location. For example, you might have files living in Amazon S3. We don't know yet whether we want to build a production pipeline with this data, so we don't want to spend a bunch of time defining a data model, like we did in chapter 3, and ingest the remote data into DuckDB's storage format. Or it might contain data that we don't want to persist for privacy reasons. However, we still want to utilize what we learned about DuckDB and SQL in the previous chapters so that we can use it to understand the shape and volume of the data. Depending on the file format and storage location, DuckDB may not even need to download the entirety of the file contents. At a later stage, we may then choose to ingest the data into DuckDB.

Most likely, you already have some kind of database in your infrastructure. DuckDB is able to use the store systems of several other databases. Most notably, there are the SQLite and Postgres integrations. The former works directly on the SQLite store files, and the latter works with the *binary transfer mode* of the Postgres client–server protocol. In either case, you don't have the data inside your DuckDB process but are still able to take advantage of DuckDB's fast query engine and SQL support. In many cases, for 22 TPC-H benchmark queries, DuckDB had been faster when using the Postgres integration than Postgres itself (and faster in all queries when using its own storage).

> **NOTE** What is the *TPC-H benchmark*? It is a decision support benchmark, consisting of a suite of business-oriented ad hoc queries and concurrent data modifications. The benchmark uses a typical star schema for sales order, with sales and line items as fact tables and a couple of dimension tables, such as products and customers. This benchmark illustrates decision support systems that examine large volumes of data, execute queries with a high degree of complexity, and give answers to critical business questions. TPC-H is the most commonly used benchmark for analytics, although many people only run the read queries, not the updates, which are also part of the specification.

5.2 Inferring file type and schema

DuckDB has two features that make it very easy to process files or sets of files. It can determine both what kind of file is being read (also referred to as *auto-inferring file types*) and the schema of the data in the file:

- *Auto-inferring files types*—With DuckDB, you can query the content of supported file formats, such as CSV, JSON, and Parquet, as simply as using

FROM `'flights.csv'`;. The functionality is provided out of the box, and it supports all SQL clauses and functions mentioned in the previous chapters. When you issue such a query, DuckDB works out first that you are not querying a table or view in your current schema. If the file exists in the filesystems, DuckDB uses its extension to determine the file type and calls an appropriate function that knows how to process that data format to read the file. Those functions provide sensible defaults for both behavior (e.g., the number of samples to take before a data type is decided) and formats (e.g., date and time formats). If those defaults don't work for you, look out for the table functions `read_csv_auto`, `read_json_auto`, and `read_parquet_auto`. These functions are called internally when you issue a query like the preceding one. They provide a plethora of arguments to change singular details but still automatically derive column names, object structures, and so on. So instead of just querying FROM `'a_file.csv'` or FROM `'data*.json'`, you would use FROM `read_json_auto('data*.json')` with the appropriate arguments you need.

- *Auto-inferring schema*—DuckDB automatically infers the schema of any data sources we ask it to process. With data formats like Parquet, this is easier, as files have an embedded schema that DuckDB can use. With others, like CSV or JSON, it will infer the schema from a configurable number of sample objects. DuckDB also infers the dialect of CSV files and detects whether they contain a header row. If we aren't completely happy with the inferences made, we can choose to override the types of all, or just some, of the columns. In such a case, you would not use a plain filename but instead use a "non-auto" function, like `read_csv`:

```
FROM read_csv(              The file
  'flights.csv',           to read
  auto_detect=true,              Use auto-detection
  columns={                      for all arguments.
    'FlightDate': 'DATE',
    'UniqueCarrier': 'VARCHAR',
    'OriginCityName': 'VARCHAR',
    'DestCityName': 'VARCHAR'
  }               Ensure the listed columns are being
);                converted into the given data types.
```

DuckDB can read multiple files of different types (CSV, Parquet, JSON files, etc.) at the same time, using either the glob syntax or by providing a list of files to read. When reading from multiple files, DuckDB must combine schemas from those files. That is because each file may have its own schema, which can differ from the other files. DuckDB offers two ways of unifying schemas of multiple files: by column position and column name. By default, DuckDB reads the schema of the first file provided, and then it unifies columns in subsequent files by column position. This works correctly as long as all files have the same schema, with the same names, at identical positions. Otherwise, you can use the `union_by_name` option for the `read_xxx` functions, which allows DuckDB to construct the schema by reading all of the names instead.

5.2.1 A note on CSV parsing

CSV parsing can be surprisingly difficult, even though the format is simple and, at first glance, straightforward. DuckDB uses sampling in all cases in which `read_csv_auto` or `read_csv` with `auto_detect` is set to `true`. A certain number of rows from the file (20,480 by default) are read to detect the following:

- The dialect of the CSV file (delimiter, quoting rule, escape, etc.)
- The types of each of the columns
- Whether the file has a header row

We consider type detection to be the most important factor in ensuring good data quality in any later step. DuckDB tries to determine the following types in descending priority:

- `BOOLEAN`
- `BIGINT`
- `DOUBLE`
- `TIME`
- `DATE`
- `TIMESTAMP`
- `VARCHAR`

To the end, everything can be cast to `VARCHAR`. This type has the lowest priority—i.e., columns are converted to `VARCHAR` if they cannot be cast to anything else.

There's a good chance you want or need to control the behavior of `read_csv_auto` or `read_csv`. The DuckDB documentation lists the most important arguments in a dedicated section (https://mng.bz/8w5B). These parameters apply to the corresponding export functions as well. Arguments we found helpful were `names`, to configure the column names in absence of header rows; `dateformat`, `timestampformat`, and `decimal_separator` for date and number formats; and `filename` when dealing with multiple files at once (this option adds an artificial column containing the filename of the processed file).

If you find yourself in a scenario in which you don't have access to the aforementioned documentation, you can always query DuckDB to give you a list of arguments to its functions:

```
SELECT distinct function_name,
       unnest(parameters) as parameter
FROM duckdb_functions()                       This can be any other
WHERE function_name = 'read_csv'    ◁──┘ function too (e.g., read_json).
ORDER BY parameter;
```

> **NOTE** JSON and Parquet processing are configurable too. The focus is different in each format. The most relevant options for JSON are the format specifications for dates and numbers, while Parquet requires some thought—especially when writing—about the size of row groups and the compression.

5.3   *Shredding nested JSON*

DuckDB's built-in JSON extension has functions to create, read, and manipulate JSON strings. This is achieved by automatically detecting the types and column names and then converting the values within the JSON into DuckDB's vectors.

We're going to explore this capability using a set of JSON files to represent shots that were taken in Premier League football matches. These files were created using the understatapi library (https://pypi.org/project/understatapi/). The source data is in JSON lines format, with one match per row. The files are stored in a subdirectory xg, which stands for *expected goals*, a term borrowed from the understat site.

We can explore the high-level structure of each JSON document by executing the following SQL query from the DuckDB CLI. The example shows that it is possible to query not only a single file but many files at once. xg/shots_*.json is a wildcard expression that will find all the files in the xg directory with the prefix shots_ and the suffix .json. Our example files have slightly different schemas, which don't work well with either union, by position or name, so we must deal with those ourselves and stick with the default: union by position. We will unnest the JSON objects into separate rows and fix any conformity problems that become apparent in the process. We recommend using the line in the DuckDB CLI mode because there are a lot of fields, which would get truncated if we were to use the default duckbox presentation mode:

```
.mode line
DESCRIBE FROM 'xg/shots_*.json';
```

> **NOTE** By default, unnest only unpacks the first level of a JSON object. If you want to unpack deeply nested objects, you can use the recursive := true parameter.

The output from running this query is shown in the following code. Please take note that we line-wrapped the output. In line mode, the DuckDB CLI will produce the type information without any line breaks. The schema that has been inferred for the expected goals JSON data looks like this:

```
column_name = h
column_type = STRUCT(
  id BIGINT, "minute" BIGINT, result VARCHAR,
  X VARCHAR, Y VARCHAR, xG VARCHAR,
  player VARCHAR, h_a VARCHAR, player_id BIGINT,
  situation VARCHAR, season BIGINT, shotType VARCHAR, match_id BIGINT,
  h_team VARCHAR, a_team VARCHAR, h_goals BIGINT, a_goals BIGINT,
  date TIMESTAMP, player_assisted VARCHAR, lastAction VARCHAR)[]
      null = YES
       key =
   default =
     extra =

column_name = a
column_type = STRUCT(
  id BIGINT, "minute" BIGINT, result VARCHAR,
```

```
X VARCHAR, Y VARCHAR, xG VARCHAR,
player VARCHAR, h_a VARCHAR, player_id BIGINT,
situation VARCHAR, season BIGINT, shotType VARCHAR, match_id BIGINT,
h_team VARCHAR, a_team VARCHAR, h_goals BIGINT, a_goals BIGINT,
date TIMESTAMP, player_assisted VARCHAR, lastAction VARCHAR) []
        null = YES
         key =
     default =
       extra =
```

From this output, we learn that each entry has h and a properties that point to STRUCT arrays, where each STRUCT represents a single event. The content is identical, but there was no way for DuckDB to create a unified schema for our input files because it couldn't match the columns by either position or name. The data will be easier to work with if we unpack those arrays. *Unpacking* here means that we turn an array of elements into individual elements so that we can easily use the LIMIT clause to restrict the number of results returned. The unnest function will unpack those arrays. We use it to create a row for each value in the arrays stored in the h and a properties. This is done in two separate SELECT statements, which are then combined using the UNION ALL clause. We also will limit the result to a small value greater than 1 (JSON documents don't have to be uniform, so one result may be too few, but a result that includes all rows will be overwhelming too):

```
FROM 'xg/shots_*.json'
SELECT unnest(h) AS row
UNION ALL          ◁──┐  This combines the results of the statements
FROM 'xg/shots_*.json'    before and after this clause, including
SELECT unnest(a) AS row   duplicates (indicated by the ALL keyword).
LIMIT 3;     ◁──┐
                │  Choose a number to limit the results returned
                │  that gives you enough results to judge
                   data quality but does not overwhelm you.
```

If we run this query, we will receive three rows. While the source of each row is a JSON object, DuckDB does return a DuckDB struct, and though it shares some similarities with JSON, it does not parse as JSON. We've reproduced one row as follows, again wrapping the lines to make the code more readable:

```
row = {'id': 54521, 'minute': 43, 'result': MissedShots,
    'X': 0.9419999694824219, 'Y': 0.52, 'xG': 0.07078909873962402,
    'player': Chancel Mbemba, 'h_a': h, 'player_id': 849,
    'situation': FromCorner, 'season': 2015, 'shotType': Head,
    'match_id': 229, 'h_team': Newcastle United, 'a_team': Liverpool,
    'h_goals': 2, 'a_goals': 0, 'date': 2015-12-06 20:00:00,
    'player_assisted': Papiss Demba Cissé, 'lastAction': Pass}
```

Before we do any further analysis, let's create a view based on the results of that query. A view is not physically materialized but instead runs the underlying query each time. The benefit of defining a view is that it provides us with a shorthand for querying the data rather than having to write out the full location of the file each time:

```
CREATE VIEW shots AS
FROM (
  FROM 'xg/shots_*.json'
  SELECT unnest(h) AS row
  UNION ALL
  FROM 'xg/shots_*.json'
  SELECT unnest(a) AS row
);
```

Next, we're going to look at the schema of that view:

```
DESCRIBE shots;
```

We should see output similar to the following:

```
column_name = row
column_type = STRUCT(
  id BIGINT, "minute" BIGINT, result VARCHAR, X VARCHAR, Y VARCHAR,
  xG VARCHAR, player VARCHAR, h_a VARCHAR, player_id BIGINT,
  situation VARCHAR, season BIGINT, shotType VARCHAR, match_id BIGINT,
  h_team VARCHAR, a_team VARCHAR, h_goals BIGINT, a_goals BIGINT,
  date TIMESTAMP, player_assisted VARCHAR, lastAction VARCHAR)
       null = YES
        key =
    default =
      extra =
```

DuckDB's inference wasn't perfect. X, Y, and xG are coordinates in the original JSON and should all have a numeric type (e.g., DOUBLE); otherwise, we won't be able to perform numeric operations on those fields. To fix this, we take the inferred STRUCT type and change the type definition of the fields in question and then cast each row to that new STRUCT.

The following listing shows how we cast row to a STRUCT, with these fields set to the DOUBLE type. Let's replace the view with one in which we've cast those fields to the correct types.

> **Listing 5.1 Using CAST on a whole STRUCT to fix the inferred types for some attributes**

```
CREATE OR REPLACE VIEW shots AS
FROM (
  FROM 'xg/shots_*.json'
  SELECT unnest(h) AS row
  UNION ALL
  FROM 'xg/shots_*.json'
  SELECT unnest(a) AS row
)
SELECT CAST(ROW AS STRUCT(
  id BIGINT, "minute" BIGINT, result VARCHAR,
  X DOUBLE, Y DOUBLE, xG DOUBLE,                     ◁— Note the different
  player VARCHAR, h_a VARCHAR, player_id BIGINT,          data type.
  situation VARCHAR, season BIGINT, shotType VARCHAR,
  match_id BIGINT, h_team VARCHAR, a_team VARCHAR,
```

```
h_goals BIGINT, a_goals BIGINT, date TIMESTAMP,
player_assisted VARCHAR, lastAction VARCHAR)) AS row;
```

Now let's look at the schema of the view again:

```
DESCRIBE shots;
```

We can see that those types have been updated to DOUBLE:

```
column_name = row
column_type = STRUCT(
  id BIGINT, "minute" BIGINT, result VARCHAR,
  X DOUBLE, Y DOUBLE, xG DOUBLE,
  player VARCHAR, h_a VARCHAR, player_id BIGINT,
  situation VARCHAR, season BIGINT, shotType VARCHAR,
  match_id BIGINT, h_team VARCHAR, a_team VARCHAR,
  h_goals BIGINT, a_goals BIGINT, date TIMESTAMP,
  player_assisted VARCHAR, lastAction VARCHAR)
       null = YES
        key =
    default =
      extra =
```

If you are lucky, as in this case, you can just cast the whole type, as DuckDB's sampling was wrong. If DuckDB's sampling, however, was right, and there truly are fields that cannot be automatically cast into a non-string type, queries on the view will be problematic. Numeric types, for example, might contain surprises, and from our experience, the representation of timestamps is often the hardest to deal with, despite the fact that there is an adequate ISO standard for formatting dates and timestamps alike.

While DuckDB does validate the property names of the JSON structure, it does not try to cast each value at the moment the view is defined, so there may be data lurking in your input that does not conform to an expected format. Additionally, if you happen to add new files to your pipeline, new, invalid data may appear. In this case, you end up with an error such as Error: Conversion Error: Could not convert string 'abc' to DOUBLE when you query for SELECT row.x FROM shots. Sometimes this is exactly what you want, but sometimes it is not.

There are two ways you can address this. Your first option is to examine each of the attributes at the field level and fix them individually (see section 5.4). If you take this approach, be sure to use one of the date formatting functions DuckDB offers (any of them will do) prior to casting. In an explorative use case, such as this, going down to the field level is a task that requires a lot of effort, which may not be worth it. Instead, we recommend switching from the cast function to try_cast (see listing 5.1, which details the use of try_cast(row AS STRUCT(…)) AS row). Any fields with data that cannot be cast to a DOUBLE will now be returned as literal NULL values.

At this point, we could start writing queries directly against this view, but one more neat feature DuckDB supports is unpacking structs into columns. This means that rather than having a single column with nested fields, each field would be its own column. As such, you can easily address that column to begin with or apply any kind of function or aggregation on it. You can compare this to the way we unnested, or flattened, the lists in the original JSON files, which meant transforming a structure like [1, 2, 3] into three rows: 1, 2, and 3. This is also supported for structs and map-shaped types; unnesting them will result in one column per attribute or key. The SELECT unnest({'x' :1, 'y':2, 'z': 3}) statement unnests, or flattens, the anonymous struct into three columns:

```
┌───────┬───────┬───────┐
│   x   │   y   │   z   │
│ int32 │ int32 │ int32 │
├───────┼───────┼───────┤
│     1 │     2 │     3 │
└───────┴───────┴───────┘
```

The * operator can be used as shorthand for expanding a struct to columns when the struct can be referenced via a variable, as in this statement. This yields the same output as our previous result:

```
WITH src AS (SELECT {'x' :1, 'y':2, 'z': 3} AS row)
SELECT row.* FROM src;
```

This technique saves you from the hassle of needing to qualify access to the elements of your struct at all times. With that knowledge, let's create a new view that flattens the rows we extracted from the lists too:

```
CREATE OR REPLACE VIEW shotsFlattened AS (
    SELECT row.*              ◁──┐  The .* syntax creates one column
    FROM shots                   │  for every top-level field in a struct.
);
```

We can then describe that new view:

```
.mode duckbox
DESCRIBE shotsFlattened;
```

We can see the new schema with individual columns. The output has been slightly truncated for readability:

```
┌─────────────┬─────────────┬─────────┐
│ column_name │ column_type │  null   │
│   varchar   │   varchar   │ varchar │
├─────────────┼─────────────┼─────────┤
│ id          │ BIGINT      │ YES     │
│ minute      │ BIGINT      │ YES     │
│ result      │ VARCHAR     │ YES     │
│ X           │ DOUBLE      │ YES     │
│ Y           │ DOUBLE      │ YES     │
│ xG          │ DOUBLE      │ YES     │
│ player      │ VARCHAR     │ YES     │
│ h_a         │ VARCHAR     │ YES     │
│ player_id   │ BIGINT      │ YES     │
│ situation   │ VARCHAR     │ YES     │
```

season	BIGINT	YES
shotType	VARCHAR	YES
match_id	BIGINT	YES
h_team	VARCHAR	YES
a_team	VARCHAR	YES
h_goals	BIGINT	YES
a_goals	BIGINT	YES
date	TIMESTAMP	YES
player_assisted	VARCHAR	YES
lastAction	VARCHAR	YES

| 20 rows |

We'll conclude our exploration of nested JSON files with a query that finds the teams with the highest number of expected goals in the 2022 season since providing data related to this metric is Understat's mission (https://understat.com):

```
SELECT CASE
        WHEN h_a = 'h' AND result <> 'OwnGoal' THEN h_team
        WHEN h_a = 'a' AND result = 'OwnGoal' THEN h_team
        ELSE a_team
        END AS team,
        round(sum(xg), 2) AS totalXG,
        count(*) FILTER(WHERE result IN ('Goal', 'OwnGoal')) AS goals
FROM shotsFlattened
WHERE season = 2022
GROUP BY ALL
ORDER BY totalXG DESC
LIMIT 10;
```

NOTE *Expected goals* (xG) is a football metric which allows you to evaluate team and player performance. In a low-scoring game, such as football, the final match score does not always provide a clear picture of each team's performance. This is why more and more sports analysts turn to advanced models, like xG, which is a statistical measure of the quality of chances to score a goal created and conceded in a match. Essentially, this is a problem field in which an analytical database like DuckDB can be very useful.

If you follow Premier League football, you won't be surprised to see that the best team in the league, Manchester City, also recorded the highest xG metric in 2022:

team varchar	totalXG double	goals int64
Manchester City	45.66	53
Arsenal	41.2	45
Liverpool	39.96	34
Newcastle United	38.17	33
Brighton	34.2	37
Manchester United	34.03	32

```
| Tottenham         |       33.49 |      40 |
| Brentford         |        31.7 |      32 |
| Fulham            |       30.12 |      32 |
| Leeds             |       27.32 |      26 |
|-------------------+-------------+---------|
| 10 rows           |    3 columns          |
```

5.4   *Translating CSV to Parquet*

A common task in data engineering is converting one data format to another. The initial tools in the space assumed that you'd need to load the entire source dataset into memory before converting it to the target data format. DuckDB lets you set a memory limit such that it will load a limited number of source data rows into memory. This is useful if you're dealing with large datasets or using a machine with limited resources.

In this section, we're going to learn how to convert CSV files to Parquet format. *Parquet* is a commonly used columnar storage file format that was designed for big data processing frameworks, like Apache Spark. Its efficient compression and encoding techniques provide the benefit of reduced storage requirements and improved query performance compared to text-based formats without metadata, like CSV and JSON. This file type also uses predicate and projection pushdown, which enable the execution of selective queries and minimize data transfer—which are especially beneficial in distributed environments. With these mechanisms, you can tell the storage layer to only fetch selected columns or specific segments of data relevant for your query and match conditions, leaving the remaining stored data completely untouched.

From the book's GitHub repository, navigate to the ch05 directory:

```
cd ch05
```

You should see an atp directory that contains a set of files with the prefix atp_rankings_. These files contain data on the rankings of professional tennis players going back to the 1970s. You'll also see a single atp_players.csv file, which contains player metadata.

Depending on your operating system, you can view this directory either in your UI or using a command-line tool, like ls or du. The latter gives you a nice, human-readable size of files to look at:

```
du -h atp/*.csv
```

Regardless of your approach, you should see the following files and approximate sizes:

```
2,1M     atp/atp_players.csv
 20M     atp/atp_rankings_00s.csv
 20M     atp/atp_rankings_10s.csv
3,3M     atp/atp_rankings_20s.csv
412K     atp/atp_rankings_70s.csv
5,7M     atp/atp_rankings_80s.csv
 16M     atp/atp_rankings_90s.csv
2,1M     atp/atp_rankings_current.csv
```

We are essentially looking at *normalized tables*—the players are stored independent of their rankings, as one would do in a relational model. Our Parquet file should contain denormalized data in the end, and we will join the rankings and players together in our pipeline.

None of the most common file browsing programs, such as du, Windows Explorer, and Finder for macOS, can give you direct insight into the files, such as the number of rows or records in each file. This is an important quality for our task of taking the content of all CSV files and converting them to one Parquet file. As a columnar format type, Parquet files group rows together. Finding a good size for the number of rows in a group is important. If the row group size is too small, compression is less effective. A significant portion of the file will be taken up with row group headers, and compression works better over larger blocks. This means the file is going to be larger, and more processing time will be spent reading headers. On the other hand, if the row group size is too large, DuckDB cannot parallelize the reads, so performance may suffer.

Let's start by writing a query that counts the number of records in each of the rankings files. The query is a nice example of how we want to use automatic structure and type inference, while changing some aspects. Therefore, we use the read_csv_auto function, which automatically infers the type of each field in the file, as FROM 'atp/ atp_rankings_*.csv'; would do, but it also allows us to pass in the filename=true flag. This will add a computed column to the result, containing the filename of each CSV file read:

```
SELECT filename, count(*)
FROM read_csv_auto(
  'atp/atp_rankings_*.csv',
   filename=true          ◁──┐  Add the filename of each
)                             │  file to the resulting rows.
GROUP BY ALL
ORDER BY ALL;
```

The individual filenames and the number of rows per file will be printed when running the statement:

filename varchar	count_star() int64
atp/atp_rankings_00s.csv	920907
atp/atp_rankings_10s.csv	915618
atp/atp_rankings_20s.csv	149977
atp/atp_rankings_70s.csv	20726
atp/atp_rankings_80s.csv	284809
atp/atp_rankings_90s.csv	725606
atp/atp_rankings_current.csv	95618

NOTE On some systems, you could use a counting utility, such as wc, using the -l option for counting lines, wc -l atp/atp_rankings_*.csv, but where's the fun in that?

We have just over 3 million records, spread across seven files. A couple of those files have almost 1 million records, and the smallest file has only 20,000. We can safely assume there will be a relatively large row group size for the Parquet file further down the road.

In contrast to CSV files, Parquet files contain a self-describing schema with dedicated data types. Whereas with CSVs, everything is typically a string by default, and each column must be sampled to determine what kind of data is actually inside, Parquet files already contain this information. Parquets only natively store a small number of data types—called *physical data types*. However, they can represent a larger number of types by adding annotations—called *logical types*. For example, Parquet files store dates as numeric values, but additional metadata tells readers they should interpret those numeric values as dates.

To create a valuable Parquet file, we should first examine the CSV file to see if each column we deal with contains the most specific and precise data type. These types will be written into the schema of the target file. Let's explore what the individual records look like by running the following query:

```
SELECT *
FROM 'atp/atp_rankings_*.csv'
LIMIT 5;
```

The output represents the rankings of several players from the first week of January 2000, limited to five records:

ranking_date int64	rank int64	player int64	points int64
20000110	1	101736	4135
20000110	2	102338	2915
20000110	3	101948	2419
20000110	4	103017	2184
20000110	5	102856	2169

The ranking_date column is recognized as a numerical value by DuckDB. Looking closely, we can be quite sure that it actually represents dates, formatted as %Y%m%d. While this looks a bit like an ISO date format, it isn't, and you can do only some operations over dates in this format, such as sort them. Otherwise, dates formatted this way are awkward to use, and you can't pass them as arguments to SQL date manipulation functions. Notably, they won't translate to the proper logical data type in Parquets either. Let's convert that column to a date, using the strptime function. strptime takes two character arguments: the string to be parsed into a date and the format. DuckDB will implicitly cast ranking_date, which is an int64, to a string before being passed to strptime. The result of strptime is then cast to a date, stripping away the time information:

```
SELECT * REPLACE (
cast(strptime(ranking_date::VARCHAR, '%Y%m%d') AS DATE)
    AS ranking_date
)
FROM 'atp/atp_rankings_*.csv'
LIMIT 5;
```

Remember * REPLACE() selects all columns and replaces some of them.

Now the result looks like this, showing the `ranking_date` as a proper date:

ranking_date date	rank int64	player int64	points int64
2000-01-10	1	101736	4135
2000-01-10	2	102338	2915
2000-01-10	3	101948	2419
2000-01-10	4	103017	2184
2000-01-10	5	102856	2169

Only the first column has changed; the others are the same as before.

> **NOTE** We could have used `FROM read_csv_auto('atp/atp_rankings_*.csv', dateformat='%Y%m%d');` to specify that dateformat for all possible columns. This feels like a bold move, as any 8-digit number would fit that format, so we decided to fix this per individual column.

At the moment, we don't know which player each row refers to, but we can work this out by joining the atp_players.csv file. We're also going to fix a problem with the `dob` field in the players CSV file, which is also formatted as a string in the `%Y%m%d` format. We end up with the following query:

```
SELECT * EXCLUDE (
        player,
        wikidata_id,
        name_first,
        name_last, player_id, hand, ioc
    )
        REPLACE (
        cast(strptime(ranking_date::VARCHAR, '%Y%m%d') AS DATE) AS ranking_
    date,
        cast(strptime(dob, '%Y%m%d') AS DATE) AS dob
        ),
        name_first || ' ' || name_last AS name
FROM 'atp/atp_rankings_*.csv' rankings
JOIN (FROM 'atp/atp_players.csv' ) players
  ON players.player_id = rankings.player
ORDER BY ranking_date DESC
LIMIT 5;
```

Exclude some columns for brevity.

Join the atp_players.csv file on the player_id column matching the player column in the rankings CSV files.

If we run this query, we'll see the following results, including the players' names!

ranking_date date	rank int64	points int64	dob date	height int64	name varchar
2022-12-26	1	6820	2003-05-05	185	Carlos Alcaraz
2022-12-26	2	6020	1986-06-03	185	Rafael Nadal
2022-12-26	3	5820	1998-12-22	183	Casper Ruud
2022-12-26	4	5550	1998-08-12	193	Stefanos Tsitsipas
2022-12-26	5	4820	1987-05-22	188	Novak Djokovic

Next, we're going to export the results to a Parquet file. We'd likely run the command to generate our Parquet file as part of a scripted data pipeline, so let's first exit the CLI by typing .exit. The amount of data we're exporting easily fits in memory, but we can restrict the amount of memory DuckDB uses by adjusting the memory_limit setting. The ability to restrict the memory being used is valuable in pipelines with a restricted amount of memory or in a serverless setting. By default, DuckDB will use 80% of all available RAM. After adjusting this setting, we'll use the COPY..TO clause to convert the contents of the CSV files into a single Parquet file; take note that the full statement we developed in this section doesn't include the LIMIT clause anymore. That was useful for our investigation and exploration, but in the end, we want all rows processed. DuckDB allows us to configure the compression algorithm to use when writing Parquet files, and we opted for the SNAPPY codec here over GZIP. While the latter generally achieves a higher compression ratio, the former is optimized for speed—which was our main concern when creating the file. The row group size appears sensible, given the sheer amount of data:

```
duckdb -s "SET memory_limit='100MB';
COPY (
  SELECT * EXCLUDE (player, wikidata_id)
          REPLACE (
            cast(strptime(ranking_date::VARCHAR, '%Y%m%d') AS DATE)
              AS ranking_date,
            cast(strptime(dob, '%Y%m%d') AS DATE) AS dob
          )
  FROM 'atp/atp_rankings_*.csv' rankings
  JOIN (
    FROM 'atp/atp_players.csv'
  ) players ON players.player_id = rankings.player
)
TO 'atp_rankings.parquet'
(FORMAT PARQUET, CODEC 'SNAPPY', ROW_GROUP_SIZE 100000);"
```

The -s flag lets us pass a command, which it will run before exiting. That should only take a few seconds to run, after which we can check the size of the generated Parquet file:

```
du -h *.parquet
```

The output is as follows:

```
36M    atp_rankings.parquet
```

NOTE Try exporting the query output to CSV and JSON formats so that you can see the difference in the file size.

5.5   *Analyzing and querying Parquet files*

Not only are Parquet files used extensively in data processing pipelines, but they can also be a great data source to query from within DuckDB. They are much closer to a database than CSV files or JSON files, as they provide a schema in their metadata. Therefore, it might be the case that you didn't create the atp_rankings.parquet file but received it from someone else. You don't know its structure or content but are tasked to create reports on it. In this section, we'll learn how to retrieve the schema and additional metadata from Parquet files, and we will use the file we just created for the sake of simplicity and adhering to our example.

If we're just interested in the column names and types contained within a Parquet file, we can use the DESCRIBE clause against the Parquet files, like you would with any other supported data source:

```
DESCRIBE FROM 'atp/atp_rankings.parquet';
```

The output of this query is shown in the following snippet. Have a close look at the ranking_date and dob columns—both have a DATE type, indicating that the type coercion we did in the previous section was successful:

column_name varchar	column_type varchar	null varchar	key varchar	default varchar	extra varchar
ranking_date	DATE	YES			
rank	BIGINT	YES			
points	BIGINT	YES			
player_id	BIGINT	YES			
name_first	VARCHAR	YES			
name_last	VARCHAR	YES			
hand	VARCHAR	YES			
dob	DATE	YES			
ioc	VARCHAR	YES			
height	BIGINT	YES			
10 rows					6 columns

All the columns from the previous section are there, and the types seem reasonable.

This schema is enough when you just want to query and analyze the data. Accordingly, you could stop here, treat the file as a table, and apply your SQL knowledge from chapters 3 and 4. If you really did just create the file using DuckDB, you may want to go deeper. Remember, Parquet has only a few physical types—Boolean, numbers of various size, and byte arrays—and needs to convert from those types to something "higher level." When working with huge datasets, numbers may be of special interest—Parquet has int32, int64, and int96 for integers. More vector-based operations can be executed in parallel over smaller, numerical data types. If optimal performance is the end goal, you should try to use the smallest data type possible that can still hold your data.

The `parquet_schema` function can be used to query the internal schema contained within a Parquet file. This is the schema stored as metadata inside the file. It will give us some insight into which columns can use an existing physical Parquet data type as well as those that don't need conversions and those that do. This function returns many fields, so let's first prefix it with `DESCRIBE` to get a list of those fields:

```
DESCRIBE FROM parquet_schema('atp/atp_rankings.parquet');
```

The resulting description of the `parquet_schema` function is as follows:

column_name varchar	column_type varchar	null varchar	key varchar	default varchar	extra varchar
file_name	VARCHAR	YES			
name	VARCHAR	YES			
type	VARCHAR	YES			
type_length	VARCHAR	YES			
repetition_type	VARCHAR	YES			
num_children	BIGINT	YES			
converted_type	VARCHAR	YES			
scale	BIGINT	YES			
precision	BIGINT	YES			
field_id	BIGINT	YES			
logical_type	VARCHAR	YES			
11 rows					6 columns

The most interesting fields, in this case, are the name and types, so let's write a query that returns only those values:

```
FROM parquet_schema('atp/atp_rankings.parquet')
SELECT name, type, converted_type, logical_type;
```

The updated results look like this:

name varchar	type varchar	converted_type varchar	logical_type varchar
duckdb_schema			
ranking_date	INT32	DATE	
rank	INT64	INT_64	
points	INT64	INT_64	
player_id	INT64	INT_64	
name_first	BYTE_ARRAY	UTF8	
name_last	BYTE_ARRAY	UTF8	
hand	BYTE_ARRAY	UTF8	
dob	INT32	DATE	

```
| ioc           | BYTE_ARRAY | UTF8    |         |
| height        | INT64      | INT_64  |         |
|---------------|------------|---------|---------|
| 11 rows                                 4 columns |
```

The `type` field describes the actual type used on disk, which is intended to be as minimal as possible. The `converted_type` and `logical_type` fields contain a description of how the `type` should be interpreted. For example, `ranking_date` is stored as an `INT32` but should be treated as a `DATE` when that field is processed. `converted_type` has been deprecated in Parquet, but as you can see, it is still written to Parquet fields for backward compatibility.

Something that stands out when looking at this metadata is that `rank`, `points`, `player_id`, and `height` are all represented as 64-bit integers. A signed 64-bit integer has a maximum value of 9,223,372,036,854,775,807. It would be surprising if the values for the `points` or `height` fields needed so much space, but we can write a query to check the maximum values being stored:

```
from 'atp/atp_rankings.parquet'
select max(rank), max(points), max(player_id), max(height);
```

We can see those maximum values in the next output:

| max(rank) | max(points) | max(player_id) | max(height) |
int64	int64	int64	int64
2271	16950	211767	211

None of these values are anywhere near the upper bound of even a 32-bit integer, so we could potentially optimize further operations on the data by casting the fields to `INT32` before exporting to Parquet format.

> **NOTE** See if you can work out how to export the data to Parquet format while using `int32` for those fields. In essence, you want to cast the relevant fields, such as `points`. We previously examined the structure of the source CSV files, seeing that the fields are recognized as `int64` or `BIGINT` in DuckDB terms. A cast can be written as `CAST(points AS INTEGER)` or `points::integer`, with `INTEGER` corresponding to Parquet's `int32`. DuckDB supports `TINYINT` (`int8`), `SMALLINT` (`int16`), `INTEGER` (`int32`), `BIGINT` (`int64`), as well as their unsigned variants and a `HUGEINT` (`int128`).

We can also explore the structure of the Parquet file itself by using the `parquet_metadata` function. This function returns one record per row group per column:

```
.mode line
FROM parquet_metadata('atp/atp_rankings.parquet')
LIMIT 1;
```

This function returns many columns, so we're using line mode again to prevent the following from being printed as a tabular result. It shows the column with an ID of 0 in the first row group of the file:

```
            file_name = atp/atp_rankings.parquet
         row_group_id = 0
   row_group_num_rows = 20726
row_group_num_columns = 10
      row_group_bytes = 2374571
            column_id = 0
          file_offset = 0
           num_values = 20726
       path_in_schema = ranking_date
                 type = INT32
            stats_min = 1973-08-27
            stats_max = 1979-12-26
     stats_null_count = 0
  stats_distinct_count =
      stats_min_value = 1973-08-27
      stats_max_value = 1979-12-26
          compression = SNAPPY
            encodings = PLAIN
     index_page_offset =
dictionary_page_offset =
       data_page_offset = 4
  total_compressed_size = 5479
total_uncompressed_size = 82934
```

This record is for the `ranking_date` column in the first row group (`row_group_id = 0`). From looking at `stats_min`, we learn that the smallest value in this row group is August 27th, 1973, and from looking at `stats_max`, we know that the largest value is December 26th, 1979.

DuckDB uses this metadata when executing queries. For example, if you wrote a query that was looking for records where the `ranking_date` was after 1980, it could safely ignore all the values in this row group since it knows that the latest value is in 1979. Parquet is an excellent file format that provides a lot of information for a database engine, allowing it to optimize its queries for you in the best way possible.

5.6   *Querying SQLite and other databases*

Another interesting feature of DuckDB is that we can attach it to other databases and query their contents. One such database is *SQLite,* an embedded OLTP database. We might want to query existing SQLite files from DuckDB if we're writing demanding analytical queries and would like the benefit of DuckDB's query engine.

While the SQL standard partially defines data types and behaviors, there may be many differences in naming and semantics between different vendors' implementations. Attaching foreign databases to DuckDB sometimes means you will have to work around mismatches. Often, the automatic inference works; sometimes, it doesn't. By that token, you may be required to complete the same conversion work as for CSV files—covered in the previous section—when querying foreign stores.

We've downloaded the Kaggle European Soccer Database (https://www.kaggle .com/datasets/hugomathien/soccer), which contains data on over 25,000 European professional football matches, players, and team attributes. It's available as a 300 MB SQLite database, which we provide in a compressed form in the example repository as well. Before you follow the next examples, you must uncompress the database using `unzip` or a Windows program of your choice. Here's how to uncompress it using `unzip`:

```
unzip database.sqlite.zip
```

To query SQLite, we'll need to first install and load the `sqlite` extension:

```
INSTALL sqlite;
LOAD sqlite;
```

Once we've done that, we can attach all the tables to the `fifa` database. The `TYPE` `sqlite` can also be inferred from the file extension:

```
ATTACH 'database.sqlite' AS fifa (TYPE sqlite);
USE fifa;
```

The tables from SQLite are registered as views in DuckDB. We can list them by running the following SQL command (or the `.tables` CLI command):

```
PRAGMA show_tables;
```

This database has several tables:

```
┌───────────────────┐
│       name        │
│      varchar      │
├───────────────────┤
│ Country           │
│ League            │
│ Match             │
│ Player            │
│ Player_Attributes │
│ Team              │
│ Team_Attributes   │
│ sqlite_sequence   │
└───────────────────┘
```

It looks like everything has been attached successfully. Let's see if we can query the `Player` view:

```
FROM Player
LIMIT 5;
```

At the time of writing, we unexpectedly got the following error:

```
Error: Invalid Error: Mismatch Type Error: Invalid type in column "height":
⇒column was declared as integer, found "182.88" of type "float" instead.
```

This may be a bug in the current DuckDB version (0.10), which may be fixed in the future. However, it is actually quite an interesting problem. SQLite is a *weakly typed database system*, which means types aren't enforced when storing data. DuckDB, on the other hand, is a *strongly typed database system* and requires all columns to have defined types. DuckDB remains faithful to SQLite's type system, which hasn't quite worked in this case—the `height` column in SQLite was defined as an `INT`, even though it contains some `float` values.

Let's inspect the `Player` view with `DESCRIBE Player;`, which returns the type of each field, as shown in the next output. We can see that `height` is a `BIGINT`, even though we saw from the previous query that it contains `float` values. It looks like we could have a problem with the `weight` field as well, although perhaps we've been lucky that there aren't any decimal values in that field:

column_name varchar	column_type varchar	null varchar
id	BIGINT	YES
player_api_id	BIGINT	YES
player_name	VARCHAR	YES
player_fifa_api_id	BIGINT	YES
birthday	VARCHAR	YES
height	BIGINT	YES
weight	BIGINT	YES

To fix this, we're going to manually create the `Player` view, but first, we'll need to detach the SQLite database:

```
USE memory;       ⟵  First, we must ensure we use a
DETACH fifa;          different database, as we cannot
                      detach the database we are using.
```

Next, we're going to have all SQLite columns converted into the `VARCHAR` type so that we don't run into any conversion errors:

```
SET GLOBAL sqlite_all_varchar=true;
```

We can now use the `sqlite_scan` command to get all the records from the `Player` table. We'll then manually cast each field to the correct type and redefine the `Player` view accordingly:

```
USE main;
CREATE OR REPLACE VIEW Player AS
FROM sqlite_scan('database.sqlite', 'Player')
SELECT * REPLACE (
  id :: BIGINT AS id,
  player_api_id :: BIGINT AS player_api_id,
  player_fifa_api_id :: BIGINT AS player_fifa_api_id,
  birthday :: DATE AS birthday,
```

```
  height :: FLOAT AS height,
  weight :: FLOAT AS weight
);
```

We can then query the `Player` view as we tried to do earlier:

```
FROM Player SELECT * EXCLUDE player_fifa_api_id
LIMIT 5;
```
◁─┐ **Exclude the player_fifa_api_id**
   field for brevity.

And this time it works! The IDs are proper `int64` columns:

id int64	player_api_id int64	player_name varchar	birthday date	height float	weight float
1	505942	Aaron Appindangye	1992-02-29	182.88	187.0
2	155782	Aaron Cresswell	1989-12-15	170.18	146.0
3	162549	Aaron Doran	1991-05-13	170.18	163.0
4	30572	Aaron Galindo	1982-05-08	182.88	198.0
5	23780	Aaron Hughes	1979-11-08	182.88	154.0

So far, so good. Now let's set the `sqlite_all_varchar` back to false and manually create the other views:

```
SET GLOBAL sqlite_all_varchar=false;

CREATE OR REPLACE VIEW Player_Attributes AS
FROM sqlite_scan('database.sqlite', 'Player_Attributes');

CREATE OR REPLACE VIEW Country AS
FROM sqlite_scan('database.sqlite', 'Country');

CREATE OR REPLACE VIEW League AS
FROM sqlite_scan('database.sqlite', 'League');

CREATE OR REPLACE VIEW Match AS
FROM sqlite_scan('database.sqlite', 'Match');

CREATE OR REPLACE VIEW Team AS
FROM sqlite_scan('database.sqlite', 'Team');

CREATE OR REPLACE VIEW Team_Attributes AS
FROM sqlite_scan('database.sqlite', 'Team_Attributes');
```

We could now, for example, write a query to find the top players, based on the most recent rankings:

```
SELECT player_name, arg_max(overall_rating, date) AS overall_rating
FROM Player
JOIN Player_Attributes PA ON PA.player_api_id = Player.player_api_id
WHERE overall_rating is not null
GROUP BY ALL
ORDER BY overall_rating DESC, player_name
LIMIT 10;
```

This query joins together two SQLite tables before finding the highest `overall_rating` for each player. The top 10 players are as follows:

```
┌─────────────────────┬────────────────┐
│    player_name      │ overall_rating │
│      varchar        │     int64      │
├─────────────────────┼────────────────┤
│ Lionel Messi        │             94 │
│ Cristiano Ronaldo   │             93 │
│ Luis Suarez         │             90 │
│ Manuel Neuer        │             90 │
│ Neymar              │             90 │
│ Arjen Robben        │             89 │
│ Zlatan Ibrahimovic  │             89 │
│ Andres Iniesta      │             88 │
│ Eden Hazard         │             88 │
│ Mesut Oezil         │             88 │
├─────────────────────┼────────────────┤
│ 10 rows             │      2 columns │
└─────────────────────┴────────────────┘
```

That all looks like it's working well, and we've successfully queried SQLite from DuckDB.

> **NOTE** DuckDB also has a `postgres` extension for querying Postgres databases. The installation is similar to the SQLite extension—just run `INSTALL postgres; LOAD postgres;` in your DuckDB session. After that, you must use the `ATTACH` command to connect to the Postgres database and provide the connection information for the instance.
>
> See the following DuckDB documentation topic for more information on the extension: https://duckdb.org/docs/extensions/postgres.html. Querying any Postgres table will be fully opaque, and all SQL features DuckDB offers will work.

5.7   *Working with Excel files*

DuckDB can read and write Excel files stored as Microsoft Office Open XML (OOXML; file extension .xlsx). This format has been used by Microsoft Office since 2007, and other applications, including LibreOffice and Google Sheets, support it as well. It requires the spatial extension to be installed in DuckDB. While this extension is primarily used to deal with spatial data, its underlying machinery supports OOXML too. The following listing shows how to install it inside the DuckDB CLI.

Listing 5.2 Installing the spatial extension

```
INSTALL spatial;
LOAD spatial;
```

The `INSTALL` statement is required only once: for the `LOAD` statement in each session in which you want to use the extension. To read Excel files, you need to use the st_read function. We took a subset of the CSV data we dealt with in section 5.4 and provided it as an Excel file in the example repository. The following statement reads the first sheet from that file:

```
SELECT ranking_date, rank, name_last
FROM st_read('atp_rankings.xlsx')
ORDER BY ranking_date limit 5;
```

The machinery for detecting types is not directly implemented in DuckDB but rather in the extension being used; it is less optimized than the type detection for CSV and JSON files. In the result of the preceding query, we notice that date columns can be read correctly, but for the rank, it picks a generic double, whereas in reality, it should be an integer:

ranking_date date	rank double	name_last varchar
1973-08-27	129.0	Gonzalez
1973-08-27	114.0	Ulrich
1973-08-27	6.0	Rosewall
1973-08-27	19.0	Emerson
1973-08-27	82.0	Phillips Moore

Excel files often contains formulas. These will be read as the raw formula string by default and will not be evaluated. Some authoring tools store the last value with the formula—in which case, that value can be read.

There is also limited support for writing Excel files. Some datatypes, such as dates and timestamps, are not supported and must be cast to a string or formatted as a string, as we do in the following statement. The statement takes about a minute to run on the author's machine and produces a hefty 299 MB Excel file (the Parquet file is just about 36 MB in size):

```
COPY (
  SELECT * EXCLUDE (player, wikidata_id)
          REPLACE (
            strftime(strptime(ranking_date, '%Y%m%d'), '%Y-%m-%d')
              AS ranking_date,
            strftime(strptime(dob, '%Y%m%d'), '%Y-%m-%d') AS dob
          )
  FROM 'atp/atp_rankings_*.csv' rankings
  JOIN (
    FROM 'atp/atp_players.csv'
  ) players ON players.player_id = rankings.player
  ORDER BY ranking_date ASC
)
TO 'atp_rankings_full.xlsx' WITH (FORMAT GDAL, DRIVER 'xlsx');
```

This is essentially the same statement that we used to create one Parquet file from our set of CSV files representing ATP rankings. If the target file already exists,

`GDAL Error (1): File extension should be XLSX` will be printed as an error message, which is a bit misleading and may be fixed in future versions of the extension.

In general, we recommend exporting Excel files to CSV before processing them with DuckDB, if that's possible for you. The general integration with DuckDB makes it easier to work with.

Summary

- You can use DuckDB's powerful query language and engine to process data, whether stored in files or flowing through a pipeline, even if you don't use its database storage functionality.
- DuckDB's query engine can be used with many different sources, such as files in different formats or the stores of other databases. DuckDB does a great job of inferring the right content and data types for JSON, CSV, and Parquet files.
- DuckDB's JSON processing capabilities allow you to query and normalize even complex, denormalized JSON documents so that they feel like a natural source of tabular data in any query.
- Data transformation with DuckDB—for example, filtering, type conversion, flattening, or enriching by joining other sources—doesn't require persistence in DuckDB.
- The vector-based DuckDB query engine deals with some workloads and queries so efficiently that using it with an external database store offers performance advantages without losing any capabilities of the external database and without requiring two different datasets to be kept in synchronization.
- Views are a helpful tool to encapsulate necessary transformation on external data types.

6

Integrating with the Python ecosystem

This chapter covers

- The differences between DuckDB's implementation of Python DB-API 2.0 and the DuckDB relational API
- Ingesting data from pandas DataFrames, Apache Arrow tables, and more via the Python API
- Querying pandas DataFrames with DuckDB methods
- Exporting data to various DataFrames formats and Apache Arrow Tables
- Using DuckDB's relational API to compose queries

Up until now, we've consistently used the DuckDB CLI to manage and execute our queries. This tool is highly effective for on-the-spot analysis and for CLI-based pipelines. Many data workflows, however, involve Python and its ecosystem to a large extent. For example, pandas DataFrames can't be ignored. In this chapter, we will learn that DuckDB's Python API goes way beyond just implementing the Python DB-API. DuckDB's Python API will let you not only use the embedded database in

123

your Python process but also query Python objects like you would tables. At the same time, you can easily convert results from queries to DataFrames. In this chapter, we focus on integrations that are directly bundled with the DuckDB Python package.

> **NOTE**   We will not cover SQLAlchemy (https://www.sqlalchemy.org), a popular Python SQL tool kit. SQLAlchemy abstracts away over many different databases and brings a full suite of well-known enterprise-level persistence patterns to Python, which are just beyond the scope of this book. You can get a driver for SQLAlchemy under the name `duckdb_engine` (https://pypi.org/project/duckdb_engine/), which supports almost all of SQLAlchemy features.

6.1   Getting started

Let's get started by installing the DuckDB Python package and learning which dependencies to import into your programs first. Next, we discuss the different options to either acquire an in-memory DuckDB connection or open a database file. Getting the idea of this is important for this chapter but also for the following ones, as we will learn about more tools in the Python ecosystem that interact with DuckDB.

6.1.1   Installing the Python package

The DuckDB Python package is published to PiPI, and we can install it by running the following command:

```
pip install duckdb
```

Once you've done that, open up a Python command prompt, and import the following libraries:

```
import duckdb
```

Next, run the following command to return the version of DuckDB:

```
duckdb.__version__
```

You should see an output similar to the following, although the exact version you see may be different:

```
'0.10.0'
```

6.1.2   Opening up a database connection

One of the questions that often comes to mind when using a database from any programming environment is, *How do I open a connection?* In the case of DuckDB, the answer is simple: *You don't have to because as an embedded database, it is already running inside your Python process.* Once you have installed the package, as shown in the preceding code snippets, you can go ahead and use `duckdb` in your Python interpreter to interact with an in-memory database. `sql` is the entry point into DuckDB's relational Python API. The following example uses the `show` method of the object returned to print the result of the statement:

```
result = duckdb.sql('SELECT 42')                          Defines an object but does
result.show()         ◄─┐                                 not execute a query yet
                        │ Executes the query
                        │ and prints the result
```

The result will be printed in a tabular fashion, similar to what the DuckDB CLI would output.

Please take note that we ran the SQL statement on the `duckdb` object we imported into our program. We didn't acquire or use a dedicated connection object. The `duckdb` object provided us with a default, in-memory connection. Of course, you can use a dedicated connection too:

- *To start an in-memory database*—`con = duckdb.connect(database=':memory:')`
- *To use a database file*—`con = duckdb.connect('my-db.duckdb')`
- *To use a database file and control whether it's read-only or not*—`con = duckdb.connect(database='my-db.duckdb', read_only=True)`

The default connection can be acquired through both `duckdb.default_connection` and `duckdb.connect(database=':default:')`, assuming you have the database name in a parameter. The important takeaway here is that without any further configuration, DuckDB will use an in-memory database that is stored globally inside the Python module.

Both the global `duckdb` and the dedicated connection object offer various methods to interact with a database. `sql()` will trigger the relational API of DuckDB as shown, and `execute()` will use the Python DB-API 2.0.

The preceding example rewritten using the DB-API looks similar but behaves like a traditional database API. It will execute the statement immediately and return an object that allows fetching one or all resulting rows:

```
result = duckdb.execute('SELECT 42')                     Executes the query and
row = result.fetchone()    ◄─┐                            returns a connection object
print(row)       ◄─┐         │ Fetches one row
                   │ Prints  │ from the connection
                   │ that row
```

There are some use cases for the DB-API, such as the ability to use prepared statements and queries that utilize named parameters, but we will focus on the relational API in this chapter. We think the latter is a unique approach to querying data, blurring the lines between relational databases and queryable objects in memory, paving the way for new, interesting solutions. The Python DB-API will appear again when we discuss querying via SQL later in this chapter.

6.2   Using the relational API

While we managed to avoid diving too deep into the mathematical concept of a relation in chapters 3 and 4, there's no way around covering some relational concepts now. We already learned that you can not only query tables but views and functions too. You can also query the result of another query. Tables, views, projections, and functions that act as tables are all relations. Relations are essentially a generalized version of tables and are composed of tuples and attributes instead of rows and columns. In a relational database, a *tuple* is defined as a list of named—and ordered—attributes. Each tuple of a relation corresponds to one record, and each attribute of a tuple corresponds to a column. Think of relations as more or less equivalent to a table.

In essence, it boils down to the fact that relations pass the duck tests—*If it looks like a duck, swims like a duck, and quacks like a duck, then it probably is a duck.* If it looks like a table, you can query it. While working in a database and running queries, this usually feels quite natural, and you don't expect it any other way. The DuckDB Python package brings this concept into Python itself and lets you query different objects as though they would be tables or views in a database. The line between having a persistent store with a relational schema and objects that just happen to behave like relations is quite blurry here.

6.2.1   *Ingesting CSV data with the Python API*

Similar to chapter 3, we have a bit of a hen-and-egg problem at hand when demonstrating different ways of querying a database: without data, there's nothing to query. So let's start again with ingesting data. We won't, however, create a relational schema for the data but instead, just use the provided objects as relations.

In this section, we're going to revisit the Populations CSV file introduced in chapter 2. As before, our approach will involve the use of the httpfs extension. However, this time around, we are not using the DuckDB SQL function `read_csv` for file processing but the function with the same name from the Python API's `read_csv`.

> **NOTE**   In the example, we are using `read_csv`, as we would like to reuse the CSV file that we prepared in chapter 2, containing countries and their relevant statistics. The same concepts and techniques apply as well to `read_parquet` and `read_json`; these functions exist both as SQL functions and as Python functions for DuckDB.

While executing SQL commands in DuckDB is powerful, using the `read_csv` function directly through the Python API offers seamless integration with Python-based workflows. This method provides a "pythonic" approach to data manipulation, bridging the gap between SQL databases and Python data structures, making it a preferred choice for Python-based projects. The object being returned can be treated as a queryable relation right from within your Python code. In the code that follows, we will use the default in-memory database, but you can easily change the connection, as shown previously.

Listing 6.1   Querying a CSV file

```
import duckdb

con = duckdb.connect(database=':memory:')

con.execute("INSTALL httpfs")
con.execute("LOAD httpfs")
```

Install the httpfs extension.
You only need to do this once.

Load the httpfs extension. You need to do
this each time you initialize a new database.

```
population = \
  con.read_csv("https://bit.ly/3KoiZR0")        ◁─┐ Read the
                                                   │ CSV files.
```

This won't print any data, but we get an object back, which we did assign to
`population`. We can check its type using Python's `type` function, which returns the
Python type of the `population` variable:

```
type(population)
```

The result is as follows:

```
<class 'duckdb.DuckDBPyRelation'>
```

`DuckDBPyRelation` is the centerpiece of DuckDB's relational API. It's a queryable relation and an API.

 If you want to query it, you can just use the `execute` method the same way you
would execute any other query from within Python against DuckDB. `execute` gives
you a new Python DB connection object, from which you can fetch the result, either
via `fetchone` until there are no more results, or via `fetchall`, like in the following
example.:

```
con.execute("SELECT * from population limit 2").fetchall()
```

`fetchall` will return the result as a list of two unformatted and difficult-to-read
Python tuples, so we won't reproduce it here. The relational API, however, is much
more and can be used as an alternative to writing SQL statements. It is essentially a fluent API, which allows incremental construction of queries. It consists of `DuckDB-
PyRelation` nodes and relations that can be seen as symbolic representations of SQL
queries. It supports the reuse of those nodes, as well as set operations, filters, projections, and aggregations. None of the objects involved hold any data, and no query is
executed until a trigger method, such as explicit fetch, showing, or similar is called.

 Let's count the number of records in our relational object. Unsurprisingly, the
builder method to count records is called `count`. The result of this method is a relational
object again. The actual query will not execute yet. We use the `show` method in the example to trigger the execution, but we could also just print the resulting object via `print`:

```
(population
  .count("*")          ◁─┐ This is the equivalent of
  .show()                │ SQL's SELECT count(*).
)
```

Both the `show` method and the implicit string representation will give us a nice rendering of the result, as shown here:

```
┌──────────────┐
│ count_star() │
│    int64     │
├──────────────┤
│          227 │
└──────────────┘
```

If you have a slow internet connection, you may notice that it takes quite a long time to return the result. This is because the CSV file is being downloaded every time we call the `show` function, which isn't ideal! We can fix this problem by persisting a DuckDB table, using the `to_table` function. This function will perform a Create Table as Select statement behind the scenes on your behalf, creating a table named `population`, selecting from the relational object:

```
population.to_table("population")
```

We now have a table called `population`, which we can access using the `table` function, like this:

```
population_table = con.table("population")
```

Bear in mind that while the `population` object created in listing 6.1 will always download and read the CSV anew, the table, once created, represents a snapshot of the data that was available at that point in time. This isn't changed by the fact that you access that table now through the relational API; it is not a view that would be recomputed when accessed.

> **NOTE** If you call `type(population_table)`, you will notice that it too is a `DuckDBPyRelation`, and it thus has the same traits and capabilities as before.

We can then rerun the code to count the number of countries, and this time, the results will be displayed instantly:

```
population_table.count("*").show()
```

With the data now being held in a table in memory, we are going to focus on composing queries with the relational API.

6.2.2   Composing queries

Up to this point, we've primarily explored how to count records in a relation using the DuckDB API. However, this is just a glimpse into its capabilities. The API offers a suite of functions for the `DuckDBPyRelation` to enhance data manipulation:

- `filter`—Only include records that satisfy a provided predicate function.
- `project`—Only return the specified columns.
- `limit`—Return the first n records.
- `aggregate`—Apply the provided aggregation expressions.
- `order`—Sort the records by the provided columns.

Using the relational API as a builder solves some problems people might run into when using plain SQL; there are many cases in which queries are generated or are based on user input. While SQL allows for parameters in queries representing values, it does not allow table or column names to be parameterized, so people often use some kind of string concatenation for building queries that select from dynamic tables. The relational API offers an advantage for creating these queries in a programmatic fashion; instead of messing with string concatenation, you can call dedicated methods that are context aware. Thus, the likelihood of creating an invalid query or a query that is prone to SQL injection decreases, and the code will be more readable and composable.

Let's have a look at what we can do if we combine a few of these functions. We'll start by finding out which countries have a population of over 10,000,000 people, returning the country and population for the first five countries. We can do this by using the `filter`, `project`, and `limit` functions. We only want to include the first five rows that have a `Population` greater than 10,000,000, and we are only interested in the country name and the actual population:

```
(population_table
  .filter('Population > 10000000')      ◁──┐  This corresponds to the filter
  .project("Country, Population")       ◁──┐  inside the WHERE clause.
  .limit(5)
  .show()                                      This will eventually turn into a SELECT
)                                              Country, Population, which is called a
                                               projection in relational terms.
```

When using the relational API, the order of the operations won't affect the performance, as no results will be materialized in between. This is different than the pandas integration we are going to discuss in the following text. When a result set gets transformed to a pandas DataFrame, that DataFrame will have pandas characteristics, which usually means values will be computed eagerly. The output of running the preceding query is as follows:

Country	Population
varchar	int64
Afghanistan	31056997
Algeria	32930091
Angola	12127071
Argentina	39921833
Australia	20264082

In our exploration, it's crucial to note that the query does not get executed until the `show` function is invoked. The object returned by the methods is still the same query builder. For example, you could still call `offset` after `limit` to specify the number of rows to skip. Now let's say we want to use another query that operates only on populations with more than 10 million people. A simple approach would involve copying the code and changing the filter criteria. However, this method lacks the elegance and efficiency inherent in the relational API of DuckDB. Instead of copy–pasting, we'll create a variable for the `filter` part of the query and create another relational object named `over_10m`. This relational object will be reused with several different queries, providing a well-defined filter that can be seamlessly and coherently reused:

```
over_10m = population_table.filter('Population > 10000000')
```

We could then find the average population of the medium to large-sized continents and regions, ordered by the largest population, using the `aggregate` and `order` functions. The relation `over_10m` just acts like a table, a view, or a common table expression would act. In the following example, we use the `aggregate` function too. This function takes in one expression, which can be made up of one or many calls to any SQL aggregate as well as zero or more columns not being part of an aggregate. DuckDB will automatically group by these columns, thus using `Region` as the grouping key while computing the average population:

```
(over_10m
  .aggregate("Region, CAST(avg(Population) AS int) as pop")
  .order("pop DESC")
)
```

Region varchar	pop int32
ASIA (EX. NEAR EAST)	192779730
NORTHERN AMERICA	165771574
LATIN AMER. & CARIB	48643375
C.W. OF IND. STATES	48487549
WESTERN EUROPE	38955933
NORTHERN AFRICA	38808343
NEAR EAST	32910924
SUB-SAHARAN AFRICA	30941436
EASTERN EUROPE	23691959
OCEANIA	20264082
10 rows	2 columns

The result underscores the demographic heft of ASIA (EX. NEAR EAST) and NORTHERN AMERICA, with both regions significantly surpassing others in their average population.

Alternatively, we might be interested in the economic standing of these populous nations. By applying an additional `filter` clause to the `over_10m` relation, we zero in on countries with a GDP per capita greater than $10,000:

```
(over_10m
  .filter('"GDP ($ per capita)" > 10000')
  .count("*")
)
```

The result reveals that 20 countries from our previously filtered set meet this economic benchmark, highlighting a subset of nations that are not only populous but also have a relatively higher economic output per individual. In the previous two examples, we have been able to use the `over_10m` relation unchanged to drive an aggregate over regions and extended by an additional filter; in both cases, we could easily reuse the original definition:

```
┌─────────────────┐
│ count_star()    │
│   int64         │
├─────────────────┤
│            20   │
└─────────────────┘
```

When working with databases, there are often scenarios where interactions between multiple relations are required. The relational API provides a suite of functions specifically designed for such multi-relation operations:

- except_—Returns all rows in the first relation that aren't in the second
- intersect—Returns all rows that appear in both relations
- join—Joins the relations on the provided keys or conditions
- union—Combines relations, returning all rows in the first relation followed by all rows in the second relation

To illustrate the capabilities of the except_ function in the relational API, consider the following scenario: you have been assigned the task of analyzing countries with populations under 10 million. The following query achieves this by excluding countries in the over_10m relation, and then it further aggregates the results by region, calculating both the average population and the number of countries in each:

```
(population_table
   .except_(over_10m)          ◁─┐  Include records that aren't
   .aggregate("""                 │  in the over_10m relation.
   Region,
   CAST(avg(population) AS int) AS population,
   count(*)
   """)            ◁─┐  Grouping by region, compute
)                    │  the average population, and
                     │  count the number of records.
```

Region varchar	population int32	count_star() int64
EASTERN EUROPE	5426538	9
OCEANIA	643379	20
WESTERN EUROPE	2407190	19
LATIN AMER. & CARIB	2154024	35
C.W. OF IND. STATES	5377686	7
NEAR EAST	2773978	11
SUB-SAHARAN AFRICA	3322228	30
NORTHERN AMERICA	43053	3
ASIA (EX. NEAR EAST)	2796374	9
BALTICS	2394991	3
NORTHERN AFRICA	3086881	2
11 rows		3 columns

The resulting table provides a breakdown by region, showcasing the average population and number of countries with fewer than 10 million inhabitants. Notably, EASTERN EUROPE stands out, with an average population of approximately 5.4 million across 9 countries, while OCEANIA has a smaller average population but encompasses 20 countries. This data offers a nuanced view of regions with smaller countries in terms of population.

Exploring further, let's consider a more specific subset of countries: those located in Eastern Europe with populations exceeding 10 million. To achieve this, we initiate by filtering out countries within the region of EASTERN EUROPE. Take note that we are using the POSIX-style operator ~ for filtering with a regular expression—in this case, an expression that finds all records with a region that contains EASTERN EUROPE:

```
eastern_europe = population_table \
  .filter("Region ~ '.*EASTERN EUROPE.*'")
```

Pattern matching

DuckDB supports four ways of pattern matching:

1 LIKE testing whether a string matches a pattern as a whole, allowing % and _ as wildcards
2 SIMILAR TO testing whether a string matches a regular expression as a whole
3 GLOB testing whether a string matches a GLOB pattern, which is useful when searching for filenames that follow a specific pattern
4 Generally applicable regular expression via functions

There are shorthands for the SQL operators: ~~ for LIKE, ~ for SIMILAR TO, and ~ for GLOB.

Having established the eastern_europe relation, the next step involves pinpointing those countries that intersect with our previously defined over_10m relation:

```
(eastern_europe
  .intersect(over_10m)        ⟵──── Keep relations that are both in
  .project("Country, Population")  ⟵── Eastern Europe and have a
)                                       population of more than 10 million.

                                    Return only the Country and
                                    Population fields.
```

```
|     Country      | Population |
|     varchar      |   int64    |
|------------------|------------|
| Czech Republic   |  10235455  |
| Poland           |  38536869  |
| Romania          |  22303552  |
```

The output table distinctly lists three countries from Eastern Europe—Czech Republic, Poland, and Romania—each with a population that breaches the 10 million mark.

This refined analysis underscores the power of DuckDB's relational API in catering to specific data requirements.

6.2.3 SQL querying

Relational objects can be treated with the same flexibility as SQL tables. This capability allows for a fluid transition between Python-based data operations and SQL-like querying. Taking a practical example into consideration, let's say our objective is to ascertain the count of medium- to large-sized nations, where the GDP per capita surpasses $10,000. The process for achieving this is illustrated as follows:

```
con.sql("""                          We're referencing over_10m,
SELECT count(*)                       which is a variable, but it's
FROM over_10m          ◁──┘           treated like a table in the query.
WHERE "GDP ($ per capita)" > 10000
""")
```

While the relational API of DuckDB offers a vast array of functionalities, there are certain scenarios, particularly those involving parameterized queries, where its innate capabilities might feel restrictive.

> **NOTE** A *parameterized query* uses placeholders in the statement text. The statement text and the actual values for the placeholders—the parameters—are passed independently to the engine. Using parameters has a couple of advantages: user input, for example, should always be passed as a parameter and never put into the statement text directly. If you just concatenate string fragments of a statement with user input, you have a high risk of so-called *SQL injection attacks,* in which a specially crafted text alters the semantics of your query. When passed as parameters to the query engine, the engine will treat input in such a way that a string will never mess up a query. Additionally, a parameterized statement may need to be parsed only once by the query engine, as its content is constant and only parameters change.

Parameterized queries allow for dynamic input, making the queries both reusable and secure by mitigating SQL injection risks. To bridge this gap in the relational API, DuckDB provides the `execute` function, adhering to the Python DB-API 2.0. This function not only facilitates the use of parameterized queries but also yields a connection object. The latter adheres to the Python Database API Specification v2.0 and exposes all the methods you expect; once the query execution is done, extracting the results can be approached in various ways. Commonly used methods in the Python DB-API 2.0 are `fetchall` and `fetchone`. The former retrieves all rows, and the latter retrieves the values of the first record in the result set. We use `fetchone` here, as the `count` aggregate used in the query returns only one row, and we can spare ourselves the effort of iterating over a list of rows:

```
con.execute("""
SELECT count(*)
FROM over_10m
```

```
WHERE "GDP ($ per capita)" > $gdp          ◁─────────┐   The GDP per capita filter is set
""", {                                               │   based on the $gdp parameter.
    "gdp":10000        ◁─────┐   Defines the parameters
}).fetchone()           ◁────┤   for the query
                             │
      Fetches the results as a tuple
   containing the first record's values
```

The result, `(20,)`, indicates that 20 countries meet the criteria. The more relevant fact is this: the query we passed to `execute` does use named parameters, and it looks like any other prepared statement. It does, however, query a relational object, `over_10m`, not an actual table. The relational object might have been built in such a way that it used parameters as well, either for the columns that should be projected or for the underlying tables to be queried. Thus, you avoid using string concatenation in all cases—the relational API and the standard DB-API complement each other here. The DB-API can only execute well-formed SQL, which does not allow tables and columns to be parameterized. The relational API allows it, and the relational objects can then be queried like any other table.

6.3   *Querying pandas DataFrames*

DuckDB's popularity in the data ecosystem is largely attributed to its robust query engine. Not limited to just file-based operations, this engine seamlessly integrates with in-memory data structures from various data infrastructure tools. One notable tool in this domain is *pandas*, a well-established open source data analysis library widely used in the data community. The combination of DuckDB and pandas allows for powerful data operations, bridging the capabilities of a database engine with the flexibility of a data manipulation library. In this section, we'll explore how to employ DuckDB to query pandas DataFrames. To kick things off, we need to ensure pandas is installed in our environment:

```
pip install pandas
```

Next, import the pandas and DuckDB libraries:

```
import duckdb
import pandas as pd
```

With the libraries in place, we proceed to create a pandas DataFrame that holds information about your authors:

```
people = pd.DataFrame({
    "name": ["Michael Hunger", "Michael Simons", "Mark Needham"],
    "country": ["Germany", "Germany", "Great Britain"]
})
```

The DataFrame `people` now contains data about three authors and the countries they live in. One of the salient features of DuckDB is its ability to interact directly with pandas DataFrames; they are treated just like any relation we've dealt with before. This means we can run SQL-like queries on `people`, just as we would a regular database table:

```
duckdb.sql("""
SELECT *
FROM people
WHERE country = 'Germany'
""")
```

```
|      name      |  country  |
|     varchar    |  varchar  |
|----------------|-----------|
| Michael Hunger |  Germany  |
| Michael Simons |  Germany  |
```

The result of the query gives us two authors living in the country `country`. This example illustrates the seamless integration and querying capabilities of DuckDB inside the Python ecosystem; it does not matter whether the relation has been created as a table, sourced from a file, or represented by a pandas DataFrame.

To query for people not living in Germany, we could use a parameterized query as in this example. Take note that we don't use `execute.fetchall` or `execute.fetchone` but `fetchdf`. This returns the result as a DataFrame instead of a Python DB-API cursor. Whether you would use a cursor to iterate the rows or a DataFrame depends on your use case—the cursor is more lightweight, while the DataFrame integrates much more efficiently in further analysis with pandas. DuckDB will take care of the dull work, creating a DataFrame from a result set for you:

```
params = {"country": "Germany"}
duckdb.execute("""
SELECT *
FROM people
WHERE country <> $country
""", params).fetchdf()

name    country
0  Mark   Great Britain
```

If the relational API suits your needs better, you can query the DataFrame as such:

```
(duckdb.sql("FROM people")        ◁──┐  Creates a new relational
  .filter("country <> 'Germany'")     │  object from the DataFrame
  .show()
)
```

Extending this capability, DuckDB also facilitates querying other in-memory data structures, like Polars DataFrames and PyArrow tables. The mechanics are akin to what we've seen with pandas. Detailed examples and implementations for these data structures can be found in the book's accompanying GitHub repository.

NOTE   The SQLAlchemy driver `duckdb_engine` supports querying DataFrames as well. You can register them on an instance of the driver (see https://mng.bz/EZpj).

6.4   *User-defined functions*

As data practitioners, we often encounter scenarios where pre-existing database functions might not cater to our specific needs. Recognizing this, DuckDB has a powerful feature: the ability to create *user-defined functions* (UDFs) within its Python package. The beauty of UDFs lies in their ability to extend the SQL language's native capabilities. With UDFs, users can define their own custom functions, benefitting from the vast ecosystem of Python libraries. Whether it's complex data manipulations, mathematical calculations, or even integrations with external tools and APIs, the possibilities become virtually limitless. In practical terms, this means that if you've ever wished for a specific function while writing an SQL query in DuckDB, you can now create it using Python and then subsequently invoke it within your SQL code.

Data ingestion, while a fundamental step in any data analysis pipeline, often comes with its own set of challenges. Raw data can be messy, and it's not uncommon to encounter errors that need rectification before any meaningful analysis can be conducted. In our current scenario, the CSV file ingested at the beginning of this chapter has presented an anomaly that needs addressing.

A discernible problem lies in the `Region` field of our dataset. This field seems to be padded with excessive space characters, making data processing and analysis cumbersome. To visualize the extent of this problem, consider the following query, which retrieves unique values of the `Region` field and computes the total character length for each distinct `Region`:

```
con.sql("""
select DISTINCT Region, length(Region) AS numChars     ⟵  Returns the region and
from population                                            number of characters
""")
```

From the following table, we can see that there are lots of trailing spaces, which is confirmed by the `numChars` column:

Region varchar	numChars int64
LATIN AMER. & CARIB	23
ASIA (EX. NEAR EAST)	29
EASTERN EUROPE	35
WESTERN EUROPE	35
NEAR EAST	35
C.W. OF IND. STATES	20
SUB-SAHARAN AFRICA	35
OCEANIA	35
NORTHERN AFRICA	35
BALTICS	35
NORTHERN AMERICA	35
11 rows	2 columns

For instance, while BALTICS comprises just 7 characters, its total length, including trailing spaces, is 35 characters. Of course, DuckDB has a built-in SQL function trim, but we are going to build our own version as an easy example that allows us to put the focus on how to define a UDF, instead of distracting with implementation details:

```
                        Defines a Python function
                          with type annotations
def remove_spaces(field:str) -> str:    ◄─┘
    if field:                       ◄──────────    Checks that the
        return field.lstrip().rstrip()  ◄─┐       field isn't null
    else:                                 └── Strips spaces from the
        return field                          beginning and end of the value
```

The function, aptly named remove_spaces, is designed to trim spaces from both the beginning and the end of the given string. Notice the type annotations: they signify that the function expects a string input and will also return a string.

Once our function is defined, we need to register it with DuckDB:

```
con.create_function('remove_spaces', remove_spaces)
```

To confirm its registration, you can query the duckdb_functions SQL function:

```
con.sql("""
SELECT function_name, function_type, parameters, parameter_types, return_type
from duckdb_functions()
where function_name = 'remove_spaces'
""")
```

The outcome is a table that provides meta-information about our function:

function_name varchar	function_type varchar	parameters varchar[]	parameter_types varchar[]	return_type varchar
remove_spaces	scalar	[col0]	[VARCHAR]	VARCHAR

You can call this function now in any SQL statement issued on the connection in which you defined the function:

```
con.sql("select length(remove_spaces(' foo '))")
```

We wrapped it in a call to length, returning the length of the new string; otherwise, spotting that the leading and trailing spaces have been trimmed might be difficult in the output of the Python program.

SQL is a typed language, so DuckDB needs to know the types of both parameters and return types of a function. DuckDB is usually able to infer those types from the Python type annotations. This inference capability, however, might not always be spot-on, especially if we had decided to not use Python type hints in our code or if the function is distributed in a third-party library without type hints. In such scenarios, it becomes necessary to explicitly define the types to ensure accurate function execution.

Explicitly specifying types is beneficial for clarity, preventing potential type infer-ence pitfalls, and ensuring consistent behavior across different environments. To redefine our function with explicit types, we first need to remove the previously regis-tered version of the function to avoid conflicts:

```
con.remove_function('remove_spaces')
```

Having done that, we can now reregister our function, but this time, we'll explicitly define the types. As shown in the following snippet, the function's parameter type and return type are distinctly specified:

- The function expects a single input parameter of type VARCHAR.
- It returns a value of type VARCHAR:

```
from duckdb.typing import *

con.create_function(
  'remove_spaces',
  remove_spaces,            The function has one
  [(VARCHAR)],       ◁──┘   VARCHAR input parameter.
  VARCHAR      ◁───┐  The function returns
)                  │  a VARCHAR.
```

Being explicit in such definitions can serve as a clear contract, stipulating how the function should be used and what to expect in return, and ensuring the system and the developers are in sync.

Next, let's use this function to write a query showing what we'll see if we remove the spaces from the Region column, shown in the following snippet. This query does two things:

- Displays the original Region values along with their character lengths (len1)
- Showcases the cleaned Region values (using remove_spaces) and their charac-ter lengths (len2):

```
con.sql("""                                    Returns the region and
SELECT DISTINCT Region, length(Region) AS len1,  ◁──  the number of characters
       remove_spaces(Region) AS cleanRegion,
       length(cleanRegion) AS len2    ◁───┐  Returns regions with no spaces
FROM population                              and the number of characters
WHERE len1 BETWEEN 20 AND 30   ◁───┐ Limited for
LIMIT 3                              brevity of output
""")
```

A glance at the difference between len1 and len2 immediately makes it evident that our function does, in fact, trim those unwarranted spaces:

Region varchar	len1 int64	cleanRegion varchar	len2 int64
ASIA (EX. NEAR EAST)	29	ASIA (EX. NEAR EAST)	20
LATIN AMER. & CARIB	23	LATIN AMER. & CARIB	19
C.W. OF IND. STATES	20	C.W. OF IND. STATES	19

With the confidence that our function is working as expected, we can then proceed to update the original dataset:

```
con.sql("""
UPDATE population
SET Region = remove_spaces(Region);
""")
```

And once that's done, let's return the unique regions and the number of characters:

```
con.sql("""
select DISTINCT Region, length(Region) AS numChars
from population
""")
```

Region varchar	numChars int64
ASIA (EX. NEAR EAST)	20
EASTERN EUROPE	14
NORTHERN AFRICA	15
OCEANIA	7
WESTERN EUROPE	14
SUB-SAHARAN AFRICA	18
LATIN AMER. & CARIB	19
C.W. OF IND. STATES	19
NEAR EAST	9
NORTHERN AMERICA	16
BALTICS	7
11 rows	2 columns

The spaces are gone! Now we have a much cleaner dataset. The extra spaces around each Region value have been eliminated, bringing more structure and uniformity to our data.

Working with data from diverse sources often introduces challenges stemming from regional disparities. An excellent example of this is the representation of decimal numbers. In the European region, a comma (,) is typically used as the decimal separator, as opposed to the period (.) used in other regions. When ingesting data into databases, these locale-specific notations can introduce complexity, especially if the system's locale doesn't align with the data's format.

For our dataset in DuckDB, we've encountered such a challenge with fields representing decimal values. Due to the European format of these values, DuckDB has interpreted them as VARCHARs, potentially hindering numerical analyses.

To rectify this, we can make use of Python's extensive library ecosystem. The locale module offers a solution to this particular challenge. We can define a function, convert_locale, that will transition these European-formatted decimal values into a format DuckDB can interpret as numeric types:

```
from duckdb.typing import *
import locale

def convert_locale(field:str) -> float:
  locale.setlocale(locale.LC_ALL, 'de_DE')
  return locale.atof(field)
```

Having defined our function, the next step is to make DuckDB aware of its existence. Registering this function allows us to use it in our SQL queries:

```
con.create_function('convert_locale', convert_locale)
```

To visualize the efficacy of this function, let's apply it to a couple of columns, namely `Coastline (coast/area ratio)` and `Pop. Density (per sq. mi.)`:

```
con.sql("""
SELECT "Coastline (coast/area ratio)" AS coastline,
       convert_locale(coastline) as cleanCoastline,
       "Pop. Density (per sq. mi.)" as popDen,
       convert_locale(popDen) as cleanPopDen
FROM population
LIMIT 5
""")
```

| coastline | cleanCoastline | popDen | cleanPopDen |
varchar	double	varchar	double
0,00	0.0	48,0	48.0
1,26	1.26	124,6	124.6
0,04	0.04	13,8	13.8
58,29	58.29	290,4	290.4
0,00	0.0	152,1	152.1

Upon examining the results, the distinction between the original and cleaned values is evident. Our function has successfully converted values like 0,00 to 0.0. It has done so not by blindly replacing a colon with a dot but with semantic awareness that it is dealing with a localization problem.

Once confident in the function's operation, it's prudent to make these changes permanent in our dataset. The ALTER TABLE clause allows us to modify column types and update values simultaneously:

```
con.sql("""
ALTER TABLE population
ALTER "Coastline (coast/area ratio)"        Updates the data
SET DATA TYPE DOUBLE                    ◁─┘ type to double         Uses our convert_locale
USING                                                              function to update all the
   convert_locale("Coastline (coast/area ratio)")  ◁──────────── values in this column
""")
```

This process underscores the importance of understanding and adapting to regional data nuances. It also highlights the flexibility and integration capabilities of DuckDB, allowing users to bridge the gap between Python's vast library ecosystem and SQL-based data manipulation.

> **NOTE** We'll leave repeating this process for the other columns that need cleaning up as an exercise for the reader. The following columns still need to be cleaned up: `Pop. Density (per sq. mi.)`, `Coastline (coast/area ratio)`, `Birthrate`, and `Deathrate`.

6.5   *Interoperability with Apache Arrow and Polars*

In the realm of data analysis, adaptability is a defining quality of a robust system. The ability to seamlessly transition between different formats or platforms allows for efficient data manipulation, storage, and visualization. One of DuckDB's strengths is its capability to interact with a diverse array of data formats, both in-memory and external. This interoperability is often invaluable, especially when integrating with other tools or exporting results for further analysis.

Now, while the data science ecosystem is replete with tools, there's a constant evolution of libraries that offer improved performance or unique features. One such emerging star is Polars. Though pandas has been the de facto standard for data analysis in Python for many years, Polars presents itself as an exciting alternative. Developed in Rust—a language known for its performance characteristics—Polars offers DataFrame operations that are both fast and memory efficient. The memory model used by Polars is based upon Apache Arrow, a cross-language development platform for in-memory data that specifies a standardized and language-independent columnar memory format for flat and hierarchical data. Arrow allows for zero-copy reads and fast data access and interchange without serialization overhead between languages and systems. As a matter of fact, Polars is not the only framework that uses Arrows as an in-memory format: pandas DataFrames and other Python libraries, such as NumPy and PySpark, do too.

Given our prior exploration of pandas in this chapter, it might be enlightening to take Polars for a spin to give yourself a chance to experience the nuances and advantages it brings to the table firsthand. Both libraries must be installed into your Python environment for the DuckDB integration to work. You want to execute the following command in a different shell without quitting the running Python interpreter so that the objects and relations we defined earlier are kept intact:

```
pip install polars pyarrow
```

We can then convert the `population` table to Polars using the `pl` function and select some columns from the first five rows:

```
import polars

population_table = con.table("population")

(population_table
    .limit(5)
    .pl()
```

Selects the first five rows (using the relational API)

Converts the population table to Polars DataFrame

```
    [["Country", "Region", "Population"]]                ⟵┐  Extracts the Country, Region, and
)                                                          │  Population for the first five rows
```

The output of this code fragment is as follows:

```
shape: (5, 3)
┌────────────────┬───────────────────────┬────────────┐
│ Country        │ Region                │ Population  │
│ ---            │ ---                   │ ---        │
│ str            │ str                   │ i64        │
╞════════════════╪═══════════════════════╪════════════╡
│ Afghanistan    │ ASIA (EX. NEAR EAST)  │ 31056997   │
│ Albania        │ EASTERN EUROPE     …  │ 3581655    │
│ Algeria        │ NORTHERN AFRICA    …  │ 32930091   │
│ American Samoa │ OCEANIA            …  │ 57794      │
│ Andorra        │ WESTERN EUROPE     …  │ 71201      │
└────────────────┴───────────────────────┴────────────┘
```

Executing this code results in a concise Polars DataFrame with just the `Country`, `Region`, and `Population` columns for the first five entries. As the output suggests, the transition from DuckDB to Polars is seamless; the DataFrame can partake in any computation Polars offers. In your code, you will want to delay the transition as long as possible, though. We could have limited the results to five rows by converting to a DataFrame first and then using `head(5)` to get the first five rows; this would have materialized all rows into the Python runtime followed by a client-side transformation. Our recommendation for both Polars and pandas is to stick to the relational or database API as long as possible and convert to a DataFrame only if you need to combine it with external data or if a computation via SQL would just not be feasible.

We could also convert the DuckDB table to an Apache Arrow table to take advantage of the myriad tools and platforms that support Arrow. To do the conversion, we can use the `to_arrow_table` function:

```
arrow_table = population_table.to_arrow_table()
```

After transforming our DuckDB table into Arrow's format, we're now in a position to harness the computational capabilities of Arrow's Python API. Suppose we are interested in countries from the NEAR EAST region. We'd like to retrieve the `country`, `region`, and `population` of each of the top five NEAR EAST entries. In the following snippet, we'll complete the following operations:

- *Filtering*—We're keen on countries that fall within the NEAR EAST region. This is our primary criterion for data extraction.
- *Column selection*—For our analysis, we require just three columns: `Country`, `Region`, and `Population`.
- *Row limitation*—To keep our output concise, we'll limit it to the top five entries:

```
import pyarrow.compute as pc

(arrow_table                                           ┌─ Only includes rows with a
    .filter(pc.field("Region") == "NEAR EAST")     ⟵┘  region in the NEAR EAST
```

```
    .select(["Country", "Region", "Population"])        Returns the Country,
    .slice(length=5)            Returns the              Region, and Population
)                                first five rows
```

The resulting table is a reflection of our specifications: compact, focusing only on the desired columns, and limited to the top five entries. The countries listed—Bahrain, Cyprus, Gaza Strip, Iraq, and Israel—are representative of the NEAR EAST region, with their respective populations displayed alongside:

```
pyarrow.Table
Country: string
Region: string
Population: int64
------
Country: [["Bahrain ","Cyprus ","Gaza Strip ","Iraq ","Israel "]]
Region: [["NEAR EAST","NEAR EAST","NEAR EAST","NEAR EAST","NEAR EAST"]]
Population: [[698585,784301,1428757,26783383,6352117]]
```

Those examples not only showcase the capabilities of Apache Arrow and Polars but also its potential to bridge the divide between data storage and computation. Having the ability to transform any result into an Apache Arrow object opens up the possibility of using all streaming, serialization, and *interprocess communication* (IPC) based on Arrow.

Summary

- DuckDB's Python API blurs the lines between tables and views in a database and objects outside.
- DuckDB enables many kinds of objects to be queried in a uniform fashion.
- Polar DataFrames, pandas DataFrames, Apache Arrow tables, and other sources can be treated as if they were a table in an SQL query.
- The relational API makes it easy to write maintainable applications utilizing reusable query fragments.
- The relational API allows the reuse of dynamic relations in a similar way to what a view would do statically.
- User-defined functions allow us to implement the functionality of the entire set of libraries in the Python ecosystem, integrating seamlessly within SQL queries, bringing more flexibility and a tailored workflow to any data analysis experience.
- Data can be exported to a variety of formats, including pandas DataFrames, Polars DataFrames, and Apache Arrow tables.
- Transitioning between various platforms becomes a lot easier with DuckDB's conversion capabilities that treat DataFrames, Apache Arrow tables, and other sources the same way.

DuckDB in the cloud with MotherDuck

This chapter covers

- The idea behind MotherDuck
- Understanding how the architecture works under the hood
- Use cases for serverless SQL analytics
- Creating, managing, and sharing MotherDuck databases
- Tips for optimizing your MotherDuck usage

Up until this point, our focus has been on using DuckDB's capabilities for querying datasets—whether they're stored locally or remotely—directly from our own computers. While this approach addresses a broad range of needs, there are specific scenarios in which a remote database server offers additional advantages.

Enter MotherDuck: a solution for enhancing SQL analytics through a simplified scale-up strategy. In this chapter, we will learn how MotherDuck enables hybrid query execution, making use of a remotely hosted DuckDB alongside one operating on our own machine.

7.1 Introduction to MotherDuck

MotherDuck (https://motherduck.com) is a collaborative serverless analytics platform that lets you query and analyze data in cloud databases and from cloud storage, using your browser or any of the DuckDB APIs. *Serverless*, in this context, means that you as a user won't have to deal with spinning up servers, clusters, or configuring database instances. Instead, you can just create a database, and the service will take care of the rest for you.

A closed beta of the platform was launched in June 2023, with general availability introduced in September 2023. MotherDuck works closely with the DuckDB Labs team to ensure the best interoperability and availability of all features in the cloud platform. You can find the documentation for the MotherDuck service at https://motherduck.com/docs/.

7.1.1 How it works

There are several ways to use MotherDuck. When you sign up for the service, you'll end up in the MotherDuck web UI running in the browser. This UI is running a special DuckDB version in the browser that knows how to communicate with Mother-Duck. The UI is both a tool to manage your MotherDuck databases and a notebook-based approach to enter and execute queries and to view their results. We will cover this later in the chapter in section 7.2.1.

The other entry points to MotherDuck are, of course, the CLI and the integrations with languages, such as Python. MotherDuck is presented as an opt-in feature to the open source database DuckDB via an extension. This extension will be automatically loaded when you open a database using the `md:` or `motherduck:` protocol and will integrate both with the query parser and engine. The parser is enhanced with functionality around database and share management. In the query engine, the extension analyzes if tables are available locally or remotely and then uses the appropriate execution engine and joins the data accordingly. If needed, parts of the local data are sent to the server for joins or filters, or data from the remote side is fetched and joined locally.

MotherDuck's architecture is shown in figure 7.1, and at the core of its operation are the following components:

- *A service layer*—Sharing, admin, services, and monitoring
- *Ducklings*—Serverless DuckDB compute instances
- *A catalog*—Database and tables
- *Storage*—Internal storage and maintenance

The service layer of MotherDuck provides capabilities like secure identity, authorization, administration, monitoring, billing, and so on. Where the serverless DuckDB "Duckling" instances execute the "remote" parts of your query, the catalog exposes the databases, tables, and views that are managed in the storage layer. The storage is durable, secure, and automatically optimized for best performance. MotherDuck—as with other modern cloud data platforms—separates storage and compute facilities, which will eventually be important for the cost that occurs when using MotherDuck.

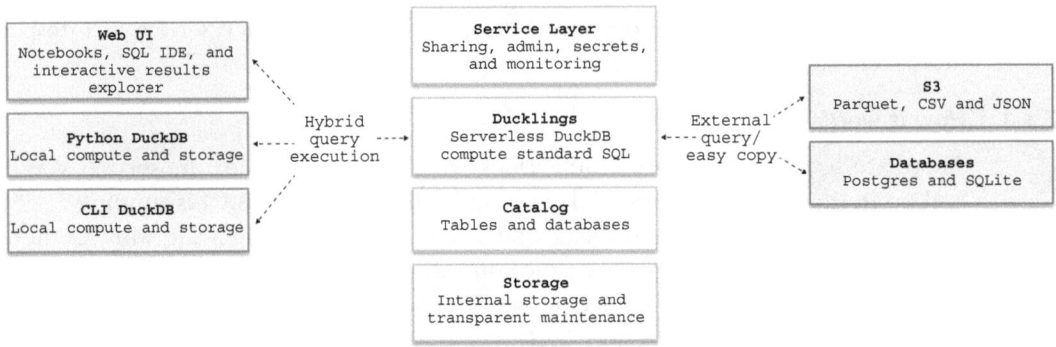

Figure 7.1   **Hybrid query execution as implemented within MotherDuck**

MotherDuck is designed so that you can focus on your queries, not on the size of the machines you need to spin up in the cloud to make the queries run quickly. The separation of the storage—and compute—layers will have some impact on the cost; we will discuss this later in the chapter in section 7.3.

7.1.2   Why use MotherDuck?

First and foremost, MotherDuck provides a simplified, performant, and efficient data warehouse based on DuckDB. Most folks are in the long tail of cloud data warehouse users and don't need analytics-processing capabilities for tens or hundreds of terabytes of hot data. Those use cases can benefit from a simpler, more efficient architecture that is not based on a distributed system but instead uses the cloud as the main data storage and DuckDB as the query engine. Think back to the fictional system presented in chapters 3 and 4, monitoring energy production. Even if you monitored several hundreds or thousands of sites and their daily output in quarterly hour measurements, you would not find anything close to a billion records per year, and most likely, they would only total a few gigabytes in size. This could hardly be considered big data, and it's something MotherDuck would be able to deal with easily.

Another way to utilize MotherDuck is as a query engine for data lakes made up of heterogeneous sources, such as cold data stored as Parquet, CSV files in S3, or data stored in Apache Iceberg. You can easily join that data with hot data stored directly in MotherDuck.

MotherDuck can serve as a serverless backend for data applications, dashboards, and APIs. Instead of running analytics queries on the main transactional database, you can use MotherDuck to run those queries on a dedicated analytics database.

Last but not least, MotherDuck allows sharing read-only snapshots of your databases to other MotherDuck users. They can use your sources, as they are shared, or join data from their instance together with your datasets as well.

Independent of what you are planning to do with MotherDuck, you will need to sign up with the MotherDuck service to use their cloud offering. We will cover this in the next section.

7.2   Getting started with MotherDuck

Throughout the book, we used the CLI or the integration with Python. To get started with MotherDuck, you will need to bring up your browser of choice first. Navigate to https://motherduck.com/, and click on the Sign Up button. You can create a free account with your GitHub account, with your Google account, or by providing an email address. Once you've done that, you'll find yourself in the MotherDuck UI. The UI shown in figure 7.2 displays your databases and their schema in a navigable tree to the left, and a query and its result, including inline bar-charts, in the main view.

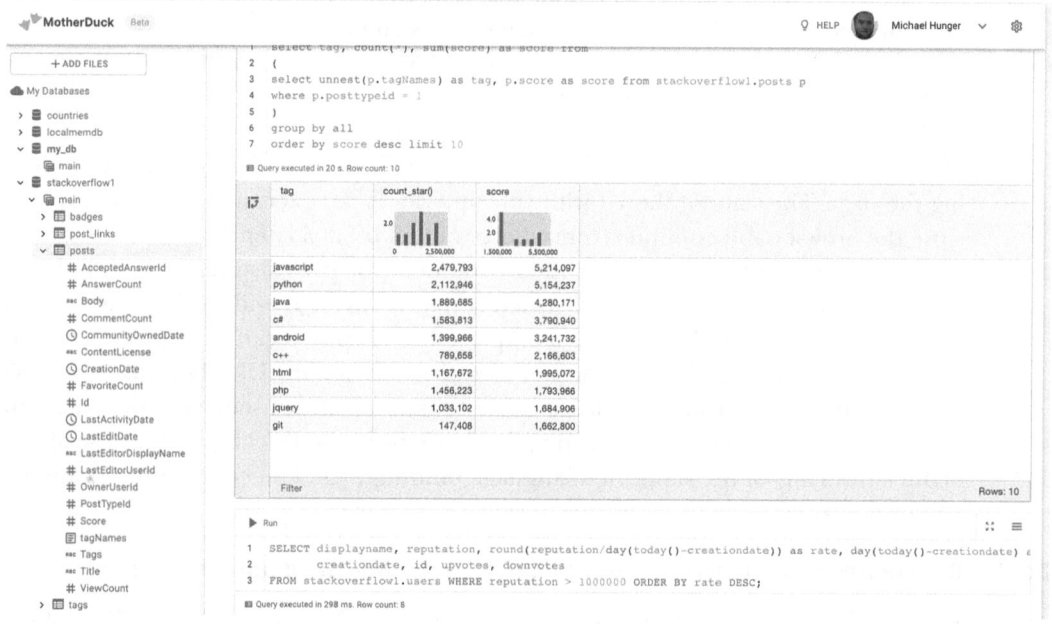

Figure 7.2   MotherDuck UI

7.2.1 *Using MotherDuck through the UI*

The web-based MotherDuck UI (https://app.motherduck.com) provides a central place for accessing and querying all your remote databases, managing your account settings, and storing any secrets necessary for querying remote data sources on S3. It also gives access to your MotherDuck API token, which is needed to access Mother-Duck outside the UI.

> **NOTE**   The database running in the web UI is actually a local, embedded database too! It is using a version of Duck that is compiled to WebAssembly (WASM), thus running locally in your browser. The queries are executed, of course, in the MotherDuck cloud, as explained earlier. Alternatively, if you don't have or want a MotherDuck account, you can visit https://shell.duckdb.org, which behaves essentially like your CLI but without being able to persist data or connect to MotherDuck.

Results of your SQL queries are cached in the DuckDB instance local to your browser, enabling you to instantly sort, pivot, and filter query results! The UI lists databases, their tables with their columns, and uploaded files on the left side. With a context menu, you can use, share, drop, detach, or copy the names of databases. The menu shown in figure 7.3 will appear as a context item when navigating the tree-like structure.

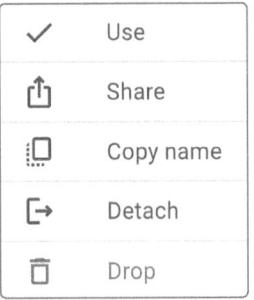

Figure 7.3   Contextual menu of the navigator

DuckDB offers a Jupyter-Notebook-like experience for running queries, which allows you to write SQL statements with auto-complete and then run them and see query results rendered in a data grid below the cell. The output data grids support local sorting, selecting output columns, showing histograms and aggregations in the column header, and pivoting and filtering the data. The state of the UI with your queries is kept across sessions, so you can close the browser and continue from where you left off at a later date.

The web-based UI is a great work environment for pre-existing, shared, and new databases. Everything that you've learned so far about SQL and writing queries and working with different data sources as explored in chapter 5 can be applied. There is support for uploading CSV and Parquet files directly from the UI. They will be accessible in any query, and you will utilize a CREATE TABLE AS SELECT statement or transform them to your needs. To import existing databases from the DuckDB CLI, or use MotherDuck from any of the supported language bindings, you'll need to authenticate the CLI or the language binding of choice with MotherDuck.

7.2.2 *Connecting to MotherDuck with DuckDB via token-based authentication*

Please make sure you have a MotherDuck account and are logged in before proceeding. DuckDB triggers the authentication process with MotherDuck at the moment you try to open a shared database instance. This can be a named database or the default one.

NOTE When you connect to MotherDuck without specifying a database, you connect to a default database called `my_db`. This is the current database. You can then query any table in this database by specifying the table name. The `USE` command allows you to switch the current database.

Let's open the default database at MotherDuck for your account by running `.open md:` in the CLI. Unless you're already authenticated, it will prompt you with the following message:

```
Attempting to automatically open the SSO authorization page in your
⇒default browser.
1. Please open this link to login into your account:
⇒https://auth.motherduck.com/activate
2. Enter the following code: XXXX-XXXX
```

If you follow through the auth flow to completion, you'll see the following lines in the terminal:

```
Token successfully retrieved [√]
You can store it as an environment variable to avoid having to log in again:
  $ export motherduck_token='eyJhbGciOiJI..._Jfo'
```

Your browser will have opened with a device confirmation message similar to that shown in figure 7.4.

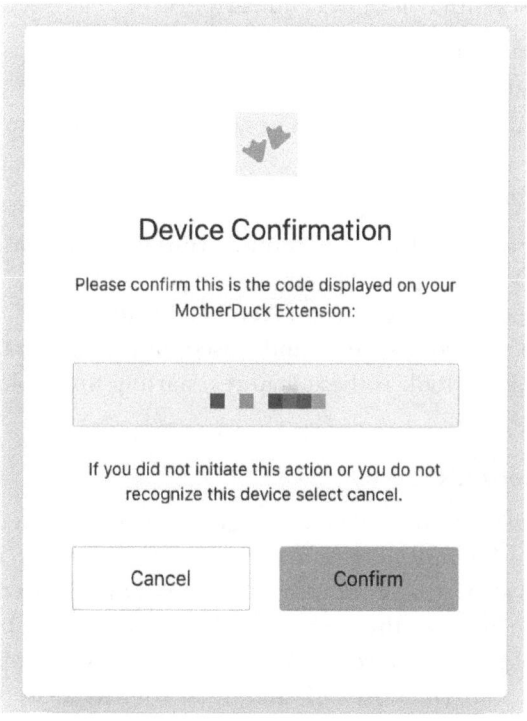

Figure 7.4
MotherDuck confirmation message

You're now able to access databases on MotherDuck, and as the message says, if you want to be automatically logged in during future sessions, you should add the Mother-Duck token as an environment variable. Alternatively, you can use the token as a parameter to the `md:` protocol like this:

```
D .open 'md:?motherduck_token=eyJhbGciOiJI..._Jfo'
```

This URL format is also applicable to the individual language bindings. Think back to chapter 6, in which we discussed connection management from within the integration with the Python ecosystem. To open a connection to MotherDuck from Python, you would use

```
import duckdb

con = duckdb.connect('md:?motherduck_token=eyJhbGciOiJI..._Jfo')
```

Next, we will discuss how to perform various tasks in MotherDuck. Whether to use the web UI or the CLI is ultimately up to you, but please make sure you set up your MotherDuck account and can access it with either the UI or the CLI.

7.3 *Making the best possible use of MotherDuck*

In this section, you will learn about the features added to DuckDB via the Mother-Duck extension that let you interact with MotherDuck and use it to its fullest potential. We start by discussing all features helping you to get your data into the cloud and potentially sharing your databases with colleagues and partners:

- Uploading databases from your local machine to the cloud
- Managing databases (creation, deletion, listing)
- Sharing databases via URL, refreshing the shares, and attaching them to your local DuckDB instance
- Accessing data from S3 buckets

After that, we will discuss how to control whether a query runs on a database that is completely remote, completely local, or partially remote and partially local.

Last but not least, MotherDuck ships a couple of AI-related features, such as functions that will automatically describe your schema and, based on that, generate or fix SQL statements for you. Let's have a look at these features, starting with uploading a local DuckDB database.

7.3.1 *Uploading databases to MotherDuck*

Think back to chapter 6, in which we used the Python integration to build up a database containing data about countries. We finished our work there, we cleaned up issues in the dataset, and now we want to share that work with colleagues. One way to do this is via the "spreadsheet way of life": just take the `countries.duckdb` store, attach it to an email or copy it to a network folder, and move on. A better, less-fragile way of sharing is MotherDuck. To begin, start your DuckDB CLI, and open your database with the following command (if you don't have that store, don't worry—the command will create it for you):

```
.open countries.duckdb
```

Let's add a `cities` table to that database, especially if you created a fresh database:

```
CREATE TABLE cities AS
SELECT *
FROM (VALUES ('Amsterdam', 1), ('London', 2)) cities(Name, Id);
```

Before we share the database, we need to detach so that all the locks will be released.

This can either be done by switching back to an in-memory database, using `.open` without arguments followed by a `LOAD motherduck;` to load the extension, or in one go by calling `.open md:`. The latter will attach the CLI to the MotherDuck default database. We can then create the remote database with the `CREATE DATABASE` statement as follows:

```
.open md:
CREATE DATABASE "countries" FROM 'countries.duckdb';
```

Depending on the size of your database and the speed of your internet connection, the upload process can take some time. In our experiments, the upload of a 16 GB database from a regular laptop accessing a 40 Mbps upstream home internet connection took about 40 minutes. At the time of writing, this is a topic MotherDuck is actively working on, and the upload performance is expected to improve in the near future. For now, it may be faster to export your database into Parquet files, upload those to cloud storage, and then create a database in MotherDuck from those files.

Once the database is uploaded, you can check whether you are able to use it. Your session is still attached to the default database in MotherDuck. That means you'll need to either prefix your tables with the database name or switch to the new database. `FROM countries.cities` uses the prefix. In the following snippet, we first switch to the database by issuing a `USE` statement. That allows us to omit the prefix to any table in that database, as we've done in all previous examples:

```
USE countries;
FROM cities;
```
⟵ The USE statement will look up the database name in the remote MotherDuck catalog.

If you happened to already leave the CLI, you can connect directly to the new database via `.open md:countries` too. Either way, we can then run a query to check that the data is there. So if we select everything from the `cities` table with `FROM cities`, we should see everything we just created:

Name varchar	Id int32
Amsterdam	1
London	2

When uploading a local database to MotherDuck, the following rule is very important to remember: *the local and remote names must always be different.* If you forget this rule and give them the same name, you risk receiving the following error:

```
create database "countries" from 'countries' ;
Error: Catalog Error: Database 'countries' has already been
➥created and attached
```

And if you try to upload your current database, you get this error:

```
Error: Binder Error: Database "countries.duckdb" is already attached
➥with alias "countries"
```

We avoided these errors in our example by calling `.open md:`, which did two things for us: it loaded the MotherDuck extension and connected to the default Mother-Duck database. Another option is using `.open`, which will switch to an in-memory database.

7.3.2   *Creating databases in MotherDuck*

In the previous section, we uploaded an existing database to MotherDuck. Alternatively, you can start building your schema from scratch directly in the cloud. If the content of your schema depends largely on files stored in another public cloud, it would be a waste of time and resources to download them first into a local DuckDB instance and then upload that database to MotherDuck. In most cases, MotherDuck will run closer to an S3 bucket than your local system, so an ingress from the cloud directly into MotherDuck may save you time and money.

You create a new database in MotherDuck using the CREATE DATABASE command. The database name can't have any special characters—only alphanumeric characters and underscores are allowed.

To create a database called `my-test`, run the following:

```
CREATE DATABASE "my-test";
```

You can confirm that the database has been created with the SHOW DATABASES command:

```
SHOW DATABASES;
```

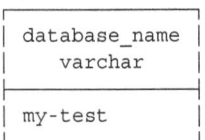

```
┌───────────────┐
│ database_name │
│    varchar    │
├───────────────┤
│ my-test       │
└───────────────┘
```

Alternatively, you can use the `.databases` CLI command. You can run either of these commands from your local DuckDB CLI, or you can navigate to the MotherDuck UI (https://app.motherduck.com/) and run them there.

The CREATE DATABASE statement just creates the database—it doesn't change your session to it—so we need to run USE 'my-test'; first. We can then check that we're connected to this database using the current_database function:

```
SELECT current_database();
```

If everything worked as expected, you should see the correct database name:

```
┌───────────────────┐
│ current_database()│
│      varchar      │
├───────────────────┤
│ my-test           │
└───────────────────┘
```

Let's now create a people table in our MotherDuck database and add a couple of rows:

```
CREATE TABLE people (name varchar, born date);
INSERT INTO people VALUES ('Mark', '1989-01-01'), ('Hannes', '1990-01-01');
```

We can then return a count of the records in the people table by running the following query:

```
SELECT count(*)
FROM people;
```

```
┌──────────────┐
│ count_star() │
│    int64     │
├──────────────┤
│            2 │
└──────────────┘
```

We can also run that same query with the database name prefixed to the table name:

```
SELECT count(*)
FROM "my-test".people;
```

And once we're happy that we've gotten the hang of how MotherDuck works, we can remove that test database. To do that, we'll need to first switch to the default my_db database before running the DROP DATABASE command.

```
USE my_db;
DROP DATABASE "my-test";
```

The my-test test database should no longer appear in the output of SHOW DATABASES;.

7.3.3 Sharing databases

MotherDuck offers the ability to share a read-only snapshot of your databases. This is great not only for sharing the data but for collaborative analysis and shared functionality. The snapshot will not only contain your data but all views, and with them all the effort you put into them during creation. Think of it as a "spreadsheet on steroids."

To make your data available to others (https://mng.bz/NRW7), you can use the CREATE SHARE statement. If you run it, you will get a shareable link that others can connect to using the ATTACH command (https://mng.bz/Ddea).

> **NOTE**   The following generated links will be different if you create the shares for the country database based on your MotherDuck account and your database.

Assuming you followed our initial instructions to create the countries database, you could share it like this:

```
CREATE SHARE shared_countries                    ◁─────┐ The name of the
FROM countries;   ◁─────┐  The name of the               shared database
                          database to share
```

You will receive a link similar to the following:

```
┌─────────────────────────────────────────────────────────┐
│                      share_url                            │
│                      varchar                              │
├─────────────────────────────────────────────────────────┤
│ md:_share/countries/1acb80cf-d872-4fab-8077-64975cce0452  │
└─────────────────────────────────────────────────────────┘
```

The amount of time it takes to create a shared database currently depends on the size of the source database. A 16 GB database took about a minute to share in our case.

To attach this database, our friend or colleague will need to have a MotherDuck account too. They can then run the following command on their DuckDB database:

```
ATTACH 'md:_share/countries/1acb80cf-d872-4fab-8077-64975cce0452'
AS shared_countries;
```

We can describe the contents of a shared database using the DESCRIBE SHARE command:

```
.mode line
DESCRIBE SHARE shared_countries;
```

This results in the following output, mirroring the source link and the original name as well as the IDs of the database and the latest snapshot:

```
share_name = shared_countries
   share_link = md:_share/countries/1acb80cf-d872-4fab-8077-64975cce0452
database_name = countries
  database_id = 9d7586ac-add9-46dc-a4fb-def6b42f0f7c
  snapshot_id = 041a5ba9-8cf4-471b-af13-1bec75a0b3ce
```

We can also list the shares that we've created:

```
LIST SHARES;
```

At the time of publication, shares are not automatically updated when you change the content of your shared database. Changes to both schema and data must be explicitly propagated through the UPDATE SHARE statement from the sharing site:

```
UPDATE SHARE shared_countries;
```

To get rid of any share you are not interested in anymore, run the DETACH statement. If you are connected to the share, you need to switch to a different database first:

```
USE my_db;
DETACH shared_countries;
```

We did actually prepare a couple of hopefully interesting shares for you, including the complete database of chapters 3 and 4, containing all tables and views we created throughout the chapters. Youc can access it with the following:

```
ATTACH
  'md:_share/duckdb_in_action_ch3_4/d0c08584-1d33-491c-8db7-cf9c6910eceb'
AS duckdb_book_ch3_and_4;
USE duckdb_book_ch3_and_4;
SHOW tables;
```

We also ingested a complete dump from Stack Overflow, which provides a great dataset to play along with:

```
ATTACH
  'md:_share/stackoverflow/6c318917-6888-425a-bea1-5860c29947e5'
AS stackoverflow_analysis;
USE stackoverflow_analysis;
SELECT count(*) FROM posts;
```

The share contains a whopping number of 58,329,356 posts and answers—an interesting corpus of data to play with. We collected some other interesting shares you can load into a sample_data database via

```
ATTACH 'md:_share/share_sample_data/23b0d623-1361-421d-ae77-62d701d471e6'
AS sample_data;
```

The tables are prefixed, and you can access them via their fully qualified names (e.g., sample_data.nyc.yellow_cab_nyc_2022_11) (see table 7.1).

Table 7.1 List of tables in the sample database

Name	Table name	Rows	Description
Hacker News	hn.hacker_news	3.9M	A sample of comments from Hacker News
NYC 311 Complaint Data	nyc.service_requests	32.5M	Requests to NYC's 311 complaint hotline via phone and web
Air Quality	who.ambient_air_quality	41k	Historical air quality data from the World Health Organization
Taxi Rides	nyc.taxi	3.3M	NYC yellow cab trips data from November 2020
Rideshare	nyc.rideshare	18.1M	Rideshare trips (Lyft, Uber, etc.) in NYC

These datasets provide many different topics, which you can use to train your SQL skills or to explore the possibilities of DuckDB and MotherDuck.

7.3.4   *Managing S3 secrets and loading Data from S3 buckets*

In previous chapters, we ingested data from files directly available over http:// or https:// protocols. Oftentimes, people use Amazon S3 for storing files, accessible via the s3:// protocol.

MotherDuck—and DuckDB—speak that protocol as well, but they need your secrets to authenticate on your behalf against Amazon S3. When using MotherDuck, you can store your secrets in their systems so that they are available in all sessions connected to MotherDuck. You do this either via the web UI or a dedicated statement— the CREATE OR REPLACE SECRET statement:

```
CREATE OR REPLACE SECRET (
  TYPE S3,
  KEY_ID 'access-key',
  SECRET 'secret-key',
  REGION 'us-east-1'
);
```

Once you've done that, you can query data in a secure S3 bucket, just like any CSV or Parquet file we queried over http or the file system before:

```
CREATE OR REPLACE TABLE mytable AS
FROM 's3://...';
```

Once you've finished working with the bucket, you'll want to remove the secret:

```
DROP SECRET (TYPE s3);
```

There are a couple of things to keep in mind when creating a secret:

- In versions of DuckDB prior to 0.10.0, you can only have one SECRET object.
- You can only use permanent S3 secrets—temporary S3 secrets, which are only valid during a session, are currently not supported.

7.3.5   *Optimizing data ingestion and MotherDuck usage*

Running a cloud-based solution incurs a variety of cost types, including, among others, the costs of compute, storage, data ingress, and data egress. The MotherDuck extension gives you close control over where a function is to be executed: in the cloud or on your local machine. If you want to process a large Parquet file you already have on your local machine, it's pointless to upload it to S3 first and then run the processing in MotherDuck, as you will pay for both the computational costs at MotherDuck and the egress cost at S3. Given a fast internet connection, you are most likely better off doing this locally and simply uploading from your machine to MotherDuck. The extension enhances all functions starting with the read_ prefix—such as read_json and read_csv_auto—to support the MD_RUN parameter. That parameter lets you control where the function will be executed, and it supports the following values:

- MD_RUN=LOCAL—This executes the function in your local DuckDB environment.
- MD_RUN=REMOTE—This executes the function in MotherDuck-hosted DuckDB runtimes in the cloud.
- MD_RUN=AUTO—This remotely executes all s3://, http://, and https:// requests, except those to localhost/127.0.0.1. This is the default option.

For example, if you wanted to query the DuckDB IP's dataset on the MotherDuck-hosted DuckDB runtime, you could execute the following query. In the example, we use .timer on to get the query execution time:

```
.timer on
SELECT count(*)
FROM read_csv_auto(
  'https://github.com/duckdb/duckdb/raw/main/data/csv/ips.csv.gz',
  MD_RUN=REMOTE
);
```

As of writing, the query took less than a second to run in the MotherDuck cloud. Using MD_RUN=LOCAL instead, it took close to 2 seconds on the author's slow internet connection.

Beyond its free tier, MotherDuck offers a Standard tier of its service for a base price of $25 per month for 100 GB storage and 100 compute hours. In the event that resources are needed beyond the standard usage allotments, users may purchase additional cold storage or compute time at rates of $0.08 per GB and $0.40 per hour, respectively. However, keep in mind that this is only for cloud usage, not your local execution (see https://motherduck.com/pricing/).

Cold storage refers to the persistent storage for your databases and files. *Hot storage*, on the other hand, is used to execute your queries, equivalent to memory usage, and it can be limited to a maximum value, fine-tuned to your needs. In DuckDB, hot storage is automatically scaled up to the upper limit and metered per second and gigabyte.

The separation actually makes a lot of sense, as studies show that a huge percentage of the data that gets processed is less than 24 hours old. By the time data gets to be a week old, it is about 20 times less likely to be queried than data from the most recent day. Additionally, the workload sizes are often smaller than overall data sizes. For example, dashboards are usually built from aggregated data: any data from the last hour can be freshly aggregated so that you won't miss out on the latest changes. Anything reaching back later than a week can be stored pre-aggregated as an additional table. The aggregate will usually have many fewer rows and consume much less storage.

If you want to keep your costs under control, avoid storing superfluous data directly in MotherDuck; instead, load or process it as needed, and set a reasonable maximum amount of hot storage you'll keep at one time. The amount of hot storage available does affect the performance of your queries.

7.3.6   *Querying your data with AI*

While SQL is somewhat similar to the English language, it's not always easy to master. And if you're new to it, some SQL constructs might be downright intimidating.

> **NOTE** An earlier name for SQL was *SEQUEL* (Structured English QUEry Language), which was a pun on QUEL, another query language based on the relational model. The name was eventually dropped due to trademark issues.

Queries in a structured language can, however, be nicely generated, and you will be delighted to hear that MotherDuck offers a generative AI feature (https://mng.bz/lMjB) that allows you to query your data using natural language. It is able to describe your data and will generate SQL statements for you or fix existing ones. The feature works by sending the database schema along with a detailed prompt and your question to a large language model (LLM) that then generates the requested SQL statement and, optionally, executes it.

From our experience, it works quite well, and you can try it out on any of the test datasets. The following example uses the StackOverflow dataset, attached with the following statements:

```
ATTACH
  'md:_share/stackoverflow/6c318917-6888-425a-bea1-5860c29947e5'
AS stackoverflow_analysis;
USE stackoverflow_analysis;
```

You can get a description of the database schema by calling the `prompt_schema` procedure:

```
.mode line
CALL prompt_schema();
```

The results of running this a couple of times are as follows:

```
summary = The database contains tables for storing data related to votes,
➥tags, posts, post links, badges, users, and comments.
Run Time (s): real 3.672 user 0.007355 sys 0.002674
```

It takes a couple seconds to run, and the result isn't all that impressive—you could have gotten the same output by looking at the table list. If you call the function a second time, you will most likely get a different response:

```
summary = The data in the database is about votes, tags, posts, post links,
➥badges, users, and comments.
Run Time (s): real 3.054 user 0.007354 sys 0.003175
```

This may initially seem surprising until we consider that an LLM is a probabilistic model that isn't guaranteed to return the same response each time.

Instead of using an SQL statement to query for the most popular tags, we will use plain English in the next example: *What are the most popular tags?* This is, of course, not a valid SQL statement, so we must indicate this via a special pragma called `prompt_query`. A *pragma* is special directive that tells a compiler or query parser how it should process its input. Here, the input should be process as a prompt:

```
.mode duckbox
pragma prompt_query('What are the most popular tags?');
```

Without showing us how, we get 10 rows back, and they are actually meaningful:

```
| TagName    | Count   |
| varchar    | int64   |
|------------|---------|
| javascript | 2479947 |
| python     | 2113196 |
| java       | 1889767 |
| c#         | 1583879 |
| php        | 1456271 |
| android    | 1400026 |
| html       | 1167742 |
| jquery     | 1033113 |
| c++        |  789699 |
| css        |  787138 |
|------------|---------|
| 10 rows    2 columns |
```

```
-- Run Time (s): real 3.763 user 0.124567 sys 0.001716
```

While this is a correct answer, you might be curious about which SQL query was used to compute the answer. We can determine this (keeping in mind that probabilistically it could have been slightly different) using the `prompt_sql` procedure:

```
.mode line
call prompt_sql('What are the most popular tags?');

query = SELECT TagName, Count
FROM tags
ORDER BY Count DESC;
Run Time (s): real 5.425 user 0.010331 sys 0.005074
```

Looks good—it's even smart enough to use the table columns along with ordering and limit to get the most popular tags. The run time for these AI prompts is between 2 and 10 seconds, with most of this time being spent inside the large language model (LLM).

Let's see how it deals with a more involved question: What are the titles and comment counts of the five posts with the most comments?

```
.mode duckbox
pragma prompt_query("Which 5 questions have the most comments, what is the
  post title and comment count");
```

```
|                                                          Title | comments |
|                                                       varchar  | int64    |
|---------------------------------------------------------------|----------|
| UIImageView Frame Doesnt Reflect Constraints                  |      108 |
| Is it possible to use adb commands to click on a view by find |      102 |
| How to create a new web character symbol recognizable by html |      100 |
| Why isnt my CSS3 animation smooth in Google Chrome (but very  |       89 |
| Heap Gives Page Fault                                         |       89 |
```

```
Run Time (s): real 19.695 user 2.406446 sys 0.018353
```

And let's check which query was used. It is interesting that it detects or knows that all entries in the `posts` table with `PostTypeId = 1` are questions and not answers. Perhaps it knows that because it was trained on the StackOverflow dataset:

```
.mode line
call prompt_sql("Which 5 questions have the most comments, what is the
   post title and comment count");

query = SELECT p.Title, COUNT(c.Id) AS comment_count
FROM posts p
JOIN comments c ON p.Id = c.PostId AND p.PostTypeId = 1
GROUP BY p.Title
ORDER BY comment_count DESC
LIMIT 5;
Run Time (s): real 4.795 user 0.002301 sys 0.001346
```

Figure 7.5 shows what this looks like in the MotherDuck UI.

Figure 7.5   MotherDuck UI with AI queries

Since the comment count is a column in the posts table, the join with the comments table isn't needed. Let's see if we can get it to generate a query using just the `posts` table by tweaking our prompt:

```
call prompt_sql("System: No joins! User: Which 5 questions have the most
  comments, what is the post title and comment count");

query = SELECT Title, CommentCount
FROM posts
WHERE PostTypeId = 1
ORDER BY CommentCount DESC
LIMIT 5;
Run Time (s): real 3.587 user 0.001733 sys 0.000865
```

Much better!

You can also use `call prompt_fixup()` to fix an SQL code for a statement (e.g., the infamous, "I forgot `GROUP BY`"):

```
call prompt_fixup("select postTypeId, count(*) from posts");

query = SELECT postTypeId, COUNT(*) FROM posts GROUP BY postTypeId
Run Time (s): real 12.006 user 0.004266 sys 0.002980
```

Or you can use it to fix an incorrect join column name or two:

```
call prompt_fixup("select count(*) from posts join users on
➥posts.userId = users.userId");

query = SELECT COUNT(*) FROM posts JOIN users ON
➥posts.OwnerUserId = users.Id
Run Time (s): real 2.378 user 0.001770 sys 0.001067
```

We think there's a lot of potential in using an LLM to generate queries for a database, especially when the model can be augmented with the database schema. While it most likely won't replace queries that are written and tuned by specialists for reports and applications, it will make database systems much more accessible to a broader audience. Notably, in early 2024, MotherDuck introduced *FixIt*—a fast SQL error fixer for the UI, based on the same technology, which fixes syntactically incorrect SQL statements or those that are directly inline in the UI (https://mng.bz/Bdar).

7.3.7   *Integrations*

MotherDuck supports a wide variety of data transfer, business intelligence, and data visualization tools, as shown in figure 7.6. Going from left to right, with optional transformations in between, MotherDuck can sit in the middle of your pipeline. Sources can either be ingested directly or via additional services and then put into storage at MotherDuck before they are queried by either business intelligence use cases or with specific data science tools. They can serve as a *retrieval augmented generation* (RAG) information retrieval component for LLM models too.

Additionally, any existing DuckDB integrations and drivers also work with MotherDuck, so everywhere you can use DuckDB, you can use MotherDuck. All it takes is

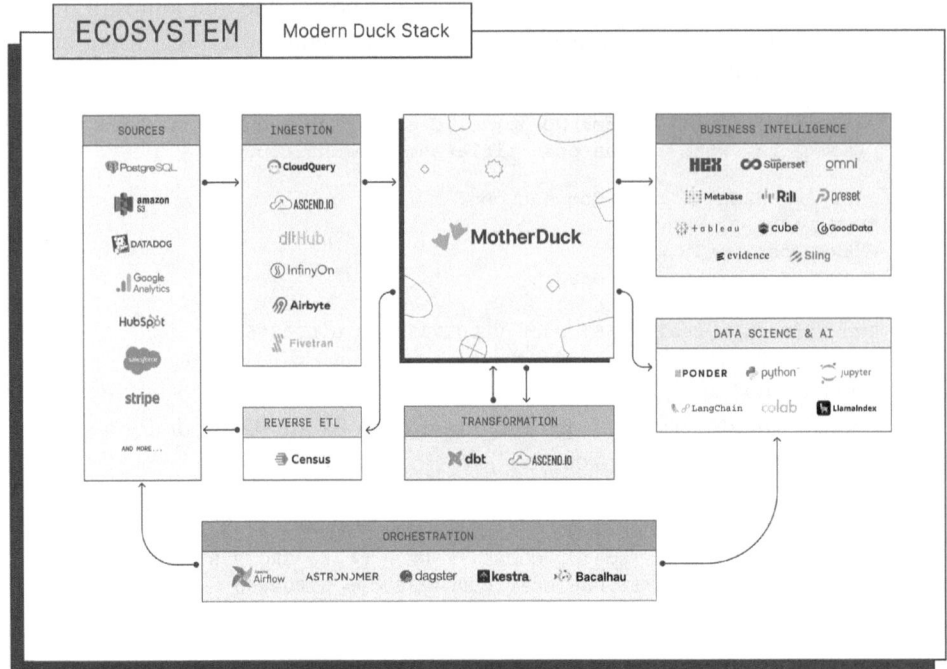

Figure 7.6   MotherDuck integrations

inserting the `md:` prefix into the database connection string and appending the `?motherduck_token=<token>` parameter.

Summary

- MotherDuck is a serverless data analytics platform that makes it easy to query and analyze data in cloud storage from the browser.
- It integrates seamlessly into the DuckDB CLI, the Python, and other language integrations using the `md:` protocol, which automatically loads the MotherDuck extension.
- MotherDuck enables you to store structured data, query that data with SQL, and share it with others.
- One key principle of the service is ease of use; you don't need to configure or spin up instances, clusters, or warehouses. You simply write and submit SQL, in the same tool or from within the same ecosystem, when working locally.
- In many cases, data can be ingested much faster at MotherDuck than locally due to its closer proximity to data sources.
- Local, remote, and shared datasets can easily be joined by using the qualified names of schema and relation.
- The MotherDuck platform also offers support for querying datasets in natural language, allowing people who are not trained in SQL to benefit from the analytical database too.

Building data pipelines with DuckDB

Having explored DuckDB's seamless integration with prominent data processing languages, such as Python, and libraries, such as pandas, Apache Arrow, and Polars, in chapter 6, we know that DuckDB and its ecosystem are capable of tackling various tasks that belong to data pipelines and can, therefore, be used within them. The combination of a powerful SQL engine, well-integrated tooling, and the potential of a cloud offering makes it more than just another database system.

In this chapter, we'll delve deeper into DuckDB's role within the broader data ecosystem, emphasizing its significance in building robust data pipelines and enhancing workflows. For this, we will first take a step back and discuss the meaning and relevance of data pipelines. Then, we are going to evaluate a couple of tools that we think are helpful when building robust pipelines. These tools cover ingestion, transformation, and orchestration. Let's start with the basics and have a look at the problems we want to solve.

> **NOTE**   As we're loading data from external live sources and repositories that have been updated, the examples in this chapter might show different outputs of records or counts than the ones you see when you run the code.

8.1   *Data pipelines and the role of DuckDB*

A *data pipeline* is usually set up to retrieve and ingest data from various sources into a data store, such as a database, a data lake stored as flat files in the cloud, or a data warehouse. Prior to storing anything, data is usually processed and transformed in many ways. These transformations include joining datasets together, filtering, aggregating, or masking, with the goal of proper integration and standardization. We've already spoken a lot about filtering and aggregations in chapters 3 and 4, but masking is new. *Masking* is about anonymizing or distorting confidential or regulated data.

It's not enough to just store the data; pipelines are about creating value. Any use of a data pipeline is eventually about creating a product, such as dashboards, APIs, machine learning (ML) models, and more. Figure 8.1 shows a potential data pipeline that demonstrates some actions taken on data and some of the directions it can take.

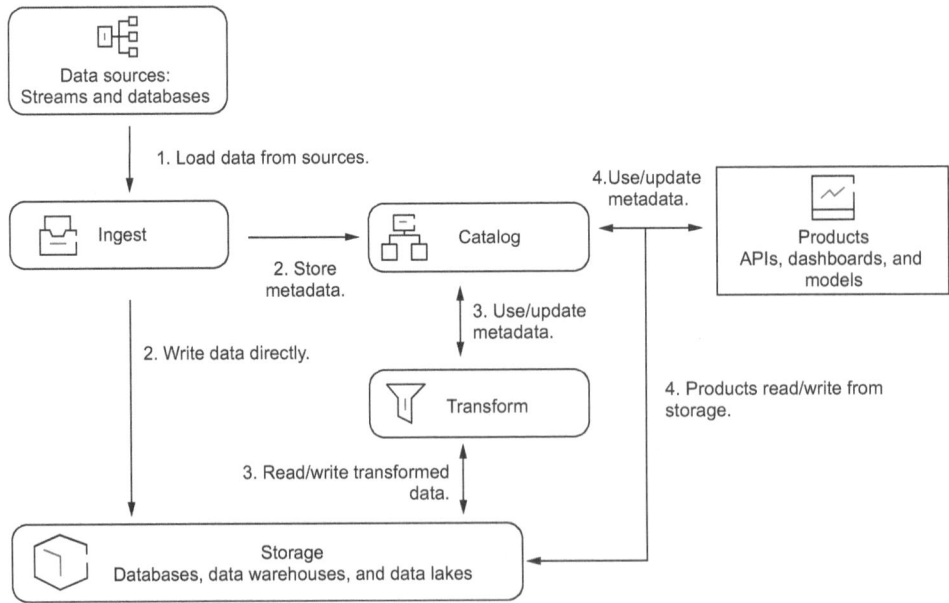

Figure 8.1   Flows in a data pipeline from data sources through transformation to storage and products

There are usually two main types of data pipelines to deal with: batch processing and streaming data. We are looking at pipelines that deal with batch processing of data in this chapter. *Batch processing* usually forms a workflow of sequences of commands, where each output of one command becomes the input to the next. Processing will be complete after the last transformation is completed and the data has been stored in the desired repository. Batch processing is appropriate when there is no immediate need to analyze each change or react to immediate changes.

> **NOTE** The flow of *extract, transform, and load* (ETL) is a subcategory of a data pipeline. Not all pipelines follow that exact sequence. While extraction, in most cases, is the first step, data can be loaded into a desired storage first and then be transformed. This sequence is known as ELT. Whether you build an ETL or an ELT pipeline is relevant when you use a cloud service like Mother-Duck in which you want to make the best possible use of resources. Sometimes, it's better to transform your data with local resources; at other times, it's more effective to transform data that is already stored in the cloud.

So what is DuckDB's role in this? While DuckDB can be used as a storage system in a pipeline, it usually sits in the transformation and processing part of a pipeline due to its simple yet powerful execution model: a single binary that is capable of dealing with large datasets, using a plethora of sources and store formats as input, providing a complete SQL engine to transform data in many different ways.

The broad support for SQL provides the first shared language to integrate with relevant processing tools like dbt, covered later in this chapter. The second shared language oftentimes—especially when storing to data lakes—uses Parquet as the output format.

Let's have a look at how a possible data pipeline with DuckDB might look. We start by ingesting some data.

8.2 Data ingestion with dlt

The data load tool (dlt; see https://dlthub.com/) is an open source Python library that lets us load data from various, and often messy, data sources into a variety of destinations. Why would you want to use dlt and not run your own Python scripts to build ingestion pipelines? The main entry to dlt, the `pipeline` function, can infer a schema from source data and load that data to the destination, creating a suitable schema there. We can use this pipeline with JSON data, DataFrames, or other iterable objects, such as generator functions, without changing any processing that comes afterward. The engine takes care of versioning as well so that a data team can focus on using the data and driving value, while ensuring effective governance through timely notifications of any changes.

dlt provides a set of predefined sources and destinations, including SQL databases, GitHub, and other interesting APIs. One of the destinations supported out of the box is DuckDB. Custom sources and destinations can be defined as well, but this topic is not covered in this book.

An interesting built-in dlt source is http://chess.com. Their API provides information about players and games. In this section, we're going to use that source to build a little chess database with DuckDB, as depicted in figure 8.2.

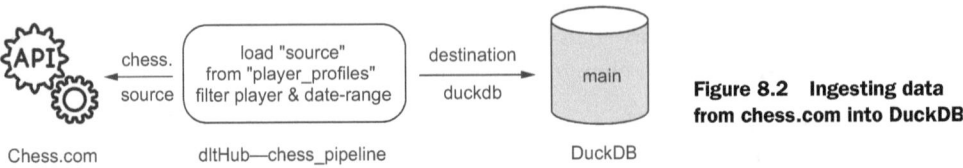

Figure 8.2 Ingesting data from chess.com into DuckDB

dlt is written in Python, and we assume you have a working Python environment with a working `pip` command. `pip` is Python's recommended package manager, and we use it to install dlt by running the following command:

```
pip install dlt
```

If you skipped chapter 6, you probably didn't install the DuckDB Python extension. It must be installed for the pipeline to work:

```
pip install duckdb
```

The full source code for the pipeline we are going to build in an interactive fashion in the following sections is also available in our examples repository on GitHub at https://mng.bz/d6pv.

8.2.1 *Installing a supported source*

Next, we're going to initialize our Chess.com pipeline (https://mng.bz/rVle). This is done via `dlt init`, which takes two arguments: the source and the destination. The source will be the built-in chess.com dlt source and the destination duckdb. As both our desired source and destination are officially supported by the tool, we can run the following command in our shell to create all necessary files and definitions for our first pipeline:

```
dlt init chess duckdb
```

This command will create some files locally, including executable scripts, so we'll need to confirm that we're happy to do that:

```
Looking up the init scripts in
➥https://github.com/dlt-hub/verified-sources.git...
Cloning and configuring a verified source chess (A source loading player
 profiles and games from chess.com api)
Do you want to proceed? [Y/n]:
```

Once it's completed, we'll see the following output:

```
Verified source chess was added to your project!
* See the usage examples and code snippets to copy from chess_pipeline.py
* Add credentials for duckdb and other secrets in ./.dlt/secrets.toml
```

```
* requirements.txt was created. Install it with:
pip install -r requirements.txt
* Read https://dlthub.com/docs/walkthroughs/create-a-pipeline
➥for more information
```

We should now have a directory called chess that contains the helper functions and a file called chess_pipeline.py that represents a working sample pipeline. You can either use it as is, as inspiration for your own experiments, or build a pipeline from scratch with us. We renamed the sample pipeline chess_pipeline.py.sample in our example repository.

8.2.2 Building a pipeline

dlt pipelines are written in Python too. You can enter the following Python snippets in a new Python file, the Python REPL, or a Jupyter notebook. We're going to use the Python REPL, and the following experiments assume you entered the Python shell from the directory into which you initialized the pipeline.

The first step is adding imports for dlt and the Chess.com source, as shown in the following listing.

Listing 8.1 Importing the required libraries for the new dlt pipeline

```
import dlt
from chess import source
```

Once we've done that, we're going to initialize a pipeline. We're going to call it chess_pipeline, and we'll also specify DuckDB as the destination. The whole definition will be stored in a variable named pipeline.

Listing 8.2 Defining a dlt pipeline

```
pipeline = dlt.pipeline(
    pipeline_name="chess_pipeline",
    destination="duckdb",
    dataset_name="main"
)
```

The name of the pipeline will be reflected in the name of the DuckDB file created.

The dataset name will be used as a schema name in DuckDB. We use main here, which is the name of DuckDB's default schema.

The DuckDB database will be written to a file named <pipeline-name>.duckdb (e.g., chess_pipeline.duckdb, in our case).

Next, we're going to create a source for four of the most popular players and their matches from November 2022.

Listing 8.3 Defining a dlt source

```
data = source(
    players=[
        "magnuscarlsen", "vincentkeymer",
        "dommarajugukesh", "rpragchess"
```

This is a function loaded from the Chess source that dlt provides.

This and the following arguments are specific to the Chess.com API.

```
    ],
    start_month="2022/11",
    end_month="2022/11",
)
```

This source contains a number of resources related to players, including profiles, games, and online statuses. To import only the players' profiles, we can write the following code.

Listing 8.4 Picking an interesting dataset from the dlt source

```
players_profiles = data.with_resources("players_profiles")
```

Until now, we've only defined what the pipeline should look like. To finally run it, we'll pass the source defined as `players_profile` to the pipelines `run` method.

Listing 8.5 Running a dlt pipeline

```
info = pipeline.run(players_profiles)
print(info)
```

We should see something like the following output:

```
Pipeline chess_pipeline completed in 0.62 seconds
1 load package(s) were loaded to destination duckdb and into dataset main
The duckdb destination used
⟜duckdb:////path/to/code/ch08/dlt_example/chess_pipeline.duckdb
⟜location to store data
Load package 1696519035.883884 is LOADED and contains no failed jobs
```

That looks like it worked. Please don't leave the Python shell yet; instead, open a second terminal, and load the database into DuckDB:

```
duckdb chess_pipeline.duckdb
```

Then check which tables have been created with SHOW TABLES:

```
┌──────────────────────┐
│         name         │
│       varchar        │
├──────────────────────┤
│ _dlt_loads           │
│ _dlt_pipeline_state  │
│ _dlt_version         │
│ players_profiles     │
└──────────────────────┘
```

dlt has also created a bunch of tables to store its own metadata, and at the bottom, we can see `players_profiles`, which presumably contains profiles for the players we specified in our script. Let's get one record from that table:

```
.mode line
FROM players_profiles LIMIT 1;

avatar = https://images.chesscomfiles.com/uploads/v1/user/
➥138850604.80351cd5.200x200o.3129ed9b015d.jpeg
   player_id = 138850604
         aid = https://api.chess.com/pub/player/dommarajugukesh
         url = https://www.chess.com/member/DommarajuGukesh
        name = Gukesh Dommaraju
    username = dommarajugukesh
   followers = 3
     country = https://api.chess.com/pub/country/IN
    location = Chennai
 last_online = 2022-07-16 19:18:02+01
      joined = 2021-05-05 10:27:46+01
      status = basic
 is_streamer = false
    verified = false
      league = Wood
_dlt_load_id = 1696519035.883884
     _dlt_id = kldRaeRA40OGBA
       title =
```

That's the profile for `Gukesh Dommaraju`, so the pipeline is working well so far.

What if we now decide we'd like to load the games as well? Quit DuckDB and return to the Python shell; rerun the pipeline with a slightly different source. Observe how we don't assign the resource like we did before but just pass it to the `run` method.

Listing 8.6   Running the pipeline with another dataset

```
info = pipeline.run(data.with_resources("players_profiles", "players_games"))
print(info)
```

The output should be similar to the following snipped, indicating it did load several archives for the players we had been interested in. Also, it did use the same storage as before:

```
Getting archive from https://api.chess.com/pub/player/
➥magnuscarlsen/games/2022/11
Getting archive from https://api.chess.com/pub/player/
➥vincentkeymer/games/2022/11
Getting archive from https://api.chess.com/pub/player/
➥rpragchess/games/2022/11
Pipeline chess_pipeline completed in 1.89 seconds
1 load package(s) were loaded to destination duckdb and into dataset main
The duckdb destination used duckdb:////path/to/code/ch08/dlt_example/
➥chess_pipeline.duckdb location to store data
Load package 1696519484.186974 is LOADED and contains no failed jobs
```

And again, let's see what data's been ingested into DuckDB. In a second terminal, run the following:

```
duckdb chess_pipeline.duckdb 'SELECT count(*) FROM players_games'
```

```
| count_star() |
|    int64     |
|--------------|
|          589 |
```

That looks good—the games have been ingested. What happens if we run the pipeline again? dlt will discover that it already ingested everything available that we asked for and won't import anything new. This is actually quite impressive; picking up batched imports where they have stopped is not an easy task. The information that dlt needs to control this capability is stored inside the three other tables (_dlt_loads, _dlt_pipeline_state, and _dlt_version) that appeared in our store. We can extract that metadata either with DuckDB or SQL, or we can use the tools dlt offers.

8.2.3   *Exploring pipeline metadata*

dlt offers the `info` command, which will inspect both the pipeline definition and the metatables inside your store to retrieve a view on the state of the pipeline itself. The command has to be invoked as follows:

```
dlt pipeline chess_pipeline info
```

Our output indicates that we've run the pipeline three times, and it describes the names of the tables that have been created. Your output will differ in date and time—and most likely in state as well:

```
Found pipeline chess_pipeline in /Home/.dlt/pipelines
Synchronized state:
_state_version: 2
_state_engine_version: 2
schema_names: ['chess']
pipeline_name: chess_pipeline
destination: dlt.destinations.duckdb
default_schema_name: chess
staging: None
dataset_name: main

sources:
Add -v option to see sources state. Note that it could be large.

Local state:
first_run: False
_last_extracted_at: 2023-11-04T19:16:35.873231+00:00

Resources in schema: chess
players_profiles with 1 table(s) and 0 resource state slot(s)
players_games with 1 table(s) and 1 resource state slot(s)

Working dir content:
Has 3 completed load packages with following load ids:
```

```
1699125395.876516
1699125399.292224
1699125402.854308
```

```
Pipeline has last run trace. Use 'dlt pipeline chess_pipeline trace'
➥to inspect
```

If you are interested in exploring the content of the data loaded with SQL, that's fine, of course. We will for now tackle transformations of datasets and put DuckDB to use not only as a store but as an integral part of transformations.

8.3 Data transformation and modeling with dbt

Data, in its raw form, often requires shaping, cleaning, and modeling to unlock its true potential. The data build tool (dbt) is an SQL-centric transformation tool designed to support the creation and management of data pipelines. It emphasizes software engineering principles, allowing data teams to ensure modularity, portability, and documentation. Integrating CI/CD within dbt facilitates the consistent and reliable deployment of data transformations.

So how do we use dbt with DuckDB? Enter the `dbt-duckdb` library, which acts as the bridge that connects dbt to DuckDB. It enables users to combine the strengths of both tools, making it possible to use DuckDB to apply transformations in dbt-powered data pipelines. The common language that both dbt and DuckDB speak is, of course, SQL.

We're going to use `dbt-duckdb` to build a straightforward data pipeline that takes some CSV files stored on GitHub, applies cleanup and data transformation, and then outputs a Parquet file with the cleaned data. Thus, DuckDB is not used as a store but only as a means of transformation, which is close to what we described in 8.1. The diagram in figure 8.3 shows what we're going to build.

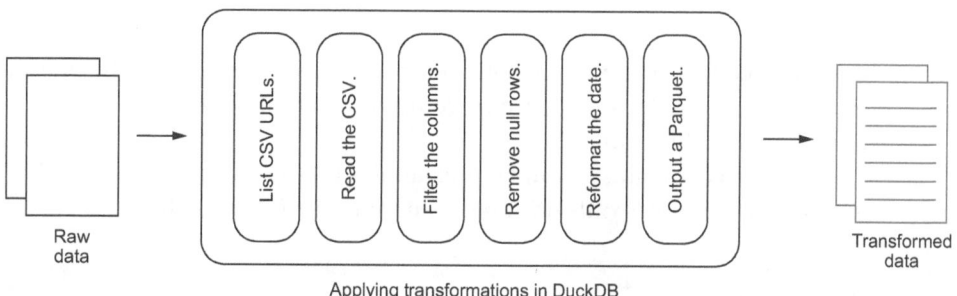

Applying transformations in DuckDB

Figure 8.3 Transforming CSVs to Parquet

Let's get to it! The first thing we need to do is install `dbt-duckdb` and `dbt` into our Python environment by running the following command:

```
pip install dbt-duckdb dbt
```

The example project we will build in the following sections is built in several iterative steps. We provide a subfolder for each step in our example repository: https://mng.bz/VxrW.

8.3.1 Setting up a dbt project

dbt thinks in projects and provides commands to create new ones. If the preceding installation succeeded, you should be able to execute the following commands in your shell, creating a new project and changing the working directory to it. If you run dbt for the first time, it will set up your profile and ask you for the database you want to use. Pick DuckDB here:

```
dbt init dbt_transformations
cd dbt_transformations
```

Let's now have a look at the directory structure. We're going to use the `tree` command to do this, but you can also navigate through the directory structure manually:

```
tree

.
├── README.md
├── analyses
├── dbt_project.yml
├── macros
├── models
│   └── example
│       ├── my_first_dbt_model.sql
│       ├── my_second_dbt_model.sql
│       └── schema.yml
├── seeds
├── snapshots
└── tests
```

We have folders for the main dbt concepts: macros, models, seeds, snapshots, and tests. For our sample project, we're going to create models and tests—we won't be using the other directories.

The project contains a couple of examples but no usable profile yet. Let's create one via a file—profiles.yml—with the content in the following listing.

Listing 8.7   Defining a dbt profile that uses DuckDB for all output

```
dbt_transformations:
  target: dev
  outputs:
    dev:                              This is the intermediate
      type: duckdb                    DuckDB store being used by
      path: '/tmp/atp.db'    ◁─────   dbt. It can have any location.
      schema: 'main'
```

NOTE YAML Ain't Markup Language (YAML) is a data serialization language designed for human readability and interaction with scripting languages. Its syntax is relatively straightforward and utilizes indentation to represent hierarchy. It exclusively uses spaces, not tabs, for this purpose.

Next, let's rename the example directory to atp and delete the existing model files:

```
mv models/example models/atp
rm models/atp/*.sql
```

Now, with the examples out of the way, we need to define new sources and models.

8.3.2 Defining sources

dbt sources provide a standardized way to reference and document raw data in external databases, data warehouses, or anywhere else. By defining sources, users ensure consistency in how raw data is accessed, while also specifying metadata and quality checks associated with the underlying datasets. We can define sources in a sources.yml file inside the models directory.

The data we're going to use is from Jeff Sackmann's tennis dataset (https://github.com/JeffSackmann/tennis_atp), which we first encountered in chapter 5. To start with, we're going to process just one of the CSV files. Create a file named models/atp/sources.yml, which creates a source that points to the atp_matches_2023.csv file on GitHub.

Listing 8.8 Defining a dbt source that fetches data from a web location

```
version:              ◁──┐ The dbt version—this needs to be 2 to work
                          │ with the version of dbt at the time of writing.
sources:
  - name: github #    ◁──┤ The name of our source—this
    meta:                 │ can be whatever we like.
        external_location: 'https://raw.githubusercontent.com/
        ➥JeffSackmann/tennis_atp/master/atp_matches_2023.csv'
    tables:
      - name: matches_file #    ◁──┐ The name we'll use to reference the
                                   │ CSV file—this can be we whatever we like.
```

We'll be able to reference this source via the combination of the source name (github) and table name (matches_file) in the model, which we'll define next.

8.3.3 Describing transformations with models

dbt models are a set of SQL queries or Python scripts that transform raw data into a desired structure. By defining these models, data analysts and engineers can create, test, and document their data transformation workflows in a consistent and version-controlled manner.

Now we're going to create our first transformation in a file named models/atp/matches.sql. We're going to pull all of the matches from the CSV file we defined in listing 8.8, but we'll exclude all the columns that start with w_ or l_. These fields contain fine-grained match data that we won't need for our use case. We'll then write the output of the query to a Parquet file. The full code snippet is shown in the following listing.

Listing 8.9   Defining a dbt model using several queries for transforming data via DuckDB

```
{{ config(
    materialized='external',
    location='output/matches.parquet',
    format='parquet'
) }}                              ◁─── Output a Parquet file
                                       in the output directory.
WITH noWinLoss AS (
    SELECT COLUMNS(col ->
      NOT regexp_matches(col, 'w_.*') AND   ◁─── Filter columns that start
      NOT regexp_matches(col, 'l_.*')       ◁───  with w_, using DuckDB's
    )                                              regexp_matches function.
    FROM {{ source('github', 'matches_file') }}   Filter columns that start
)                                                  with l_, using DuckDB's
                                                   regexp_matches function.

SELECT * REPLACE (
    cast(strptime(tourney_date, '%Y%m%d') AS date) as tourney_date   ◁───
)
FROM noWinLoss                                    Coerce tourney_date
                                                  field to date type.
```

Annotations: "Query the source we defined in the previous section." points to the WITH noWinLoss AS (... FROM {{ source('github', 'matches_file') }}) block.

Next, let's create the output directory so that dbt will be able to write the Parquet file there:

```
mkdir output
```

The pipeline we defined will run the following steps:

1 dbt will grab the CSV data from GitHub.
2 It will pass the content to DuckDB.
3 Run the transformations written in SQL.
4 Store the outcome as a Parquet.

Let's run it with

```
dbt run
```

The process will print something along the following lines:

```
...
09:48:35  Found 1 model, 1 source, 0 exposures, 0 metrics, 351 macros,
         0 groups, 0 semantic models
09:48:35
09:48:35  Concurrency: 1 threads (target='dev')
09:48:35
09:48:35  1 of 1 START sql external model main.matches_2023
         ........................ [RUN]
```

```
09:48:37  1 of 1 OK created sql external model main.matches_2023
➥..................... [OK in 1.16s]
09:48:37
09:48:37  Finished running 1 external model in 0 hours 0 minutes
➥and 1.20 seconds (1.20s).
09:48:37
09:48:37  Completed successfully
09:48:37
09:48:37  Done. PASS=1 WARN=0 ERROR=0 SKIP=0 TOTAL=1
...
```

It looks like everything worked. We can look in the output directory for the generated Parquet file using the du command-line tool:

```
du -h output/*

120K    output/matches.parquet
```

We can then open up a DuckDB CLI session to inspect the contents of the file:

```
SELECT count(*) FROM 'output/matches.parquet';
```

```
┌──────────────┐
│ count_star() │
│    int64     │
├──────────────┤
│         2986 │
└──────────────┘
```
◁─── **At the time of writing, you'll see 2,986 records, but more matches are added all the time, so it's possible this number may be higher!**

```
.mode line
FROM 'output/matches.parquet' LIMIT 1;

tourney_id = 2023-9900
    tourney_name = United Cup
         surface = Hard
   tourney_level = A
    tourney_date = 2023-01-02
       match_num = 300
       winner_id = 126203
     winner_seed = 3
    winner_entry =
     winner_name = Taylor Fritz
     winner_hand = R
       winner_ht = 193
      winner_ioc = USA
      winner_age = 25.1
        loser_id = 126610
      loser_seed = 5
     loser_entry =
      loser_name = Matteo Berrettini
      loser_hand = R
        loser_ht = 196
       loser_ioc = ITA
       loser_age = 26.7
```

```
            score = 7-6(4) 7-6(6)
          best_of = 3
            round = F
          minutes = 135
      winner_rank = 9
winner_rank_points = 3355
       loser_rank = 16
loser_rank_points = 2375
```

That looks pretty good—we've successfully written our first dbt pipeline. We've extracted the data from the CSV file, removed some of the fields, and then written the result out to a Parquet file. But how do we know if the data in the Parquet file is correct?

8.3.4 *Testing transformations and pipelines*

dbt tests are assertions applied to data models to ensure data quality and consistency. By defining these tests, we can validate our transformations, catching problems like NULL values, duplicates, or violations of referential integrity.

One place we can define tests is in the schema.yml file, which lives in models/atp/schema.yml, next to our model files. We're going to create tests for just a few of the columns, but in a production pipeline, you'd want to create tests for all the fields to make sure the transformation worked as expected.

We'll test the following assertions:

- tourney_id is not NULL.
- winner_id is not NULL.
- loser_id is not NULL.
- surface is not NULL and only contains one of the following values: Grass, Hard, or Clay.

Create the file models/atp/schema.yml, and enter the contents of the following listing.

Listing 8.10 A dbt schema asserting various qualities of our dataset

```
version: 2

models:
  - name: matches
    description: "ATP tennis matches schema"
    columns:
      - name: tourney_id
        description: "The ID of the tournament."
        tests:
          - not_null
      - name: winner_id
        description: "The ID of the winning player."
        tests:
```

```
            - not_null
        - name: loser_id
          description: "The ID of the losing player."
          tests:
            - not_null
        - name: surface
          description: "The surface of the court."
          tests:
            - not_null
            - accepted_values:
                values: ['Grass', 'Hard', 'Clay']
```

You don't need to create a test for every field—only the ones that are necessary for your use case. You don't need to create tests for fields where the data might be dirty or where it doesn't matter if it's dirty.

NOTE   If you're feeling adventurous, you can try to add assertions for some of the other fields.

To run the tests, we can run the following command:

```
dbt test

...
10:57:39  Found 1 model, 5 tests, 1 source, 0 exposures, 0 metrics,
➥351 macros, 0 groups, 0 semantic models
10:57:39
10:57:39  Concurrency: 1 threads (target='dev')
10:57:39
10:57:39  1 of 5 START test accepted_values_matches_surface__Grass__Hard
➥Clay ....... [RUN]
10:57:39  1 of 5 PASS accepted_values_matches_surface__Grass__Hard__Clay
➥............. [PASS in 0.14s]
10:57:39  2 of 5 START test not_null_matches_loser_id
➥............................. [RUN]
10:57:39  2 of 5 PASS not_null_matches_loser_id
➥................................. [PASS in 0.12s]
10:57:39  3 of 5 START test not_null_matches_surface
➥............................. [RUN]
10:57:39  3 of 5 PASS not_null_matches_surface
➥.................................... [PASS in 0.12s]
10:57:39  4 of 5 START test not_null_matches_tourney_id
➥............................. [RUN]
10:57:39  4 of 5 PASS not_null_matches_tourney_id
➥................................. [PASS in 0.12s]
10:57:39  5 of 5 START test not_null_matches_winner_id
➥............................. [RUN]
10:57:39  5 of 5 PASS not_null_matches_winner_id
➥................................. [PASS in 0.12s]
10:57:39
10:57:39  Finished running 5 tests in 0 hours 0 minutes and 0.66
➥seconds (0.66s).
...
```

Everything looks good so far.

While dbt comes with several built-in assertions, we will sometimes want to do finer-grained tests than this. For example, we might want to test the range of the values in the `tourney_date` column.

To do this, we'll need to install a package, like dbt_expectations, that offers more assertions. At the top level of the project, create the packages.yml file, and add the following:

```
packages:
  - package: calogica/dbt_expectations
    version: 0.10.1
```

To install the package, we can run the following command:

```
dbt deps
```

We should see the following output:

```
19:30:56   Running with dbt=1.6.7
19:30:56   Installing calogica/dbt_expectations
19:30:56   Installed from version 0.10.1
19:30:56   Up to date!
19:30:56   Installing calogica/dbt_date
19:30:57   Installed from version 0.10.0
19:30:57   Up to date!
```

We can then update models/atp/schema.yml to add an assertion that checks that the values for `tourney_date` are between January 1, 2023 and December 31, 2023, as shown in the following listing.

Listing 8.11 Adding tests to the schema defined in listing 8.10

```
models:
  - name: matches
      # Keep the original assertions, too
      - name: tourney_date
        description: "Verify that the tournament started in 2023"
        tests:
          - dbt_expectations.expect_column_values_to_be_of_type:
              column_type: date
          - dbt_expectations.expect_column_min_to_be_between:
              min_value: "CAST('2023-01-01' AS DATE)"
              max_value: "CAST('2023-12-31' AS DATE)"
```

If we rerun `dbt test`, this new assertion will be picked up, and we will see it in the test output.

8.3.5 *Transforming all CSV files*

So far, we've only worked with the 2023 matches, but there is a list of other CSV files going back to 1968 that we need to process. We started with only one file to keep our waiting times low, getting immediate feedback regarding whether our schema and models work or not.

Let's change the sources for our pipeline first, starting with models/atp/sources.yml. We're going to change the `external_location` to return a function that iterates over the years from 1968 to 2023, creates a list of all the CSV file URLs, and reads them using the `read_csv_auto` function. This is a prime example of how DuckDB is used as a processing tool in this pipeline, not as storage.

Listing 8.12 Computing a list of CSV files as sources for the pipeline

```
version: 2

sources:
  - name: github
    meta:
      external_location: >
        (FROM read_csv_auto(
          list_transform(
            range(1968, 2023),
            y -> 'https://raw.githubusercontent.com/JeffSackmann/
            tennis_atp/master/atp_matches_' || y || '.csv'
          ),
          types={'winner_seed': 'VARCHAR', 'loser_seed': 'VARCHAR'}
        ))
      formatter: oldstyle
    tables:
      - name: matches_file
```

> Transforms each year into a URL that ends with atp_matches_<year>.csv

> Generates a list of all the years from 1968 to 2023

> We need to use the oldstyle formatter so that we can use the {} characters in the query used by the external_location property.

Once we've done that, we can run `dbt run` again to generate a new Parquet file. Let's quickly explore the contents of our new Parquet file:

```
SELECT count(*) FROM 'output/matches.parquet';
```

```
┌──────────────┐
│ count_star() │
│    int64     │
├──────────────┤
│      188934  │
└──────────────┘
```

That's a lot more rows than we had before, so we can assume that it worked. Let's run `dbt test` to see if our assertions still pass:

```
12:58:05  Finished running 7 tests in 0 hours 0 minutes and 1.49
seconds (1.49s).
12:58:05
12:58:05  Completed with 3 errors and 0 warnings:
12:58:05
12:58:05  Failure in test accepted_values_matches_surface__Grass__Hard
Clay (models/atp/schema.yml)
12:58:05    Got 1 result, configured to fail if != 0
12:58:05
12:58:05    compiled Code at target/compiled/dbt_transformations/models/
atp/schema.yml/accepted_values_matches_surface__Grass__Hard__Clay.sql
```

```
12:58:05
12:58:05  Failure in test dbt_expectations_expect_column_min_to_be
➥between_matches_tourney_date__CAST_2023_12_31_AS_DATE___CAST_2023
➥01_01_AS_DATE_  (models/atp/schema.yml)
12:58:05    Got 1 result, configured to fail if != 0
12:58:05
12:58:05    compiled Code at target/compiled/dbt_transformations/models/
➥atp/schema.yml/dbt_expectations_expect_column_3a4294205f95862ee31c
➥ce05b1e1ebf7.sql
12:58:05
12:58:05  Failure in test not_null_matches_surface (models/atp/schema.yml)
12:58:05    Got 2937 results, configured to fail if != 0
12:58:05
12:58:05    compiled Code at target/compiled/dbt_transformations/models/
➥atp/schema.yml/not_null_matches_surface.sql
12:58:05
12:58:05  Done. PASS=4 WARN=0 ERROR=3 SKIP=0 TOTAL=7
```

Hmm, not this time. We've got three broken tests:

- not_null_matches_surface—This means there are NULL surfaces.
- accepted_values_matches_surface*Grass*Hard__Clay—This means there are surfaces that aren't Grass, Hard, or Clay.
- dbt_expectations_expect_column_min_to_be_between_matches_tourney_ date*CAST_2023_12_31_AS_DATECAST_2023_01_01_AS_DATE*—This means some matches have a date that isn't in 2023.

Let's debug them, starting with the surface field, which now has some NULL values, although it was only supposed to have the values Grass, Hard, and Clay:

```
FROM 'output/matches.parquet' SELECT surface, count(*) GROUP BY ALL;
```

| surface | count_star() |
varchar	int64
Clay	67537
Carpet	20900
Hard	74814
Grass	22746
	2937

Carpet looks like a valid value, but there are also almost 3,000 rows that don't have a surface. We're going to update schema.yml to allow Carpet as a valid value and update the matches.sql model to filter out the matches that have a NULL surface.

We also have a perhaps more predictable problem in the tourney_date field, where we now have dates that aren't necessarily in 2023. This has happened because we're now ingesting data from all years rather than just 2023. We'll update schema.yml to allow a range of dates from December 1967 to December 2023. Our new models/atp/schema.yml file looks like the following listing.

Listing 8.13 Adding details to our schema

```
version: 2

models:
  - name: matches
    description: "ATP tennis matches schema"
    columns:
      - name: tourney_id
        description: "The ID of the tournament."
        tests:
          - not_null
      - name: winner_id
        description: "The ID of the winning player."
        tests:
          - not_null
      - name: loser_id
        description: "The ID of the winning player."
        tests:
          - not_null
      - name: surface
        description: "The surface of the court."
        tests:
          - not_null
          - accepted_values:
              values: ['Grass', 'Hard', 'Clay', 'Carpet']   ⟵  Carpet is allowed
                                                                  now too.
      - name: tourney_date
        description: "The date when the tournament started"
        tests:
          - dbt_expectations.expect_column_values_to_be_of_type:
              column_type: date
          - dbt_expectations.expect_column_min_to_be_between:
              min_value: "CAST('1967-12-01' AS DATE)"
              max_value: "CAST('2023-12-31' AS DATE)"
```

The transformation in models/atp/matches.sql now gets an additional WHERE clause to exclude all matches without a surface, as shown in the following listing.

Listing 8.14 Updating our transformations to deal with oddities in some of the new files

```
{{ config(
    materialized='external',
    location='output/matches.parquet',
    format='parquet'
) }}

WITH noWinLoss AS (
    SELECT COLUMNS(col ->
      NOT  regexp_matches(col, 'w_.*')
      AND NOT regexp_matches(col, 'l_.*')
    )
    FROM {{ source('github', 'matches_file') }}
)
```

```
SELECT * REPLACE (
    cast(strptime(tourney_date, '%Y%m%d') AS date) as tourney_date
)
FROM noWinLoss                          | Filtering out NULL
WHERE surface IS NOT NULL      ◁───┘ values for surface
```

Due to the changes in the model, we must first run the pipeline again with `dbt run` before running `dbt test` to make all tests pass, ensuring our pipeline is working end to end. We started out with CSV files on GitHub and have successfully transformed them into a single Parquet file and cleaned up the data as part of the process.

> **NOTE** The next step would be to set up a production pipeline to go along with the dev one. It would be fairly similar, but perhaps, we'd write the Parquet file to an S3 bucket, rather than the local file system. We'll leave that as an exercise for the reader.

8.4   *Orchestrating data pipelines with Dagster*

So far in this chapter, we've learned about tools that can load data into DuckDB from external sources or transform data between formats using DuckDB. These are important tasks, but we are still missing a piece of the data pipeline puzzle: How do we trigger or orchestrate the transformation or ingestion code?

In a world with no orchestration tools, we would need to write our own manual scheduling and execution code. We'd need to set up cron jobs to run dbt commands and write custom scripts to handle the sequencing and dependencies of dbt tasks.

Luckily for us, tools like Airflow, Luigi, Kestra, Prefect, and Dagster (the tool we'll be using in this chapter) do exist. These tools control the orchestration of data pipelines, which is what we'll be exploring in this section. As in the previous section, we provide the pipeline we are building here in our GitHub repository as several steps: https://mng.bz/x2og.

Dagster is a cloud-native tool built to manage and organize data flows in modular pipelines. One of its core concepts is the (software-defined) asset, which is an object in persistent storage, such as a table, file, or machine learning model. A software-defined asset is a description, in code, of an asset that should exist and how to produce and update that asset. Assets form parts of data processing jobs, which can then be scheduled.

Like dlt and dbt, Dagster is written in Python. It aims to make it easier for developers to work with data throughout different stages, such as creating, deploying, and monitoring data assets by using Python functions to describe the data assets. These functions tell Dagster what data assets to create or update as well as which dependencies an asset has. Describing assets with Python function lets us describe any dependencies and interactions as verifiable code, which is a big advantage over configuration-based tools, especially for developers. We will show how to create these asset functions in the following sections with our concrete pipeline. Dagster offers especially good support for data lineage and data provenance, as those are important aspects of data pipelines for auditing, debugging, and tracing. It has an integration with DuckDB, called `dagster-duckdb`, which we'll be using in this section.

We're going to use the same tennis dataset we used in the previous section, but this time, we're going to load the data into DuckDB, rather than create a Parquet file. In addition to loading tennis matches, we'll also import player profiles, and we'll see how to load static data from pandas DataFrames.

Let's start by installing the main dependencies required to use Dagster and DuckDB:

```
pip install dagster dagster-duckdb
```

We'll also install `dagster-webserver`, which is required to run the Dagster UI and can be used to visualize pipelines:

```
pip install dagster-webserver
```

> **Possible error when installing dagster-webserver**
>
> At the time of writing, you may see the following error, which results in the Dagster server shutting down when trying to install the dagster-webserver package:
>
> ```
> ImportError: cannot import name 'appengine' from
>   'requests.packages.urllib3.contrib'
> ....
>     raise Exception(
> Exception: dagster-webserver process shut down unexpectedly
>   with return code 1
> ```
>
> If you see this error, you'll need to pin the dependencies `urllib3` and `requests-toolbelt` to the following versions:
>
> ```
> pip install urllib3==1.26.15 requests-toolbelt==0.10.1
> ```

8.4.1 Defining assets

With those dependencies installed, we're ready to create our pipeline. Let's create a directory called atp and add the following files:

- atp/__init__.py—Orchestration code will go in here.
- atp/assets.py—Asset definition code will go in here.

We're going to start by creating a Python function to define the asset in assets.py called `atp_matches_dataset`, which loads the atp_matches_*.csv files into the `matches` table in DuckDB.

> **NOTE** You can also copy the code for these two files from the GitHub repository: https://mng.bz/AdMg.

It constructs the list of CSV URLs based on the year range (1968 to 2024) in Python code and then uses the DuckDB Python API to load the CSV files into DuckDB. During loading, it also converts the `tourney_date` column into a date type.

Listing 8.15 Defining the first asset we want to process in our Dagster pipeline

```
from dagster_duckdb import DuckDBResource
from dagster import asset

@asset
def atp_matches_dataset(duckdb_resource: DuckDBResource) -> None:
    base = "https://raw.githubusercontent.com/JeffSackmann/tennis_atp/master"
    csv_files = [                              ◁──┐ Constructs the
        f"{base}/atp_matches_{year}.csv"          │ list of CSV files
        for year in range(1968,2024)
    ]

    create_query = """
    CREATE OR REPLACE TABLE matches AS                Imports the CSV files
    SELECT * REPLACE(                                        into DuckDB
        cast(strptime(tourney_date, '%Y%m%d') AS date) as tourney_date
    )                                                              ◁──┐
    FROM read_csv_auto($1, types={    ◁──┐ $1 refers to the first parameter
      'winner_seed': 'VARCHAR',            │ passed to the execute function,
      'loser_seed': 'VARCHAR',            │ which is the list of CSV files.
      'tourney_date': 'STRING'
    })                              Converts tourney_date │
        """                                  to date type │
                                                           Passes in the list of CSV
    with duckdb_resource.get_connection() as conn:  ◁──┘  files as a parameter
        conn.execute(create_query, [csv_files])  ◁──┘
```

Next, we're going to update __init__.py to configure `atp_matches_dataset` as an asset and specify the location where the DuckDB database should be created. This file essentially controls the available libraries, determines when jobs should be run, and uses information from the environment when necessary. We're also going to create a job that contains our assets and a schedule that will run the job once an hour.

Listing 8.16 Defining the Dagster job in __init__.py

```
from dagster_duckdb import DuckDBResource

from dagster import (
    AssetSelection,
    ScheduleDefinition,
    Definitions,
    define_asset_job,
    load_assets_from_modules,
)                                                            The job
                                                          definition
from . import assets

atp_job = define_asset_job("atp_job", selection=AssetSelection.all())  ◁──┘
```

```
atp_schedule = ScheduleDefinition(
    job=atp_job,
    cron_schedule="0 * * * *",
)

all_assets = load_assets_from_modules([assets])
defs = Definitions(
    assets=all_assets,
    jobs=[atp_job],
    resources={"duckdb": DuckDBResource(
        database="atp.duckdb",
    )},
    schedules=[atp_schedule],
)
```

This is a schedule that runs once an hour. See crontab.guru (https://crontab.guru) for a primer on the Cron syntax.

Dagster picks up all the functions that have the @asset annotation.

The definitions tie everything together—assets, jobs, resources, and schedules.

The location of the DuckDB database relative to the location where Dagster is run

8.4.2   Running pipelines

We can then launch the Dagster UI by running the `dagster dev` command with the
`-m` flag pointing at the atp directory to find our definitions:

```
dagster dev -m atp
```

Then, navigate to http://localhost:3000 in your web browser, where you'll see the diagram in figure 8.4, which shows the job, schedule, and asset we defined.

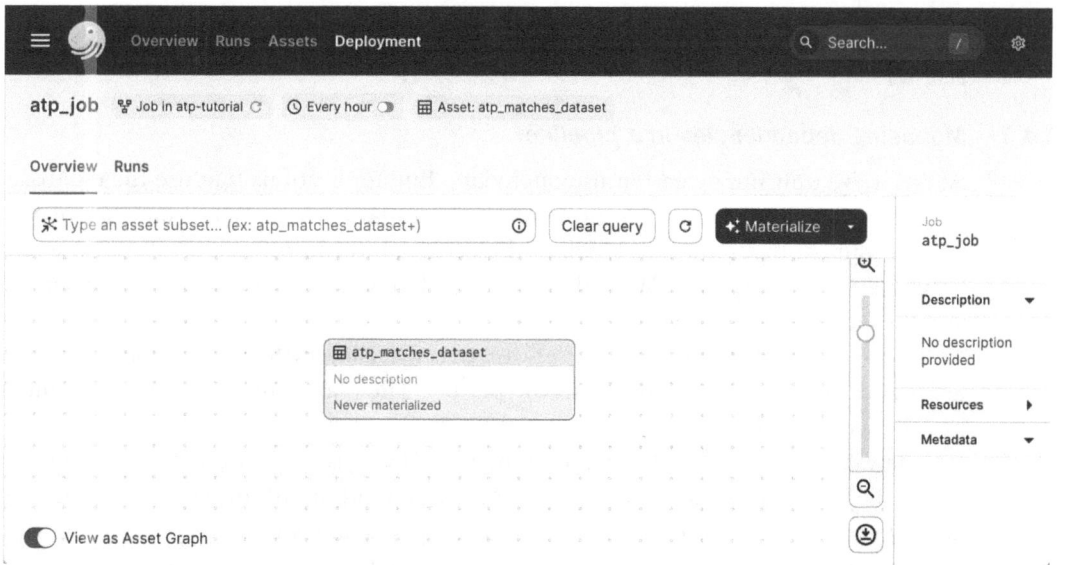

Figure 8.4   The initial Dagster job and asset graph in the Dagster UI

We can manually run the pipeline by clicking on Materialize at the top of the screen.
It will take a few seconds to run, but if we click the Refresh button, we'll see that our
asset has now materialized, as seen in figure 8.5.

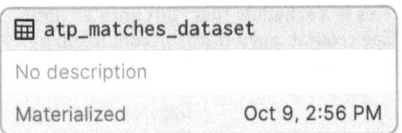

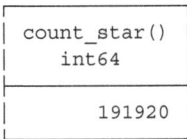

Figure 8.5   The state of the dataset in Dagster will change from never materialized to materialized.

We can check that the matches have been successfully loaded by querying the DuckDB database. As Dagster does not keep the database open or locked after materializing a pipeline, we don't have to stop any process prior to accessing the DuckDB database:

```
duckdb atp.duckdb 'SELECT count(*) FROM matches'
```

```
┌──────────────┐
│ count_star() │
│    int64     │
├──────────────┤
│       191920 │
└──────────────┘
```

> **NOTE**   At the time of writing, there are `191920` matches in the dataset, but this number will likely have increased by the time you try out this code sample. As long as it's more than 0, the import has likely worked!

We've now successfully loaded the roughly 200,000 tennis matches into DuckDB using Dagster.

8.4.3   Managing dependencies in a pipeline

So far, we've only imported tennis match data. But applications that use the database might also need other data on the tennis players that participated in matches, so we need to import that data too. Loading the actual player information will be an additional part of our pipeline. We'll then create a dependency between the players asset and the `matches` asset we've already created.

To do this, we'll add two more assets to assets.py, using Python functions. First up is `atp_players_dataset`, which ingests the players. The player information is contained in a file named atp_players.csv.

The values in the `dob` column are in the format `yyyymmdd`, but there are some rows where the last four digits are `0000`. Since `00` isn't a valid month or day, we're going to default each to `01` instead so that we can coerce the values to a date type, using the `strptime` function. The asset we are about to add not only queries the source but also applies some transformation. It is defined as follows and must be added to assets.py, as shown in the following listing.

> **NOTE**   As with the first step, you can copy the code from the GitHub repository: https://mng.bz/ZEn5.

Listing 8.17   A Dagster asset that uses DuckDB to transform data from an external source

```
@asset
def atp_players_dataset(duckdb: DuckDBResource) -> None:
    base = "https://raw.githubusercontent.com/JeffSackmann/tennis_atp/master"
    csv_file = f"{base}/atp_players.csv"

    with duckdb.get_connection() as conn:
        conn.execute("""
        CREATE OR REPLACE TABLE players AS
        SELECT * REPLACE(
            CASE
                WHEN dob IS NULL THEN NULL
                WHEN SUBSTRING(CAST(dob AS VARCHAR), 5, 4) = '0000' THEN
                    CAST(strptime(
                        CONCAT(SUBSTRING(CAST(dob AS VARCHAR), 1, 4), '0101'),
                            '%Y%m%d'
                    ) AS date)
                ELSE
                    CAST(strptime(dob, '%Y%m%d') AS date)
                END AS dob
        )
        FROM read_csv_auto($1, types = {
            'dob': 'STRING'
        });
        """, [csv_file])
```

Annotations:
- Some dates have month and day set to 00. This code sets both to 01 so that strptime can parse them.
- Leaves the NULL dates as they are
- Parses dates in the correct format with strptime
- Passes in the CSV files as a parameter

The atp_players.csv file contains columns for `name_first` and `name_last`, but for easier filtering by a user, we'd like the resulting `players` table to have an additional `name_full` column that concatenates the other two fields.

To achieve that, we add another asset, `atp_players_name_dataset`, which has a dependency on `atp_players_dataset`, which we just defined, and adds the `name_full` column to the `players` table. The `name_full` column will be a result of concatenating `name_first` and `name_last`, separated by a space.

Listing 8.18   A Dagster asset that transforms existing data

```
@asset(deps=[atp_players_dataset])
def atp_players_name_dataset(duckdb: DuckDBResource) -> None:
    concatenate_query = """
    ALTER TABLE players ADD COLUMN name_full VARCHAR;
    UPDATE players
    SET name_full = name_first || ' ' || name_last
    """

    with duckdb.get_connection() as conn:
        conn.execute(concatenate_query, [])
```

Annotations:
- Declares a dependency on the atp_players_dataset
- Concatenates the name_first and name_last columns

Creating a dependency on the `atp_players_dataset` means that Dagster will give us a warning if we try to materialize `atp_players_name_dataset` without first materializing `atp_players_dataset`, and when running the pipeline, Dagster orders the execution of the assets accordingly. This makes sense, as we can't update the `players` table to add the `name_full` column if the `players` table doesn't exist! This kind of dependent asset operation can be used for many different use cases, such as data refactoring, cleaning, or augmentation, where one or more assets are used as input to execute the operation.

To see the new assets, we'll need to stop and start the `dagster dev` command. After we've done that, we'll see the asset graph shown in figure 8.6.

Figure 8.6 Dagster asset graph with players included

We can then materialize all the assets via the UI, or we can do it from the terminal by running the following command:

```
dagster job execute -m atp --job atp_job
```

A truncated version of the output from this command is as follows:

```
atp_matches_dataset - STEP_START - Started execution of step
➥"atp_matches_dataset".
atp_players_dataset - STEP_START - Started execution of step
➥"atp_players_dataset".
atp_matches_dataset - STEP_SUCCESS - Finished execution of step
➥"atp_matches_dataset" in 413ms.
atp_players_dataset - STEP_SUCCESS - Finished execution of step
➥"atp_players_dataset" in 1.51s.
atp_players_name_dataset - STEP_START - Started execution of step
➥"atp_players_name_dataset".
atp_players_name_dataset - STEP_SUCCESS - Finished execution of step
➥"atp_players_name_dataset" in 49ms.
```

We can see that `atp_matches_dataset` and `atp_players_dataset` both start running immediately, but `atp_players_name_dataset` only starts running once `atp_players_dataset` has completed, as it has a dependency on that asset. We can check that the players have loaded correctly by running the following query, which only returns columns with the `name_` prefix:

```
duckdb atp.duckdb \
  'SELECT COLUMNS(col -> col LIKE "name_%") FROM players LIMIT 5'
```

We can see from the output that the `name_full` column has been successfully added to each record:

name_first varchar	name_last varchar	name_full varchar
Gardnar	Mulloy	Gardnar Mulloy
Pancho	Segura	Pancho Segura
Frank	Sedgman	Frank Sedgman
Giuseppe	Merlo	Giuseppe Merlo
Richard	Gonzalez	Richard Gonzalez

You might have noticed that the asset named `atp_players_name_dataset` did not use any external source data but transformed data that had already been ingested into the store. Dagster enables many more transformations in assets. You can use all functionality and libraries that are available in Python, such as pandas.

8.4.4 Advanced computation in assets

As we learned in chapter 6, DuckDB can query pandas DataFrames, and we can use that functionality in Dagster as well. The following asset ingests a DataFrame that provides the tennis tournament levels metadata.

> **NOTE** Tennis tournaments are categorized by the amount of prize money and the number of rankings points available. `Grand Slam` is the most valuable tournament category, followed by `Tour Finals`, `Masters 1000s`, `Other Tour Level`, `Challengers`, and `ITFs`.

While this example is more of a demonstration, imagine an actual computation you can do in Python with all the statistical and numerical features pandas has to offer. By being able to integrate DuckDB and Dagster assets through Python and its capabilities, even doing complex computations and operations as part of data pipelines becomes possible and easy for Python developers.

Let's add the asset in the following listing to assets.py.

Listing 8.19 Deriving new data by computing new values in a Dagster asset

```
import pandas as pd

@asset
def atp_levels_dataset(duckdb: DuckDBResource) -> None:
    levels_df = pd.DataFrame({
        "short_name": [
```

```
                "G", "M", "A", "C", "S", "F"
            ],
            "name": [
                "Grand Slam", "Tour Finals", "Masters 1000s",
                "Other Tour Level", "Challengers", "ITFs"
            ],
            "rank": [
                5, 4, 3, 2, 1, 0
            ]
    })

with duckdb.get_connection() as conn:
    conn.execute("""
    CREATE TABLE IF NOT EXISTS levels AS
    SELECT * FROM levels_df
    """)
```

The updated asset graphs can be seen in the Dagster UI in figure 8.7.

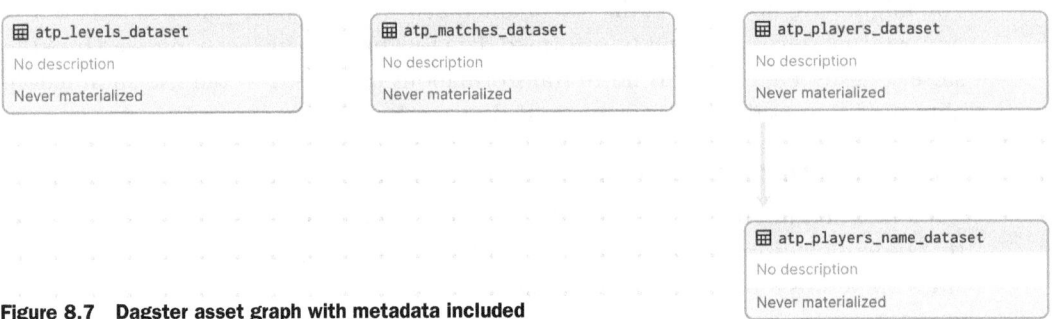

Figure 8.7   Dagster asset graph with metadata included

We can then materialize these assets again via the command line:

```
dagster job execute -m atp --job atp_job
```

Taking a look at the levels with

```
duckdb atp.duckdb 'FROM levels'
```

confirms that our ingestion of the DataFrame worked correctly:

short_name varchar	name varchar	rank int64
G	Grand Slam	5
M	Tour Finals	4
A	Masters 1000s	3
C	Other Tour Level	2
S	Challengers	1
F	ITFs	0

Everything looks good, and our Dagster pipeline has successfully ingested all the data required, but at the moment, the DuckDB database resides only on our machine. A complete data pipeline would publish your data to the cloud so that your application could use it from there.

8.4.5   Uploading to MotherDuck

If we want to make the newly created tennis database available to an application, we may choose to upload it to MotherDuck, a service we learned about in chapter 7. If you want to try out this last step of orchestrating a pipeline with Dagster, make sure you created a MotherDuck account and have your MotherDuck token set as an environment variable in your shell. As discussed in chapter 7, we can take the local database, publish and share it to MotherDuck, or transport the data directly into a cloud instance.

To keep things concise, we'll focus on the changes needed to publish the data to MotherDuck directly instead of writing to a local DuckDB database. Let's open atp/__init__.py and go down to the `defs` variable, which should read as follows.

> **Listing 8.20   Adding a new definition to our Dagster job inside atp/__init__.py**

```
defs = Definitions(
    assets=all_assets,
    jobs=[atp_job],
    resources={"duckdb": DuckDBResource(
        database="atp.duckdb",
    )},
    schedules=[atp_schedule],
)
```

To have the pipeline uploaded to MotherDuck, we need to change the database string to use the MotherDuck syntax. We'll also need to provide our MotherDuck token, as shown in the following code listing.

> **Listing 8.21   Changing the location of the DuckDB store to point to MotherDuck**

```
import dotenv          ◁──┐  This is only necessary for running from the
import os                 │  CLI. The Dagster UI automatically picks up
dotenv.load_dotenv()      │  properties defined in the .env file.

mduck_token = os.getenv("motherduck_token")

defs = Definitions(
    assets=all_assets,
    jobs=[atp_job],
    resources={"duckdb": DuckDBResource(
        database=f"md:md_atp_db?motherduck_token={mduck_token}",
        schema="main"         ◁──┐  Connects to the md_atp_db
    )},                          │  database in MotherDuck
    schedules=[atp_schedule],
)
```

If we now run the `atp_job`, the data will be uploaded to MotherDuck into a database named `md_atp_db`. Make sure you exported the necessary token to your shell first:

```
dagster job execute -m atp --job atp_job
```

Once the job has finished, we can confirm the database has been created from the MotherDuck UI at https://app.motherduck.com. We should see something similar to figure 8.8.

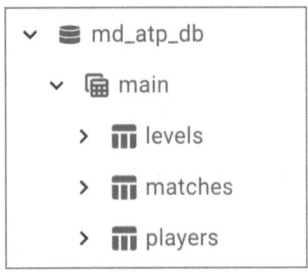

Figure 8.8   The ATP dataset on MotherDuck

Dagster orchestrated data loading and transformation as well as computing additional information. As a final step, it published the result to a cloud data store, ready to build a product upon, which we'll do in the next chapter.

Summary

- Data pipelines let us load and transform data in an automated and consistent way.
- DuckDB can be easily integrated into various data pipeline tools, like dlt, dbt, and Dagster.
- DuckDB can play many roles in a data pipeline: data loading, transformation, and storage.
- Data transformation and filtering can be done both with SQL and Python APIs.
- Data can be loaded remotely from a set of CSV files (and other sources and formats) and pandas DataFrames.
- Using Python for data pipelines allows for powerful transformations and computations.
- Declaring dependencies helps orchestrate the order of operations in a pipeline.
- MotherDuck is a suitable destination for DuckDB data in the cloud.

9

Building and deploying data apps

In section 8.4, we learned how to build a pipeline that ingested data into a local DuckDB database and into one running on MotherDuck. While many data analysts will be happy to interact with the data in DuckDB with SQL queries, other users will prefer to have an interface that doesn't require them to write code. To provide value for those users, we want to create applications that retrieve the information from DuckDB—either via SQL queries or by any of the other means we've learned so far, such as the relational Python API. Of equal importance, we aim to present this process in an accessible fashion and in a way that readers find meaningful.

Some datasets can be represented in a tabular fashion; more often, it is helpful to visualize and summarize that data as charts. This also makes the data more accessible and allows users to answer questions, offer insights, or support decisions, which is critical for most data-informed use cases. Creating ideal charts that don't skew the meaning of a dataset is a topic for another book, though. We are going to focus on the technical side of things here and explore DuckDB's integration with some of the existing tools for building accessible frontends. First, we create an end-user-facing application with Streamlit and later a business intelligence (BI) dashboard with Apache Superset. While interactive applications usually focus on ready-made reports and restrict interactivity on filtering those reports, *BI dashboards* usually aggregate data from many possible sources in such a way that they allow a holistic overview, usually not based on raw numbers but dedicated charts.

9.1   *Building a custom data app with Streamlit*

We already dealt with Association of Tennis Professionals (ATP) data in chapters 5 and 8. In chapter 5, we aggregated ATP rankings from several CSV sources into one table and, eventually, only one Parquet file. Later, in chapter 8, we consumed player data from web resources as part of a data pipeline. Eventually, we stored everything in a DuckDB database, as you can see in figure 9.1.

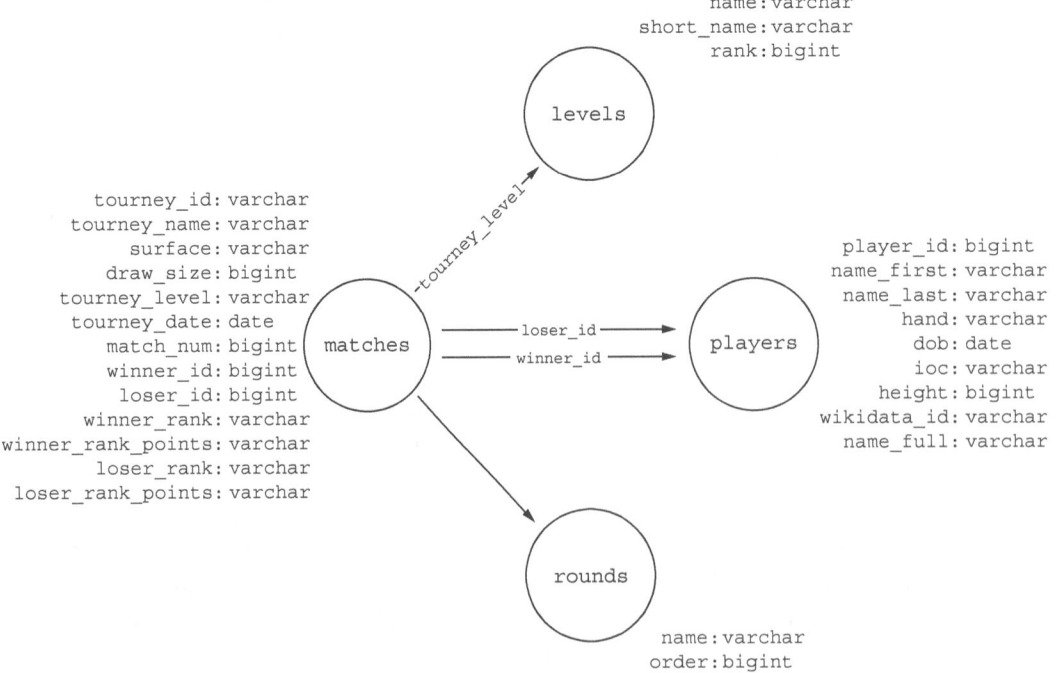

Figure 9.1   ATP database schema

By now, you know how to use the database, but that is not necessarily true for your users. They might not know SQL or have direct access to the database. An application can help them navigate the data and structure, while combining interactive filters with useful visualizations. Let's build an application for that instead. Our goal is to provide a platform where users can search for and analyze head-to-head player statistics. We are going to use a tool called Streamlit for crafting an interactive web interface. And, of course, we'll use DuckDB to handle all database tasks. Through this exercise, you will learn how to combine Streamlit and DuckDB to develop a data app with an emphasis on simplicity and ease of deployment.

9.1.1 What is Streamlit?

Streamlit is a library that makes it possible to create interactive web apps using only Python—no knowledge of JavaScript-based frontend libraries or frameworks is required. For data engineers, data scientists, and backend developers, who are often not full-stack engineers, this is a good way to prototype and build quick, data-driven applications. Unlike other visualization tools in the data and BI space that are low-code, visual builders, Streamlit is a code-first tool. You write your apps using Python and the tools and libraries, such as pandas, scikit-learn, matplotlib, and DuckDB, that you're already familiar with. For all of these reasons, Streamlit is especially useful for creating frontends for data or machine learning (ML) apps. In addition, Snowflake Inc.—the company behind Streamlit—offers the Streamlit Community Cloud, a platform where you can deploy and manage your apps for free.

9.1.2 Building our app

Streamlit comes as a Python package, so you need to install that first in your terminal:

```
pip install streamlit
```

We'll also need to make sure we have the DuckDB Python package installed if we haven't already done that:

```
pip install duckdb
```

Streamlit does not generate a skeleton for your application. Instead, you create an application, represented by a Python script, that will act as your canvas, on which you'll draw charts, text, widgets, tables, and more. Let's start with that. Create a file named app.py containing the following code, which will define a wide layout and render a title when run via Streamlit.

Listing 9.1 Writing a minimal Streamlit app

```
import streamlit as st

st.set_page_config(layout="wide")
st.title("ATP Head to Head")
```

If we then go back to the terminal, we can run the following command to launch the app. As soon as you run the script as shown, a local Streamlit server will spin up, and your app will open in a new tab in your default web browser:

```
streamlit run app.py
```

In the terminal, you'll see something like the following output:

```
You can now view your Streamlit app in your browser.

  Local URL: http://localhost:8501
  Network URL: http://192.168.86.207:8501
```

The initial page is shown in figure 9.2.

Figure 9.2   Initial Streamlit app

This is not all that interesting so far, but it's a start!

Next, we're going to connect the Streamlit app to the atp.duckdb database we created in section 8.4, which you can also find in the book's GitHub repository under https://mng.bz/RZDD.

The following snippet that will be part of our app.py script will bring in the DuckDB Python package and connect to the database stored in atp.duckdb, as described in chapter 6. We're opening the database in read-only mode since we don't intend to change the data:

```
import duckdb

atp_duck = duckdb.connect('atp.duckdb', read_only=True)
```

Remember that this setup is different from a client–server-based database deployment. The database runs embedded in the same process as the Streamlit application. As a result, the frontend to be rendered will not require any remote database connection.

Next, we create a function inside the application named search_players that will search for the provided player name in the matches table. The function takes in a search term and then uses it as part of a query string to find records from the matches table we populated in chapter 8. The query is about finding all rows that contain the search term either in the winner_name or loser_name columns. In both WHERE clauses, we make use of the fact that we can refer to aliases given to a column later. As shown in listing 9.2, we use prepared statements with parameterized queries (https://mng.bz/2K29) to pass the search term as a named parameter to the query, avoiding the possibility of an SQL injection (we spoke about how to avoid SQL injections in more detail in chapter 6.2.3).

> **Listing 9.2 A function that uses a prepared statement**

```
def search_players(search_term):
    query = '''
    SELECT DISTINCT winner_name AS player
    FROM matches
    WHERE player ilike '%' || $search_term || '%'
    UNION
    SELECT DISTINCT loser_name AS player
    FROM matches
    WHERE player ilike '%' || $search_term || '%'
    '''
    values = atp_duck.execute(query, {"search_term":search_term}).fetchall()
    return [value[0] for value in values]
```

Streamlit is all about writing out data in various forms; it supports lists, maps, DataFrames, and more. We use the st instance we imported from the streamlit package, as shown in the following code, to write out the result of the search_players function, producing HTML that looks as shown in figure 9.3:

```
st.write(search_players("Novak"))
```

So far, we have created a simple, yet fully functional page that displays a list of matches in which a specific player appeared. This gives us the groundwork to make things interactive for the users.

Figure 9.3 The result of calling search_players with Novak as parameter

9.1.3 *Using Streamlit components*

The app would be pretty boring if it only displayed matches for a specific player. Let's create an input field for the search term.

Streamlit thinks in *components*. Instead of writing individual HTML fragments and JavaScript code for client-side interactivity, you declare the use of a component, parameterize it, and rely on the component to then render the necessary pieces onto your web page. One such component is the streamlit-searchbox, published as a library on GitHub under m-wrzr/streamlit-searchbox (https://github.com/m-wrzr/streamlit-searchbox) and providing all the usual features users expect these things to have, such as autocomplete.

We can install `streamlit-searchbox` by running the following command from the terminal:

```
pip install streamlit-searchbox
```

Once we've done that, we'll import `st_searchbox` in our Python code:

```
from streamlit_searchbox import st_searchbox
```

Then, we'll use that function to create a couple of search boxes, with the initial selection defaulted to Roger Federer and Rafael Nadal. We don't have to think about how to write HTML to create a two-column-wide layout; we can just ask Streamlit to do so. How the components are positioned in that layout is also taken care of for us using the Python keyword `with`. Having previously defined both the variables `left` and `right`, we create two scopes in which the components will be positioned. The search boxes created within these scopes will be labeled with `Player 1` and `Player 2`, respectively, and they will show different default values.

The most important part, however, is the first argument to `st_searchbox`, which is the actual `search_players` function defined in the following listing. That function will be called when the user modifies the content of the rendered search box. Add the following code to app.py.

Listing 9.3 Parameterizing a Streamlit component with Python

```
left, right = st.columns(2)          ◁——  Creates two columns
with left:                                 on the page
    player1 = st_searchbox(search_players,  ◁——  Creates a searchbox
        label="Player 1",                         component, using
        key="player1_search",                     search_players as a
        default="Roger Federer",                  data source
        placeholder="Roger Federer"
    )
with right:
    player2 = st_searchbox(search_players,
        label="Player 2",
        key="player2_search",
        default="Rafael Nadal",
        placeholder="Rafael Nadal"
    )
```

Returning to the browser, our UI should now look like figure 9.4.

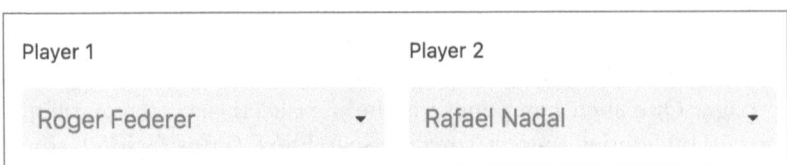

Figure 9.4 Streamlit components rendered as search boxes with default values

The search box controls are already fully functional. The moment we type *Murr* to search for *Andy Murray*, the underlying `search_players` will be called, and the results will be passed back into the UI. This will eventually render as shown in figure 9.5. The moment we click on a result, it will be assigned to the `player1` variable, which represents both the component and the rendered search box.

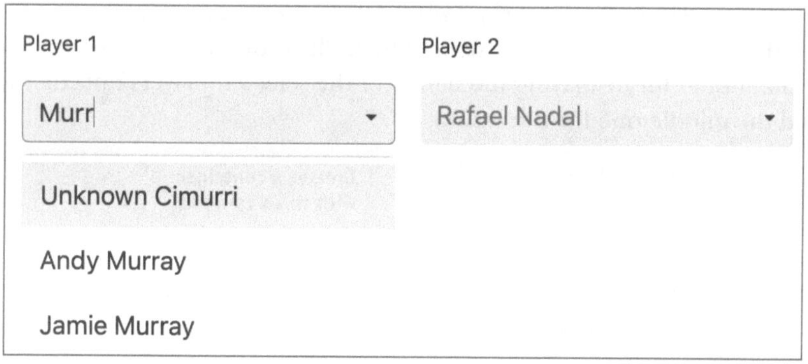

Figure 9.5   Searching for Andy Murray

So far, we can retrieve player names from the database and assign them to variables in our script. While a list of players is nice, it is most likely not what the user is interested in. They probably want to have a report containing all the matches between the selected players, along with information about the level of tournament and round in which the match was played.

Streamlit is a great support for rendering pandas DataFrames as interactive tables, without any further coding required. In chapter 6, we learned that DuckDB also has native support for DataFrames. We can write a query that takes both player names as parameters, queries the `matches` table again to retrieve the desired information, and returns the result as a DataFrame via DuckDB's `fetchdf` method, as shown in the Python code in the following listing.

Listing 9.4   Querying the database and returning a DataFrame

```
matches_for_players = atp_duck.execute("""
SELECT                                       ⭠──────────────   Returns the match, tournament level,
    tourney_date,tourney_name, surface, round,                and round metadata for each match
    rounds.order AS roundOrder,
    levels.name AS level, levels.rank AS levelRank,           Joins the levels table
    winner_name, score                                        to get the level of
FROM matches                                                  the tournaments for
JOIN levels ON levels.short_name = matches.tourney_level  ⭠─  the matches
JOIN rounds ON rounds.name = matches.round
WHERE (loser_name  = $player1 AND winner_name = $player2) OR     Joins the rounds table
      (loser_name  = $player2 AND winner_name = $player1)        to get round metadata
                                                                 for the matches
```

```
ORDER BY tourney_date DESC
""", {"player1":player1, "player2":player2}).fetchdf()
```
Passes in player1 and player2 as parameters and returns a DataFrame

Let's first add a heading about the list of matches that shows the players' names and the number of wins they have. We can compute the number of wins by filtering `matches_for_player` to find the rows where the `winner_name` matches each player's name. In the following code, we instruct Streamlit to define a set of three columns, with the outer ones for displaying the names of the selected players outside the search boxes and the middle one for the result:

```
left, middle, right = st.columns(3)         Creates a container
with left:                                   with three columns
      st.markdown(
          f"<h2 style='text-align: left; '>{player1}</h1>",
          unsafe_allow_html=True
      )
with right:          Renders the name of the second player
      st.markdown(
          f"<h2 style='text-align: right; '>{player2}</h1>",
          unsafe_allow_html=True
      )
p1_wins = matches_for_players[        Computes the
      matches_for_players.winner_name == player1].shape[0]   wins for player 1
p2_wins = matches_for_players[                          Computes the
      matches_for_players.winner_name == player2].shape[0]   wins for player 2
with middle:          This renders the wins per player. We're using
      st.markdown(     custom Markdown, so it styles nicely!
          f"<h2 style='text-align: center; '>{p1_wins} vs {p2_wins}</h1>",
          unsafe_allow_html=True
      )
```

Renders the name of the first player → (annotation pointing to `with left:` / `st.markdown(` block)

Markdown

Markdown is a lightweight markup language with plain-text formatting syntax, designed to be easy to write and read. This markup is then converted into structurally valid HTML. It is usually used to format the documentation of README files, but it is also supported in Streamlit via the `markdown` function.

In this case, we're using it to render the player names and the number of wins in three headings: left, right, and center aligned, with custom-styled HTML inside the Markdown. That's why we also have to set `unsafe_allow_html=True`.

Let's now render this DataFrame on the page. We're going to drop the `roundOrder`, `level`, and `levelRank` fields from the DataFrame we render to the page because they create a bit too much clutter; those fields will come in handy later but aren't required just yet:

```
st.markdown(f'### Matches')
st.dataframe(
    matches_for_players.drop(["roundOrder", "level", "levelRank"], axis=1)
)
```

The result of querying the database, asking for a DataFrame, and rendering that is shown in figure 9.6. When the user selects a different pair of players, the content will automatically be refreshed.

	tourney_date	tourney_name	surface	round	winner_name	score
0	2016-05-02 00:00:00	Madrid Masters	Clay	SF	Andy Murray	7-5 6-4
1	2016-04-11 00:00:00	Monte Carlo Masters	Clay	SF	Rafael Nadal	2-6 6-4 6-2
2	2015-11-15 00:00:00	Tour Finals	Hard	RR	Rafael Nadal	6-4 6-1
3	2015-05-03 00:00:00	Madrid Masters	Clay	F	Andy Murray	6-3 6-2
4	2014-05-26 00:00:00	Roland Garros	Clay	SF	Rafael Nadal	6-3 6-2 6-1
5	2014-05-11 00:00:00	Rome Masters	Clay	QF	Rafael Nadal	1-6 6-3 7-5
6	2012-03-21 00:00:00	Miami Masters	Hard	SF	Andy Murray	W/O
7	2011-10-03 00:00:00	Tokyo	Hard	F	Andy Murray	3-6 6-2 6-0
8	2011-08-29 00:00:00	US Open	Hard	SF	Rafael Nadal	6-4 6-2 3-6 6-2
9	2011-06-20 00:00:00	Wimbledon	Grass	SF	Rafael Nadal	5-7 6-2 6-2 6-4

Andy Murray   8 vs 17   Rafael Nadal

Matches

Figure 9.6 Matches between Andy Murray and Rafael Nadal

That all looks good, and now we can browse through the Murray–Nadal matches to our heart's content. While some people will be happy with a tabular representation of the match data, others will prefer a more visual way to present that data.

9.1.4 Visualizing data using plot.ly

Great charts are important in both data-centric applications and dashboards, but creating great charts is difficult both technically and content-wise. You don't have to reinvent the wheel, though, as there are various ready-made solutions available for rendering charts and diagrams, both under commercial and open source licenses.

One of our favorite libraries for creating interactive visualizations is plot.ly (https://plotly.com/). plot.ly is a data visualization tool that lets users create visually appealing charts and diagrams with an intuitive API. Streamlit provides direct support for using plot.ly charts.

We can install plot.ly by running the following in the terminal:

```
pip install plotly
```

Next, back in app.py, import `plotly.express`, which is a module that makes it easier to quickly construct a chart:

```
import plotly.express as px
```

The visualization we have in mind will be a scatterplot that has the tournament names (ordered by the month and day held) along the *y* axis and dates along the *x* axis. The points on the chart will represent a match, and we'll color them differently, depending on the winner.

The first thing we need to do is create a new DataFrame that has the tournaments ordered by the month and day held. We'll sort the data using the `strftime` function in DuckDB:

```
sorted_matches_for_players = atp_duck.sql("""
FROM matches_for_players                          Orders the matches
ORDER BY strftime(tourney_date, '%m-%d')   ◁──┘  by month and day
""").fetchdf()
```

We can then create a scatterplot based on `sorted_matches_for_players`, with the size of the points based on the importance of the round in which the players played:

```
fig = px.scatter(sorted_matches_for_players,        The color tones used for the points. The
    x="tourney_date",                               default is two light blues, which we find
    y="tourney_name",                               difficult to distinguish in print. See
    color="winner_name",                            https://plotly.com/python/discrete-
    size="roundOrder",                              color for more options.
    color_discrete_sequence=px.colors.qualitative.Plotly,  ◁──
    category_orders={
        "tourney_name": (                           ◁──┐  Ensures plot.ly
            sorted_matches_for_players['tourney_name']  │  doesn't reorder the
            .drop_duplicates()                          │  tournament names
            .tolist()
        )
    },
)
```

We can then render the chart using Streamlit's built-in support for rendering plot.ly charts:

```
st.plotly_chart(fig, use_container_width=True)
```

> **NOTE** Streamlit also has functions for rendering charts created by other data visualization tools, such as Altair, Bokeh, PyDeck, and more.

The resulting chart is shown in figure 9.7.

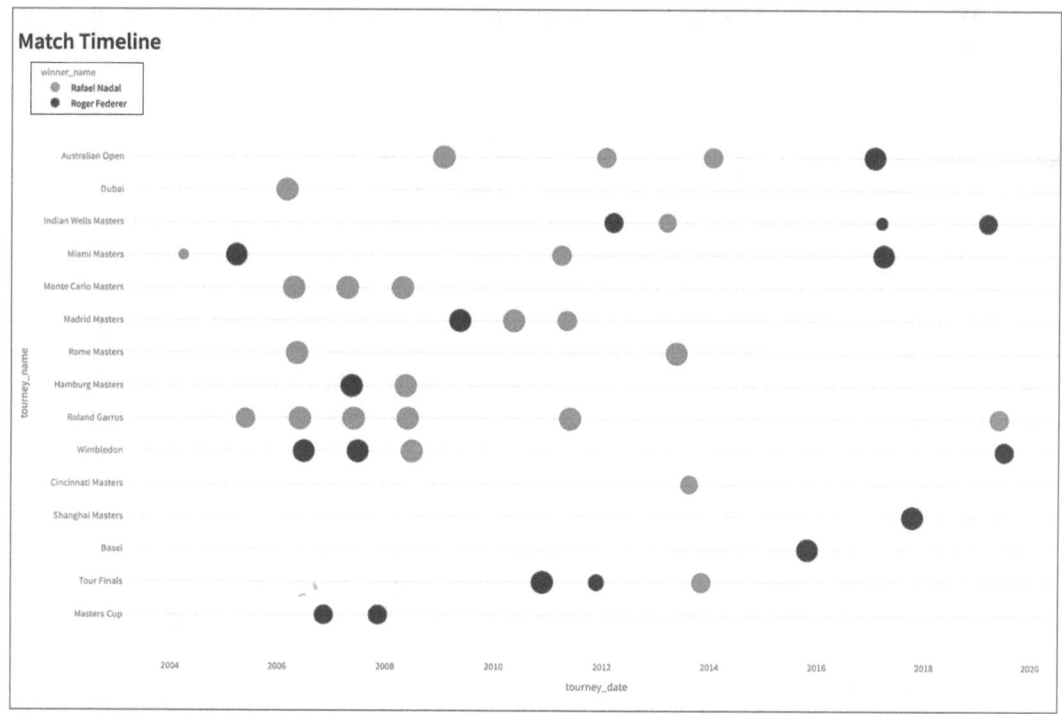

Figure 9.7 The timeline of matches between Murray and Nadal, visualized as a scatterplot by plot.ly

This looks pretty cool, but we need a grid that makes it easier to see the years in which the matches took place. We can do this by computing the minimum and maximum years and then drawing a vertical line for each year:

Computes the minimum year from the matches between the players

Computes the maximum year from the matches between the players

```
min_year = sorted_matches_for_players['tourney_date']
    .dt.year.min()
max_year = sorted_matches_for_players['tourney_date']
    .dt.year.max()
unique_years = list(range(min_year, max_year+2))
```

Constructs a list that contains all the years from the minimum year until one year after the maximum year

```
for year in unique_years:
    fig.add_shape(
        type="line",
        x0=f"{year}-01-01", x1=f"{year}-01-01",
        y0=0, y1=1,
        yref="paper",
        layer="below",
        line=dict(color="#efefef", width=2)
    )
```

Adds a vertical line for each year

Iterates over each of the years

We can then return to the Streamlit app to see the new and improved version of the chart in figure 9.8.

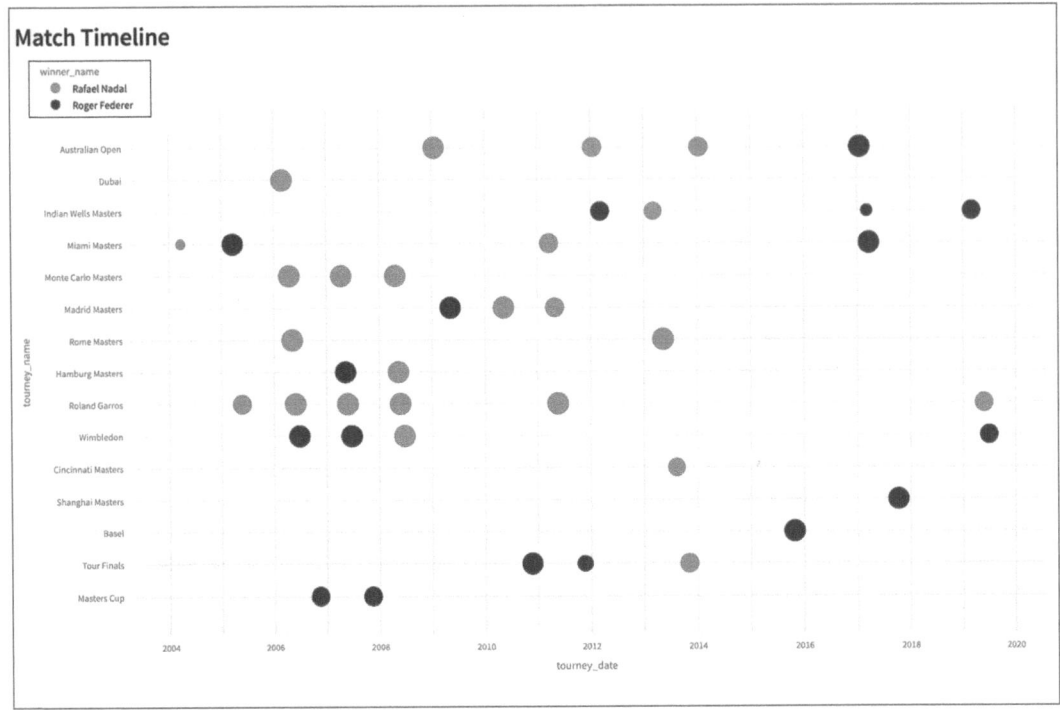

Figure 9.8   Murray vs. Nadal timeline with vertical lines

That makes it much easier to see when they've played each other over the last 15 years or so. Most of their matches took place in 2008–2009 and 2010–2011, with the rest scattered out. This was difficult to see when we looked at the table of results. We already knew that Nadal dominated the rivalry, but that fact is emphasized even further by this visualization.

Whether we want to represent a DataFrame as a table or a chart does not change the way that we retrieve said DataFrame from DuckDB. It's a matter of choice to either pass it directly to Streamlit for rendering a tabular representation or to plot.ly first, creating a chart which then is passed to Streamlit. This is similar to the experience we saw in chapter 6, where we switched from pandas to Apache Arrow to Polars Data-Frame without changing the way we interacted with the database technology.

9.1.5   *Deploying our app on the Community Cloud*

Deploying an application can be as simple as copying static files onto a web server or as complicated as setting up containers, a service, and, in general, a lot of movable parts. Sometimes, there are good reasons for any of the extremes, but often, there's most likely a middle ground. Maybe someone else already set up the whole complicated infrastructure and provided a "push-to-run" scenario for your application. The Streamlit Community Cloud, which is backed by Snowflake Inc., provides exactly that.

If you agree to their terms, you can directly push your new application to production, right from within the local Streamlit server, by clicking on the Deploy button in the top-right-hand corner of the UI. You'll then see the modal window shown in figure 9.9.

You might need to add requirements.txt with the four dependencies to your repository if it doesn't exist yet.

Listing 9.5   requirements.txt

```
streamlit
duckdb
streamlit-searchbox
plotly
```

The tooling gives you a choice between the Community Cloud and a custom deployment (figure 9.9).

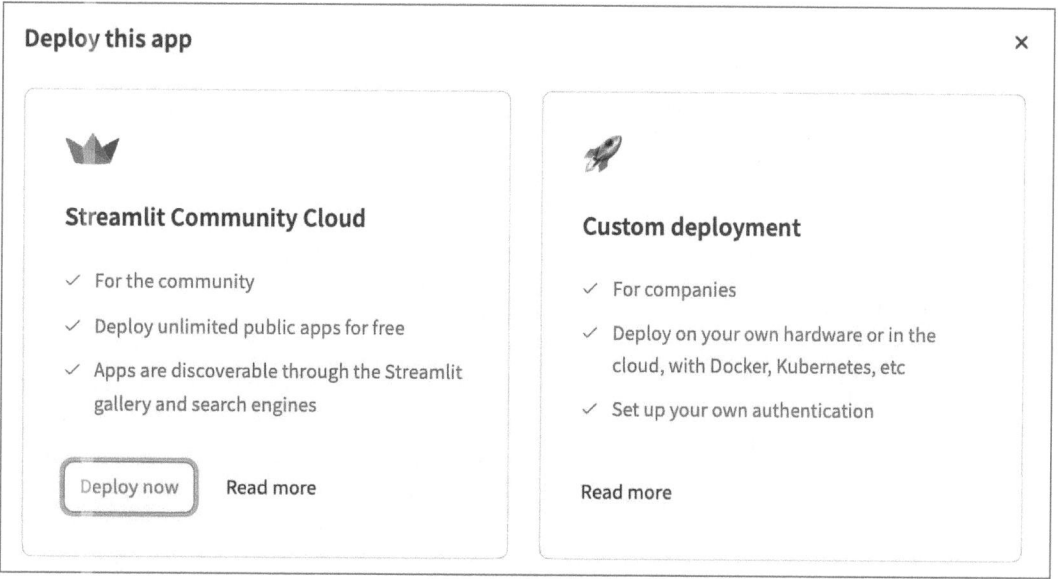

Figure 9.9   Choosing how to deploy your new application to production

You'll need to have your project connected to a remote GitHub repository; otherwise, you'll see the error in figure 9.10.

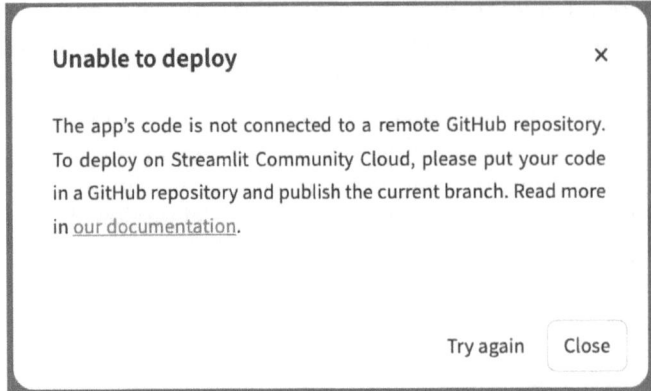

Figure 9.10   The error message received when trying to deploy an app not connected to a remote GitHub repository

Once we've got our app connected to a GitHub repository, if we click through the deploy flow again, we'll see the screen shown in figure 9.11.

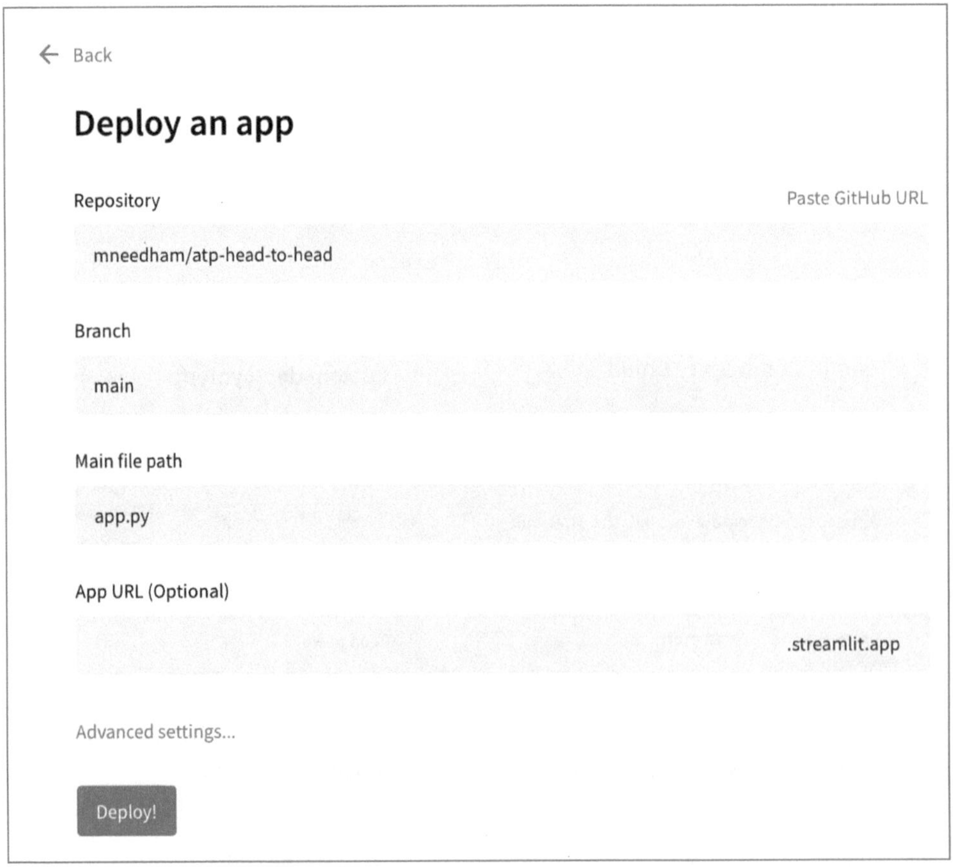

Figure 9.11   Deploying our app

We can then choose a URL for the app and adjust the branch or main file path if those need changing. We can also change the version of Python that will be used via the Advanced Settings.

As you can see from the screenshot, the completed version of this app lives in the mneedham/atp-head-to-head repository (https://github.com/mneedham/atp-head -to-head), and it's been deployed to atp-head-to-head.streamlit.app (https://atp -head-to-head.streamlit.app/). Without diving into the world of frontend frameworks, we have been able to build an interactive web application by using a handful of Stream-lit components—all in one language we already know (Python)—connecting to DuckDB in a way we already understand and by passing data as DataFrames, a familiar data format.

But admittedly, we did still have to write some code to get all this working! In case you're not that comfortable with writing code, or you just want to get something up and running quickly for yourself or your users, there are other options. If, rather than an interactive application, you want to create a dashboard, you can achieve this with a low-code or BI tool. We'll still get interactivity in terms of zooming, panning, and otherwise changing the representation of charts, but we won't have to write any application code. This is where a tool such as Apache Superset comes in.

9.2   Building a BI dashboard with Apache Superset

While Streamlit gives us a lot of control over our application without requiring special-ist frontend knowledge, sometimes we don't want to spend so much time writing custom code for a frontend. DuckDB integrates with a variety of BI tools, including Hex, Tableau, and the one that we'll be using in this chapter: Apache Superset.

9.2.1   What is Apache Superset?

Apache Superset is an open source data exploration and visualization platform devel-oped by Maxime Beauchemin, who is best known for creating Apache Airflow. Super-set has integrations with a large number of databases (including DuckDB!), and everything can be configured through its UI. It has preinstalled visualization types, which should cover most use cases, but you can also create custom visualizations in JavaScript.

Superset has support for SQLAlchemy, a Python library that provides a high-level, object-oriented interface for interacting with databases. It manages database connec-tions, defines database schemas, and performs queries against these databases.

While there are many BI tools, many of them are cloud services that require you to register for an account. Superset, on the other hand, can be tried out on our machine, and if we later decide to deploy to production, we have the option of using the Preset (https://preset.io/) hosted service.

There are a variety of ways to install Superset (https://mng.bz/1G2y), including Docker Compose scripts and a Helm repository for deploying to Kubernetes. These would be good options if we were deploying Superset to production, but to install

Superset on our machine, we're going to follow the instructions found on the "Installing from PyPI" documentation page (https://mng.bz/PZEg).

We start by installing the following library. All the following commands are executed from your terminal:

```
pip install apache-superset==3.1.2
```

NOTE   At the time of writing, Superset only works with Python 3.10.

Now we need a way to connect Superset to DuckDB. duckdb_engine (https://pypi .org/project/duckdb-engine/) is DuckDB's SQLAlchemy driver, and we're going to use it to get these two tools to play nicely together.

We can install the driver by running the following command:

```
pip install duckdb-engine
```

Next, we need to configure some environment variables, without which Superset won't run. You need to set these variables whenever you have a new terminal session before running any of the following commands. Superset contains a Flask application, so we need to set the FLASK_APP variable to define the name of the file that Flask should look for. We also need to specify a secret key (https://mng.bz/JZ0P), with a random string of characters, for a more secure installation:

```
export SUPERSET_SECRET_KEY="sYBpNA2+bQHvmXcojOVp53b8xbmN3ZQ"
export FLASK_APP=superset
```

Next, we're going to initialize Superset's database. This stores all the metadata that Superset uses, and it won't work without it:

```
superset init
superset db upgrade
```

The next step is to create an admin user. We're going to create a user called admin with the same password, but you should use more secure credentials when you do this yourself and your machine is exposed to the internet. Flask app builder (FAB) is the framework Superset is built on top of. It provides authentication, user management, permissions, and roles:

```
superset fab create-admin \
  --username admin \
  --firstname Superset \
  --lastname Admin \
  --email admin@example.com \
  --password admin
```

We should see the following output:

```
logging was configured successfully
...
Recognized Database Authentications.
Admin User admin created.
```

Now we can launch the Superset web server on port 8088 by running the following command:

```
superset run -p 8088 \
  --with-threads \
  --reload \
  --debugger
```

We can then navigate to the Superset UI at http://localhost:8088 and log in with the admin/admin username and password we just created.

9.2.2 *Superset's workflow*

Before we create anything, it's probably helpful to understand the terms Superset uses and how they relate to each other. The following are important concepts to understand:

- *Database*—The underlying data source (DuckDB, in our case)
- *SQL Saved Query*—A custom SQL query against one or more tables in the database
- *Dataset*—A wrapper around an SQL-saved query or a database table
- *Chart*—A visualization based on a dataset
- *Dashboard*—A collection of charts

The tables that comprise a database aren't one of Superset's concepts, but they are used by datasets.

So when we're using Superset, we'll need to first create a database. It will then automatically detect the schema, and therefore tables, that comprise that database. We can then create datasets based on those tables or write SQL queries and turn those into datasets. And finally, we create charts on top of those datasets, which are used in dashboards. Figure 9.12 contains a visual representation of the Superset workflow.

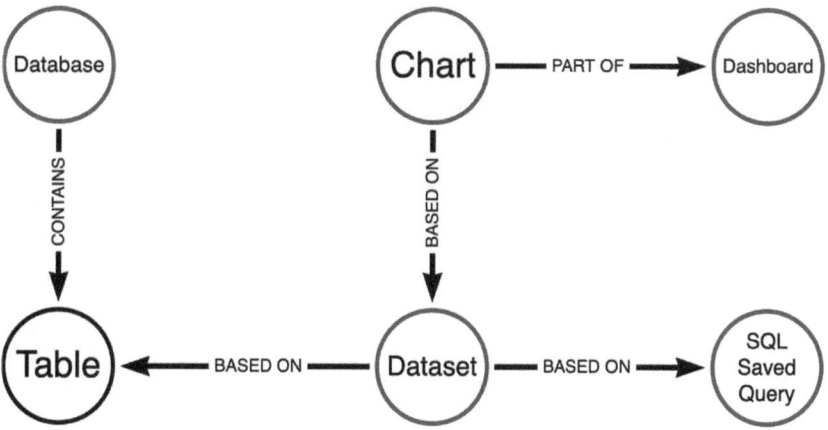

Figure 9.12   Terms used by Superset and their relationships

9.2.3 Creating our first dashboard

In this section, we're going to learn how to create a dashboard. Dashboards are used to help visualize important business metrics so that we can quickly get a picture of the state of things. We'll also want to be able to interact with the dashboard so that we can dig deeper into the data if there are any problems.

NOTE Any dashboard we create over a tennis dataset won't be as important as one over a business dataset, but hopefully, you'll see how to apply these techniques to your own data.

+
Settings
Security
List Users
List Roles
Action Log
Row Level Security
Data
Database Connections

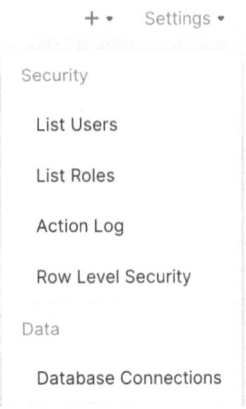

Figure 9.13 Database connections

Let's create our first dashboard, starting by connecting Superset to DuckDB. Click on the Settings button in the top right, as shown in figure 9.13.

Once you've done that, click on the `+ Database` button, which will result in the modal window shown in figure 9.14.

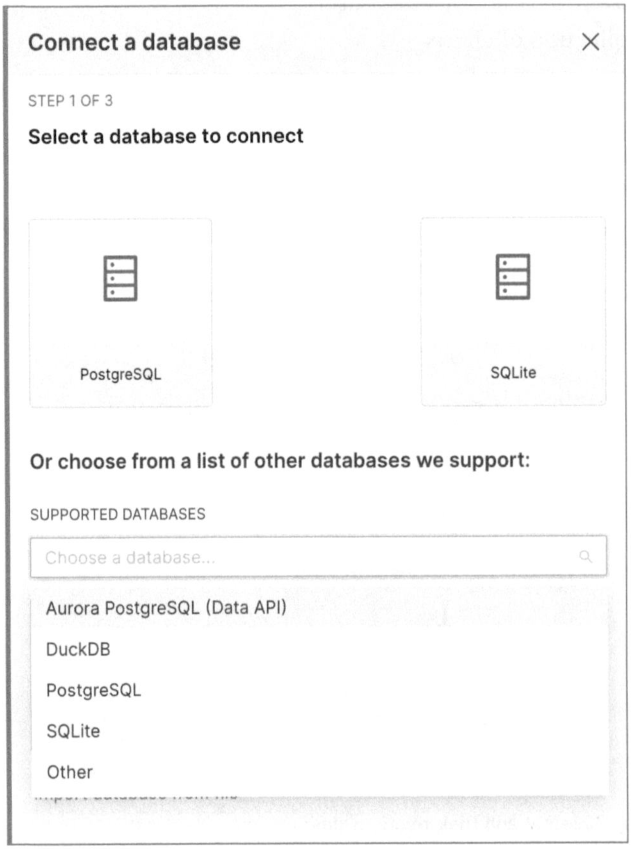

Connect a database
STEP 1 OF 3
Select a database to connect
PostgreSQL
SQLite
Or choose from a list of other databases we support:
SUPPORTED DATABASES
Choose a database...
Aurora PostgreSQL (Data API)
DuckDB
PostgreSQL
SQLite
Other

Figure 9.14 Connecting to a new database

Click on DuckDB, and then in the `SQL Alchemy URI` field, enter the connection string, which has the format of `duckdb:///<your-database>`. For us, that will be `duckdb:/// atp.duckdb`, as shown in figure 9.15.

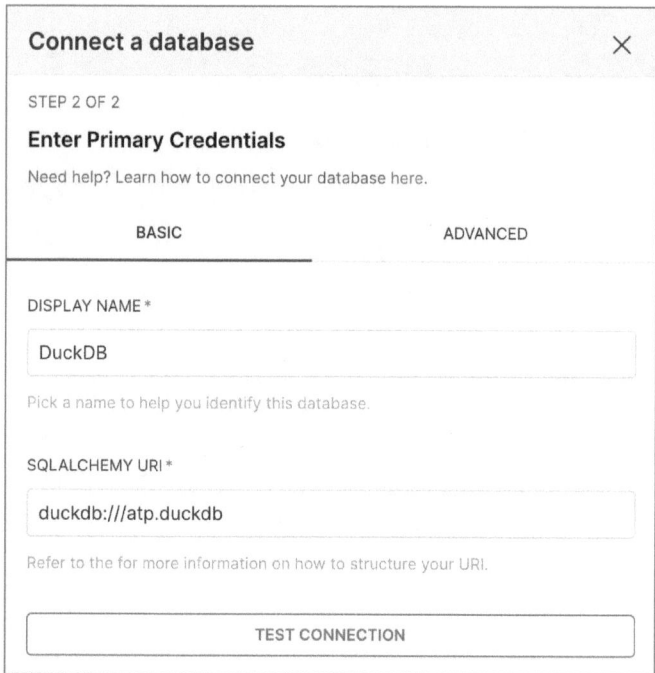

Figure 9.15
Connecting to the ATP
DuckDB database

If your Streamlit application from the previous section is still running, you need to close it first to release the lock on the database file. Click on the Test Connection button to confirm that everything is wired up correctly.

> **NOTE** You can also connect to a Mother-Duck database using `duckdb:///md:<my_ database>?motherduck_token=<my_token>`.

Once you've done that, click on the Data link at the top of the screen and then on the Create Dataset button. We'll then see the screen in figure 9.16, where we can select the database, schema, and table that we want to use.

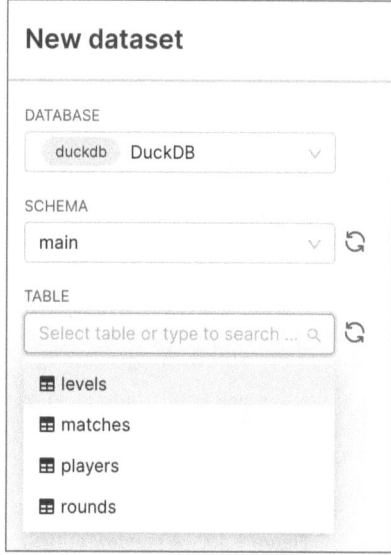

Figure 9.16   Choosing a table
to make up a dataset

We're going to select the `matches` table. Once we select that, we'll see a UI that shows all fields in that table, as shown in figure 9.17.

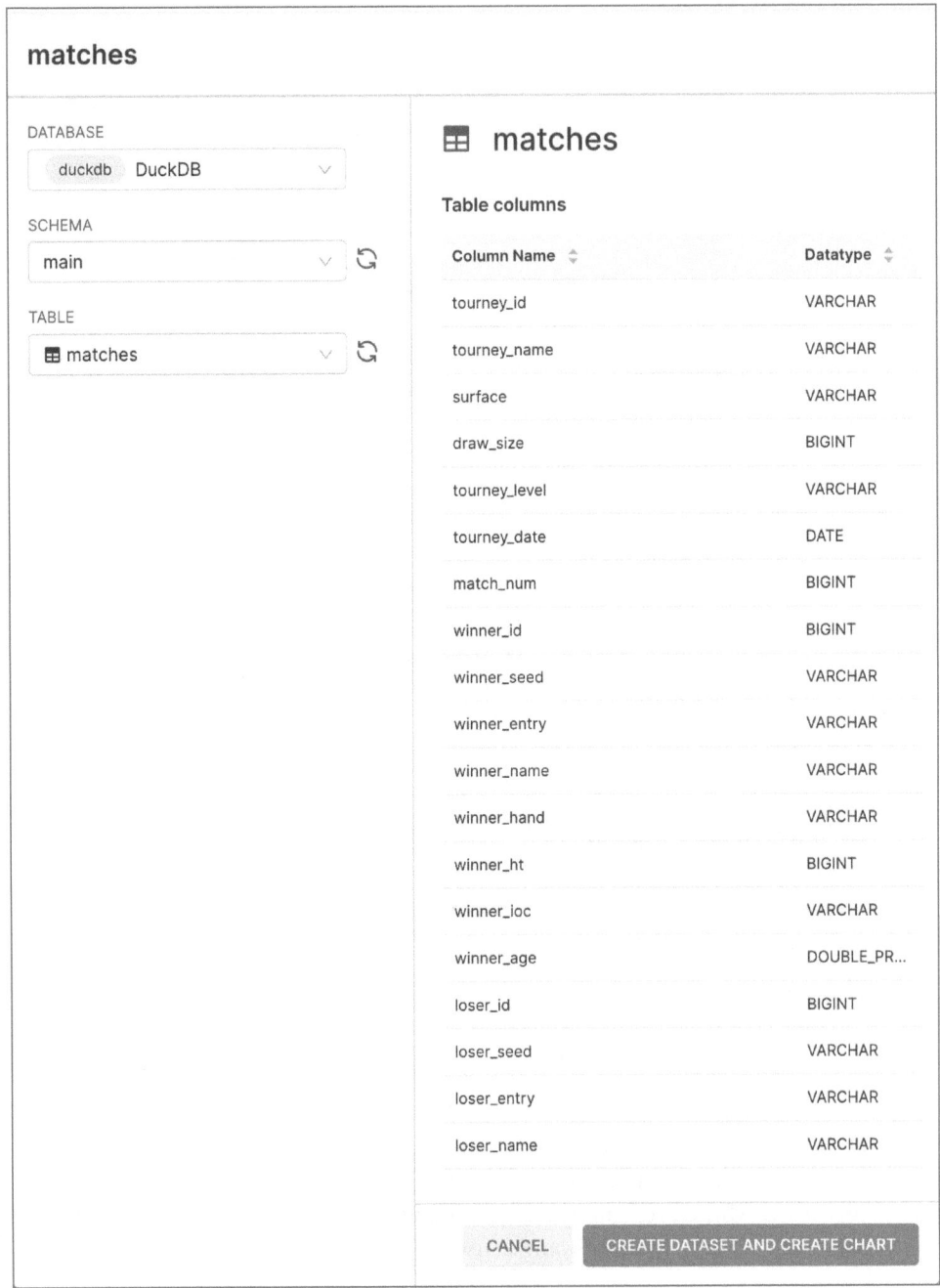

Figure 9.17   **A preview of the `matches` table**

If we're happy with our selection, we can click on Create Dataset and Create Chart, after which we'll be asked which chart we'd like to create from the screen shown in figure 9.18.

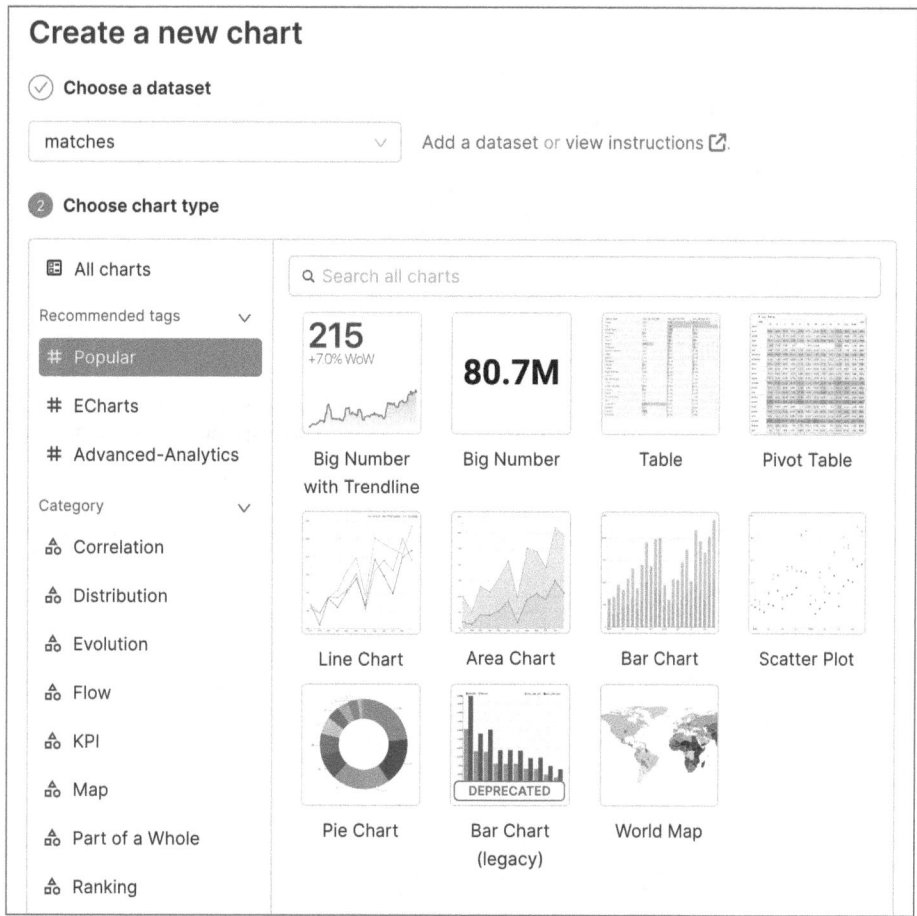

Figure 9.18 Choosing a chart for a specific dataset

Let's select Bar Chart; we'll then create a chart that shows the number of matches played per year from 1967 to 2023. It's often said that there are a lot more tennis matches played nowadays than there used to be, so it'll be interesting to see what the data shows us.

To create this chart, we'll need to configure the following sections:

- X-Axis is `tourney_date`.
- Time Grain is `Year`.
- Metrics is `COUNT(*)`.

You can see a screenshot of how to do this in figure 9.19.

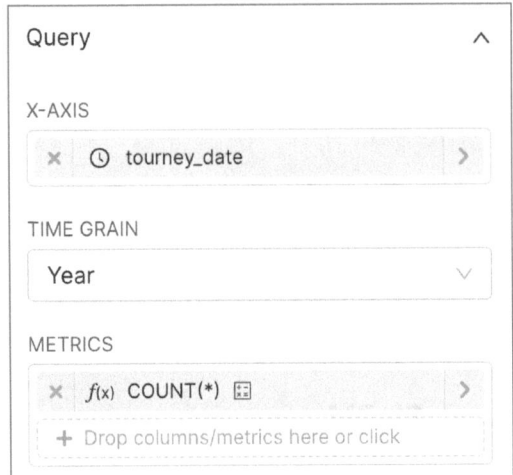

Figure 9.19 Configuring a bar chart showing matches played per year

If we create the chart, we'll see a preview on the right-hand side. It should look like figure 9.20.

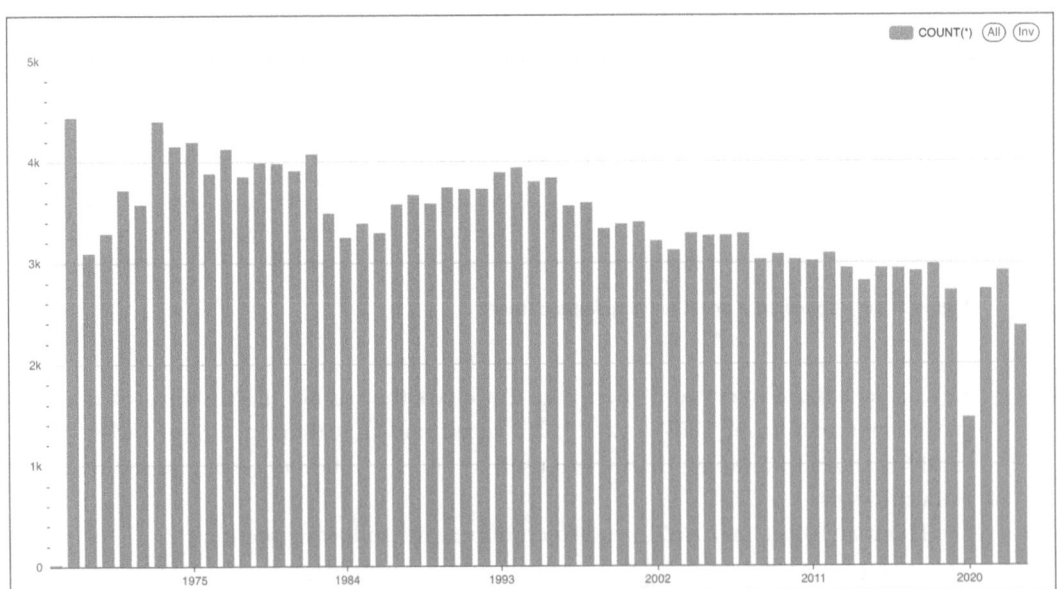

Figure 9.20 A preview of the bar chart showing matches played per year

There doesn't seem to be any evidence that more matches are being played nowadays. If anything, there seems to be a slight downward trend in the number of matches being played. There's also an outlier in 2020, caused by the COVID-19 pandemic, which resulted in the tennis season being paused from March to August 2020.

If we're happy with the chart, we can save it via the screen shown in figure 9.21. We'll be asked if we want to add the chart to an existing or new dashboard. Let's add it to a new dashboard called ATP Dashboard.

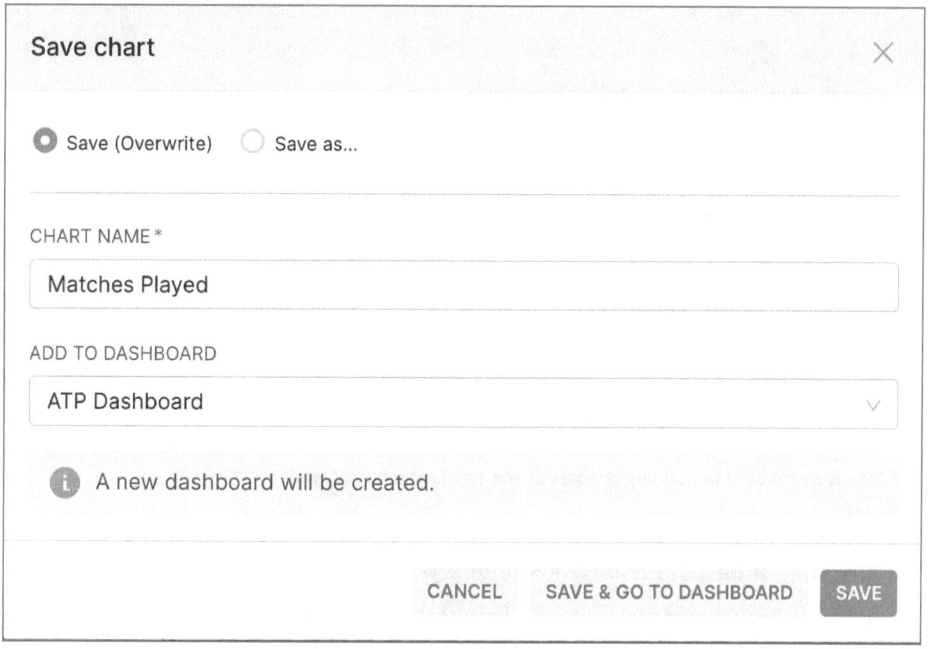

Figure 9.21 Saving the chart

NOTE   If we don't type anything into the dashboard field, the chart won't be assigned to a dashboard, but we can always add it to a dashboard afterward.

If we click Save & Go to Dashboard, we should now see a dashboard containing our chart, as shown in figure 9.22. Success! We've created our first dashboard.

We can repeat the process described in this section if we want to add more charts based on individual tables, but if we want to create a chart based on data from multiple tables, we'll need to do something slightly different.

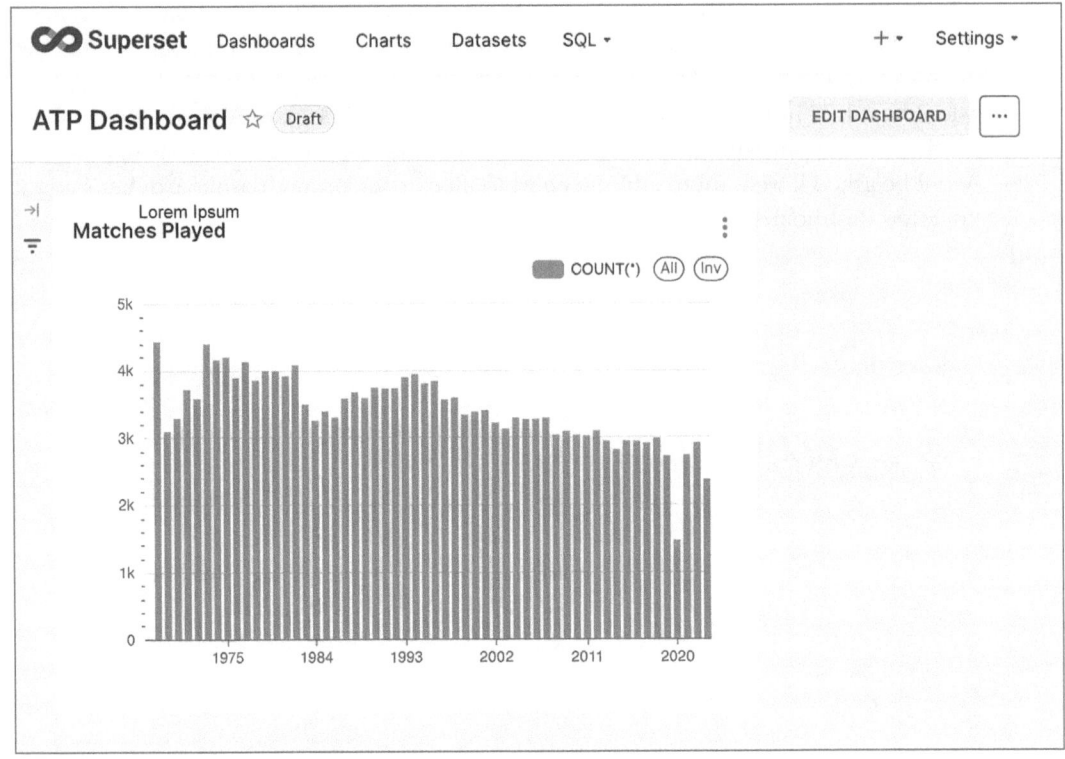

Figure 9.22   A dashboard containing a chart of the total matches played

9.2.4   *Creating a dataset from an SQL query*

In addition to creating datasets from tables, we can also create them from SQL queries. To do this, when we add a new dataset, we'll need to click on the **SQL Lab** link
from the top menu.

Next, we need to add a new query tab, select the database and schema, and then
enter a query. For example, let's say we want to work out whether grand slam winners
have been getting older over time. We need to get data from both the `matches` and
`players` tables to answer this question. The following query computes the cumulative
count of grand slam winners aged 30 and over:

```
SELECT
    winner_name,
    tourney_date,
    (tourney_date - dob)/365 AS age,          Computes the age        Computes the
    COUNT(*) OVER (ORDER BY tourney_date) AS cumulative_count    of the winner     cumulative count
FROM matches                                                                        of winners
JOIN players ON players.player_id = matches.winner_id         Filters to only return the Final
WHERE round='F'                                               match in each tournament
AND tourney_level = 'G'         Filters to only include
                                Grand Slam events
```

```
AND age >= 30
ORDER BY tourney_date;
```
⊲─┐ **Filters to only return**
   │ **winners aged 30 or older**

Let's paste that query, and then click on the Run button. We should see the output shown in figure 9.23. Once we're happy with our query, we can select the Save Dataset option and click on the Save button to give the dataset a name.

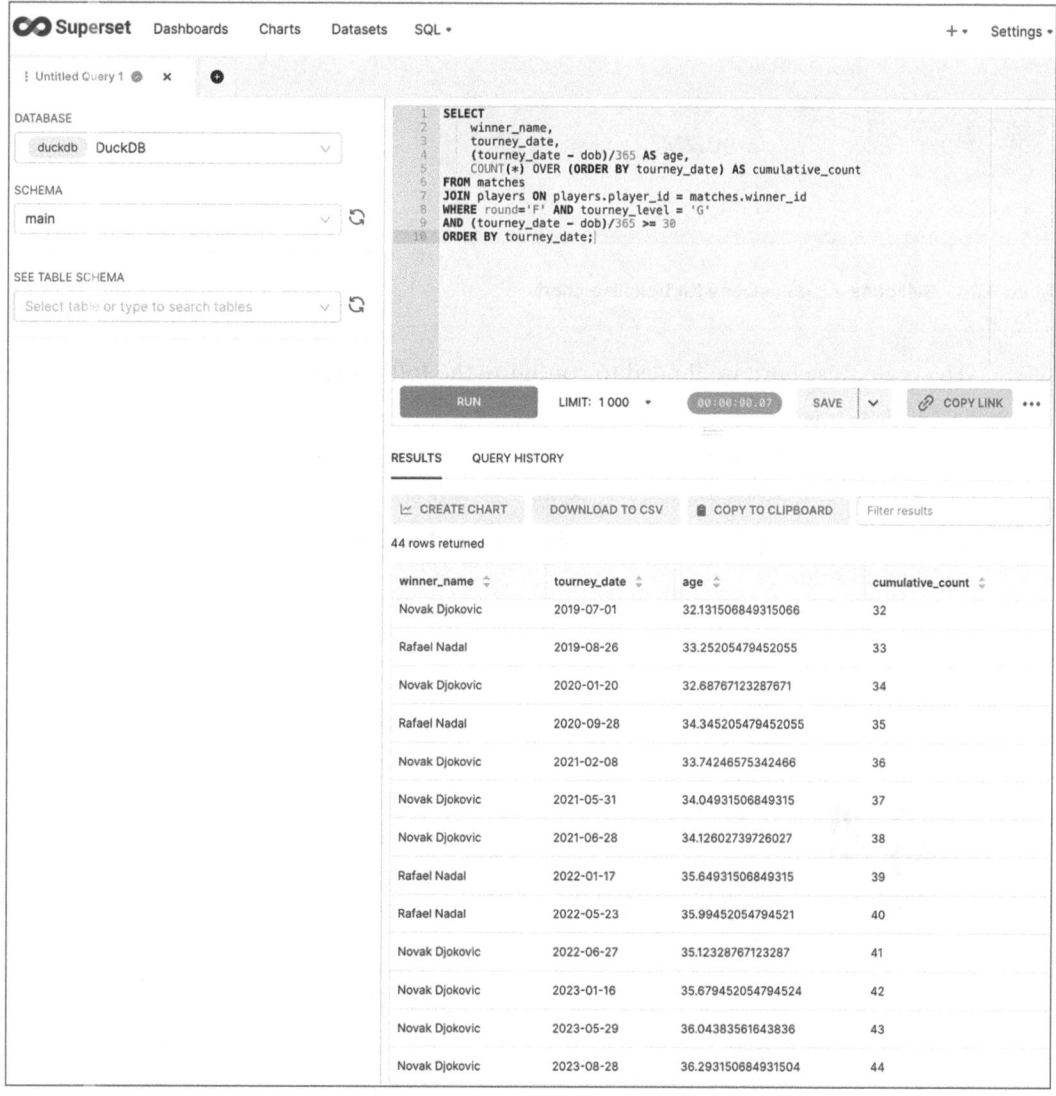

Figure 9.23   Grand slam winners aged 30 and over

Let's now return to the Charts page; this time, we'll choose Big Number with Trendline as our chart. We'll also select our new dataset, as shown in figure 9.24.

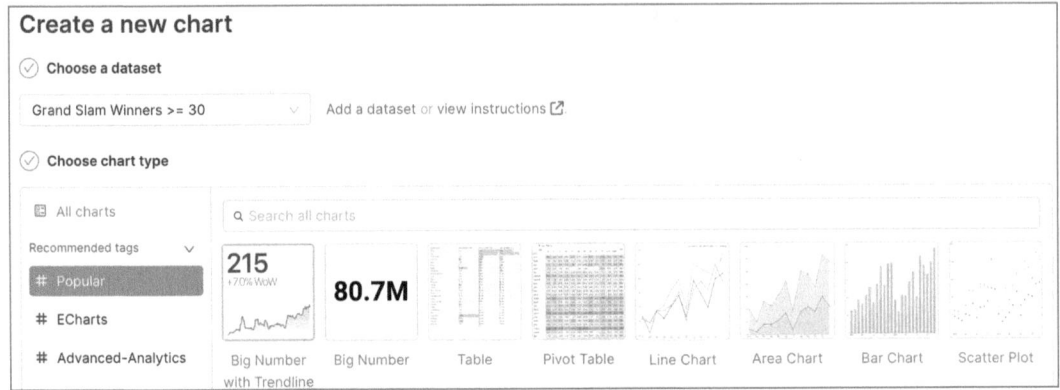

Figure 9.24   Selecting a big number with trendline chart

To create this chart, we'll need to configure the following sections:

- X-Axis is `tourney_date`.
- Time Grain is `Day`.
- Metrics is `SUM(cumulative_count)`, which is a custom metric.

If we then click Update Chart, we should see the visualization shown in 9.25 on the right-hand side.

Figure 9.25   The number of grand slam winners aged 30 and over

Let's save the chart and add it to the ATP Dashboard we created earlier. If we navigate to the dashboard, we should see something that looks like figure 9.26.

Figure 9.26 A dashboard with the over 30 Grand Slam winners included

Hopefully, this has given you a good idea of how to construct a dashboard using Superset. We've added a few more charts to the dashboard following the approach described in this section and the previous one. You can see the final result in figure 9.27.

Figure 9.27 The ATP Dashboard

We've used a few different chart types to give you an idea of what you can do with Superset. In the next section, we'll explain how you can import a copy of this dashboard so you can explore the various elements.

9.2.5   *Exporting and importing dashboards*

We generally configure databases, datasets, charts, and dashboards, using Superset's UI. But if we want to deploy those dashboards elsewhere (or, say, share them with the readers of a book), we probably don't want to have to go through the whole process from scratch. This is where Superset's export and import dashboard features come into play.

We can export dashboards from the Dashboard page. If we hover over the Actions column of the Dashboards row, we'll see an export button, as shown in figure 9.28.

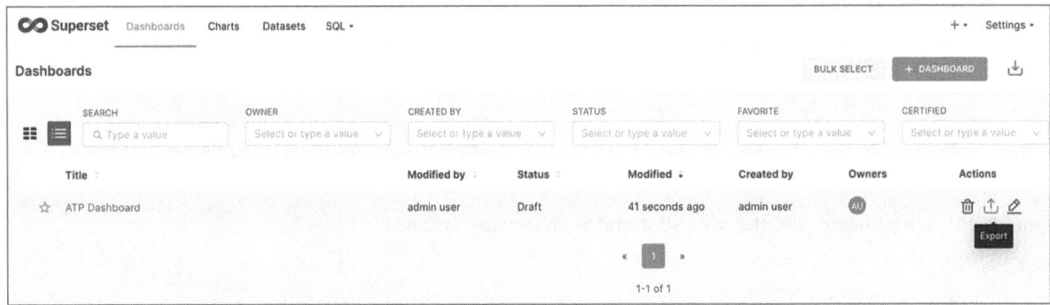

Figure 9.28   Exporting a dashboard

If we click on this button, Superset will generate a ZIP file that contains our databases, datasets, charts, and dashboards. We've included the ZIP file in the book's GitHub repository (https://github.com/duckdb-in-action/examples), and if we navigate to ch09, we can unzip that file:

```
unzip dashboard_export_20231203T162310.zip
```

In a Linux-based terminal, we can use the tree command (tree /f /a on Windows or find dashboard_export_20231203T162310 on MacOS) to list all the included files:

```
tree dashboard_export_20231203T162310

dashboard_export_20231203T162310
├── charts
│   ├── Grand_Slam_Winners__30_11.yaml
│   ├── Grand_Slam_winners__25_9.yaml
│   ├── Lowest_Ranked_Grand_Slam_Winners_8.yaml
│   ├── Matches_Played_7.yaml
│   └── Multi_Title_Winners_6.yaml
├── dashboards
```

```
|     └── ATP_Dashboard_1.yaml
├── databases
|     └── DuckDB.yaml
├── datasets
|     └── DuckDB
|           ├── Grand_Slam_Winners__30.yaml
|           ├── Multi_Title_Winners.yaml
|           ├── Young_Grand_Slam_Winners.yaml
|           └── matches.yaml
└── metadata.yaml
```

There's a directory for each of the concepts we learned about at the start of this section:

- The config to connect to the database is in databases/DuckDB.yaml.
- Datasets are defined in datasets/DuckDB.
- Charts are defined in charts.
- The config for the dashboard is in dashboards/ATP_Dashboard_1.yaml.

You can import this dashboard from the dashboard page by clicking on the down arrow button in the top-right corner of the Dashboard page, as shown in figure 9.29.

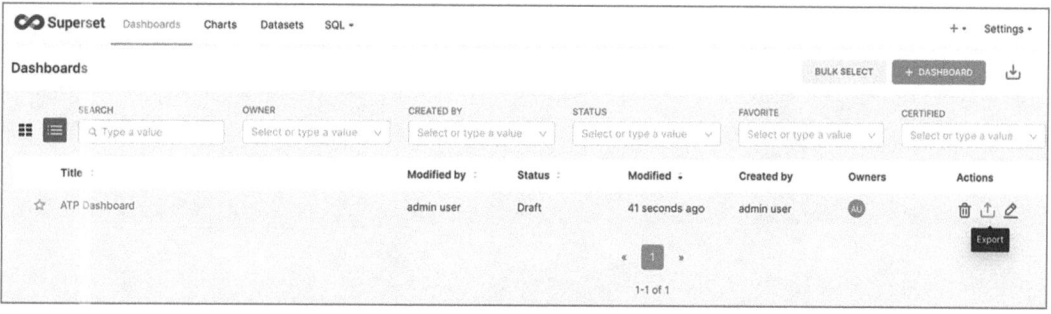

Figure 9.29 Importing a dashboard

If we then select the ZIP file, it will import the setup into Superset, and we should see the dashboard from figure 9.27.

Summary

- Streamlit is a low-code environment that provides various ready-made and reusable components solving recurrent tasks when writing web applications.
- Streamlit is written in Python and thus integrates in various ways with DuckDB's Python API via the DB-API 2.0, the relational API, or DataFrames.
- In contrast to a no-code and purely declarative environment, you can write custom Python in your Streamlit application to enhance its capabilities.

- plot.ly provides a similar low-code approach for creating visually appealing, interactive visualizations that can be used seamlessly with Streamlit.
- Apache Superset is at the other end of the spectrum: it is basically a no-code, drag-and-drop alternative for building a visually appealing dashboard.
- The only code you usually need to write using Apache Superset are custom SQL queries that feed into the visualizations.

Performance considerations for large datasets

10

This chapter covers

- Preparing large volumes of data to be imported into DuckDB
- Querying metadata and running exploratory data analysis (EDA) queries on large datasets
- Exporting full databases concurrently to Parquet
- Using aggregations on multiple columns to speed up statistical analysis
- Using `EXPLAIN` and `EXPLAIN ANALYZE` to understand query plans

So far in this book, we've seen how to use DuckDB with a variety of datasets, but most of them have been small or medium in size. This isn't unusual, as those datasets are representative of many of those we'll come across in our daily work.

However, huge datasets do exist, and we wouldn't want you to think that you need to use another data processing tool when you encounter these! In this chapter, we're going to look at two datasets: the first contains data about Stack Overflow, the popular coding question-and-answer website, and the second contains data about taxi trips in New York City. With these two datasets, we can teach you tips and tricks when working with bigger datasets in DuckDB.

For each one, we'll show how to prepare and then import it into DuckDB. Once we've done that, we'll run some queries on the data before exporting the database into a portable format.

10.1 Loading and querying the full Stack Overflow database

Stack Overflow is an online, community-driven question-and-answer website designed for developers and programmers to ask and answer technical questions. It was created in 2008 and uses a reputation system, where users earn points and privileges by contributing useful answers and content.

If you're like us, you've probably spent a lot of time on Stack Overflow looking for the answers to technical questions. And if you've been a good citizen, perhaps you've answered some questions as well! But have you ever stopped to consider the system and data behind this useful site?

If not, it's time to change that by analyzing a dump of Stack Overflow data with DuckDB. The dataset size is 11 GB in compressed CSV format and contains 58 million posts, 20 million users, and 65 thousand tags. It's not quite "Big Data" (see https://motherduck.com/blog/big-data-is-dead/), but it's big enough to put DuckDB through its paces.

In this section, we will explore the Stack Overflow dataset, using DuckDB both locally and on MotherDuck. First, we're going to download and transform the raw data, and then we'll load it into DuckDB and inspect it with some EDA queries before exporting it to Parquet.

10.1.1 Data dump and extraction

If you want to do some basic exploratory analysis of the Stack Overflow data, the site provides the Stack Exchange Data Explorer (https://mng.bz/wx6W), which is a website for executing SQL queries on the Stack Overflow data. It is great for getting a feel for the dataset, but it is limited in the number and complexity of queries you can run so that usage doesn't overload the service.

We want to have more control over the queries that we run though, so we want access to the raw data. In this section, we're going to show how to download and transform the raw data, but we know this isn't the most fun part of the process, so don't feel like you need to follow all the steps in the section.

> **NOTE**   If you just want to access the final tabular data, you can either download the Parquet files from S3 (s3://us-prd-motherduck-open-datasets/stack-overflow/parquet/2023-05/) or mount the MotherDuck share (md:_share/stackoverflow/6c318917-6888-425a-bea1-5860c29947e5) to focus on querying the data. Alternatively, you can pick one of the smaller stack exchange communities, like math or biotechnology, if the Stack Overflow data is too big.

For the bravehearted among you, let's get this dataset ready to load into DuckDB. Stack Exchange publishes all their data publicly on the Internet Archive Stack Exchange dump (https://archive.org/download/stackexchange) under a Creative Commons license. We're going to use the largest set of files for the Stack Overflow site itself. We can use the `curl` command-line utility for that task as shown, which stores the files under the same name that they have on the server:

```
curl -OL "https://archive.org/download/stackexchange/stackoverflow.com-\
{Comments,Posts,Votes,Users,Badges,PostLinks,Tags}.7z"
```

The Internet Archive's bandwidth is limited, so downloading the data can be a frustrating and slow process, with frequent aborts of the connection likely. We will end up with seven compressed XML files with a total size of 27 GB:

```
19G stackoverflow.com-Posts.7z
5.2G stackoverflow.com-Comments.7z
1.3G stackoverflow.com-Votes.7z
684M stackoverflow.com-Users.7z
343M stackoverflow.com-Badges.7z
117M stackoverflow.com-PostLinks.7z
903K stackoverflow.com-Tags.7z
```

After the download finishes, you will need to extract the files using 7-Zip (https://7-zip.org/) or p7zip (https://p7zip.sourceforge.net/), as shown.

The files are in the SQL Server export format, where each `Row` element has all columns as attributes. Here is an example of the file contents:

```
<?xml version="1.0" encoding="utf-8"?>
<users>
...
  <row Id="728812" Reputation="41063" CreationDate="2011-04-28T07:51:27.387"
  DisplayName="Michael Hunger" LastAccessDate="2023-03-01T14:44:32.237"
  WebsiteUrl="http://www.jexp.de" Location="Dresden, Germany" AboutMe=
  "&lt;p&gt;&lt;a href=&quot;http://twitter.com/mesirii&quot; rel=&quot;
  nofollow&quot;&gt;Michael Hunger&lt;/a&gt; has been passionate about
  so?ware development for a long time. If you want him to speak at your
  user group or conference, just drop him an email at michael at jexp.de"
  Views="7046" UpVotes="4712" DownVotes="24" AccountId="376992" />
...
```

Unfortunately, DuckDB doesn't support parsing XML yet, so we will have to use some external tools to get this data into a format that DuckDB supports. While the process is time-consuming, it is a reliable way of converting the XML to CSV.

We are using `xidel` (https://www.videlibri.de/xidel.html), an XML processing command-line tool that outputs JSON. We'll then convert the JSON output to CSV, using the `jq` (https://jqlang.github.io/jq/) command-line JSON processor. You can find download and installation instructions for `xidel` and `jq` on their respective websites. Finally, we'll compress the CSV file with `gzip` to save space.

Let's have a look at how to do this for the comments. First, we extract the contents of the zip file before piping the output to `xidel`, as you can see in listing 10.1.

The process is as follows:

1 Extract relevant fields from the XML, for instance, the post ID, score, text, creation date, and user ID.
2 Convert the XML to JSON.
3 Convert the JSON to CSV.
4 Output the header.
5 Compress the CSV to a file called Comments.csv.gz.

We could have also used the built-in functionality of DuckDB to load the JSON files from `xidel` directly, but it can be useful to have the CSV around for other tools that don't support it. Additionally, the files are a bit smaller without the repeated key names.

Listing 10.1 Converting the XML file via JSON to CSV

```
7z e -so stackoverflow.com-Comments.7z | \
xidel -se '//row/[(@Id|@PostId|@Score|@Text|@CreationDate|@UserId)]' - | \
(echo "Id,PostId,Score,Text,CreationDate,UserId" &&
jq -r '. | @csv') |
gzip -9 > Comments.csv.gz
```

Each file will be processed similarly, but for brevity's sake, we won't include all the commands inline. If you want to see the code so that you can try it yourself, you can find it in the book's GitHub repository.

Once we're done, we'll have the following list of CSV files, with a total size of 11 GB:

```
5.0G    Comments.csv.gz
3.2G    Posts.csv.gz
1.6G    Votes.csv.gz
613M    Users.csv.gz
452M    Badges.csv.gz
137M    PostLinks.csv.gz
1.1M    Tags.csv.gz
```

10.1.2 *The data model*

Before we start exploring, let's look at the data model of the Stack Overflow dataset. To remind ourselves of the UI, figure 10.1 shows a screenshot of the Stack Overflow site with most information visible.

In the downloaded and converted files previously listed, we have the following entities, which correspond also to the filenames:

- Questions (Post with postTypeId=1) with a title, body, creationDate, ownerUserId, parentId, acceptedAnswerId, answerCount, tags, upvotes, downvotes, views, and comments. The maximum of six Tags define the topics of the question.
- User with displayName, aboutMe, reputation, last login date, and so on.

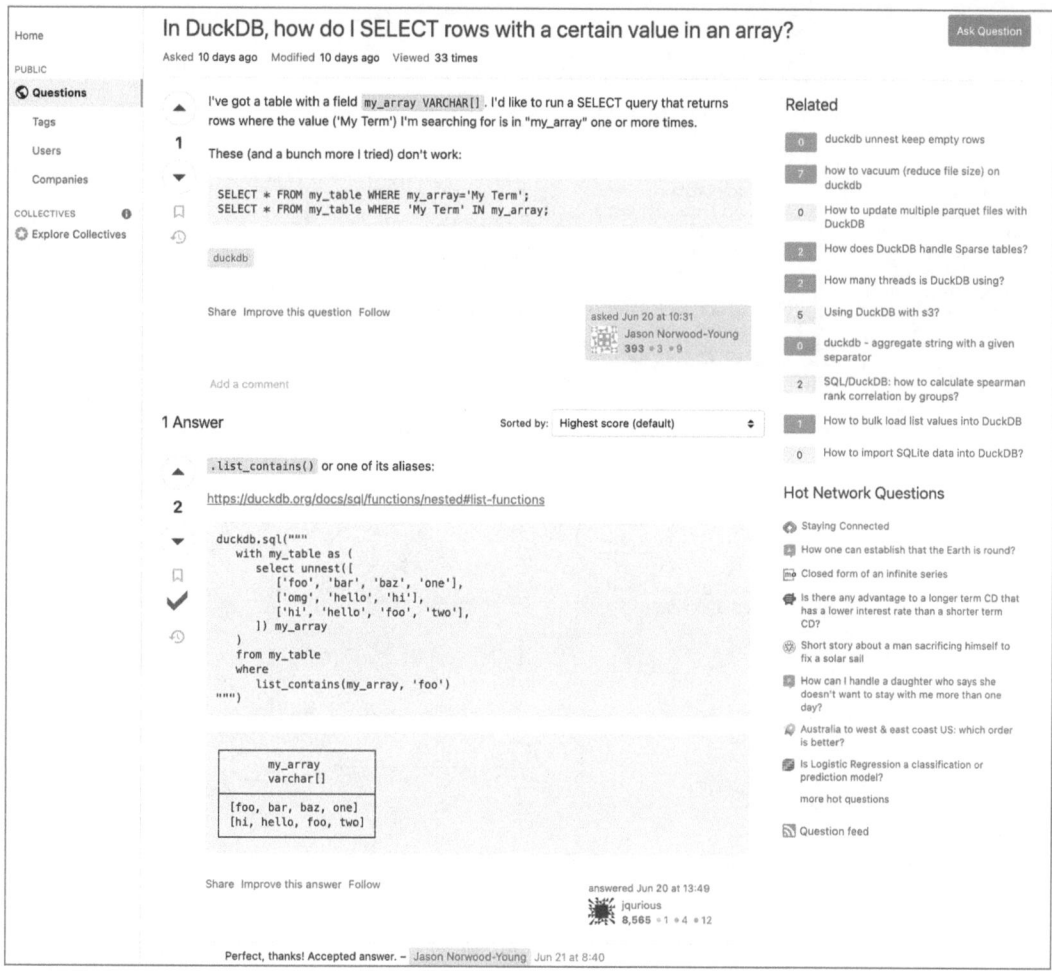

Figure 10.1   The Stack Overflow UI showing a user question and an accepted answer

- Answers (`Post` with `postTypeId=2`) with their own `ownerUserId`, upvotes, down-votes, and `comments`. One of the answers can be accepted as the correct answer.
- `Questions` and `Answers` can have comments with their own `text`, `ownerUserId`, and `score`.
- `Badges` with `class` columns that users can earn for their contributions.
- `Posts` can be linked to other `Posts` (e.g., duplicates or related questions as `PostLinks`).

The files don't have any information about indexes or foreign keys; we need to recreate those references manually. For that purpose, we drew the data mode shown in figure 10.2, which is a simplified version of the Stack Overflow data model with the most important columns listed above as attributes and foreign keys as arrows.

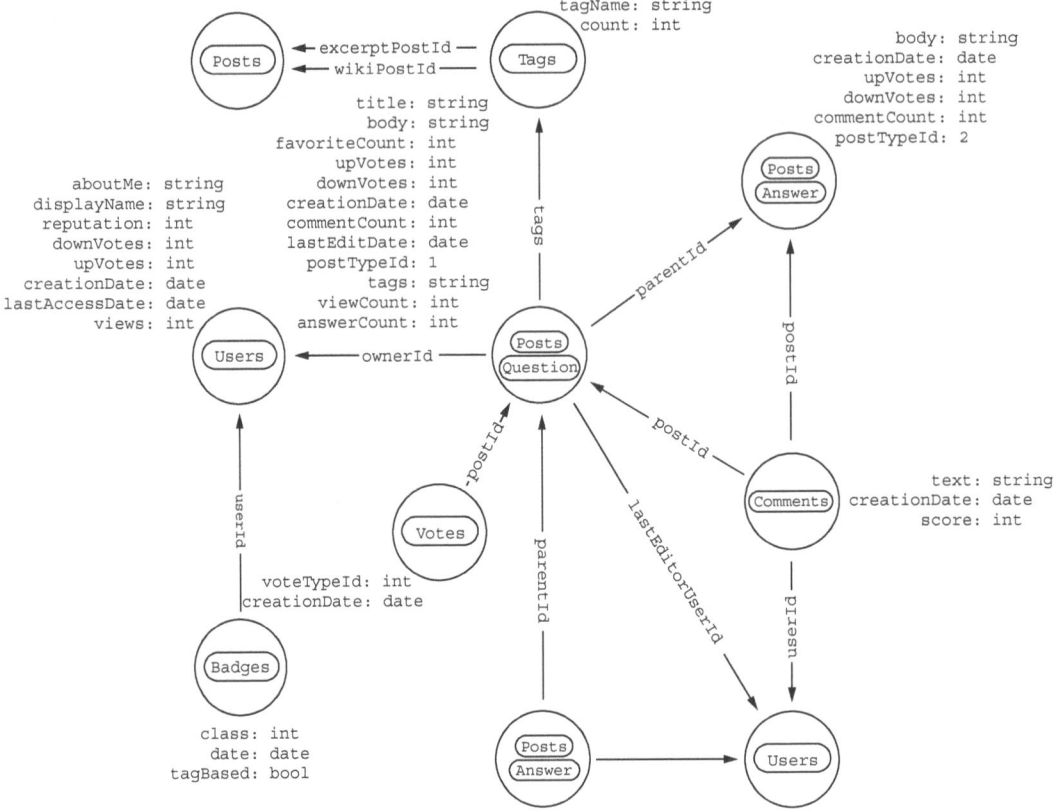

Figure 10.2   Stack Overflow data model

You can see how the Post (Question or Answer) connects to the User who has written it via the ownerId. Comment, Vote, and Answer refer to the original Post via postId, and the accepted Answer–Post is linked from the Question–Post via accepted-AnswerId. The Badge connects to the User via userId, and the PostLink connects two Post entities via postId and relatedPostId.

10.1.3 Exploring the CSV file data

Now that we've got the data prepared, we're back in familiar territory when it comes to importing the data into DuckDB. As we covered in earlier chapters, DuckDB has the read_csv function, which we can use to load data directly from the compressed gzipped CSV files. read_csv will automatically try to infer column types, which we've found works well for the Stack Overflow dataset.

Let's look at the Tags file first and query it for structure and content. We're going to start with the following query, which counts the number of tags with

```
SELECT count(*)  FROM read_csv('Tags.csv.gz')
```

We've got just under 65,000 tags, which seems like a lot, but there are many different technologies people can get stuck on, so it makes sense! Next, let's have a look at the structure of the data in the `Tags` file, using the `DESCRIBE` function, which gives us the name and type of each column.

Listing 10.2 Describing the metadata of the `Tags` file

```
DESCRIBE(FROM read_csv('Tags.csv.gz'));
```

The `DESCRIBE` command returns the metadata of the tags files, and we can see the names and types of the available columns:

```
┌───────────────┬─────────────┐
│  column_name  │ column_type │
│    varchar    │   varchar   │
├───────────────┼─────────────┤
│ Id            │ BIGINT      │
│ TagName       │ VARCHAR     │
│ Count         │ BIGINT      │
│ ExcerptPostId │ BIGINT      │
│ WikiPostId    │ BIGINT      │
└───────────────┴─────────────┘
```

The `TagName` and `Count` fields are the ones we need to determine the most popular tags. Let's find the top five most popular tags with a query that just runs perfectly fast, even on the compressed, large file.

Listing 10.3 Selecting the top `Tags` from the CSV file

```
SELECT TagName, Count
FROM read_csv(
    'Tags.csv.gz',
    column_names=['Id', 'TagName', 'Count'])
ORDER BY Count DESC
LIMIT 5;
```

We can see that these are the usual suspects when it comes to programming languages (i.e., the most popular ones):

```
┌────────────┬─────────┐
│  TagName   │  Count  │
│  varchar   │  int64  │
├────────────┼─────────┤
│ javascript │ 2479947 │
│ python     │ 2113196 │
│ java       │ 1889767 │
│ c#         │ 1583879 │
│ php        │ 1456271 │
└────────────┴─────────┘
```

To see how tags distribute across their usage, we can bucket the counts into powers of 10 and then count the number of tags in each bucket, as shown in the following listing.

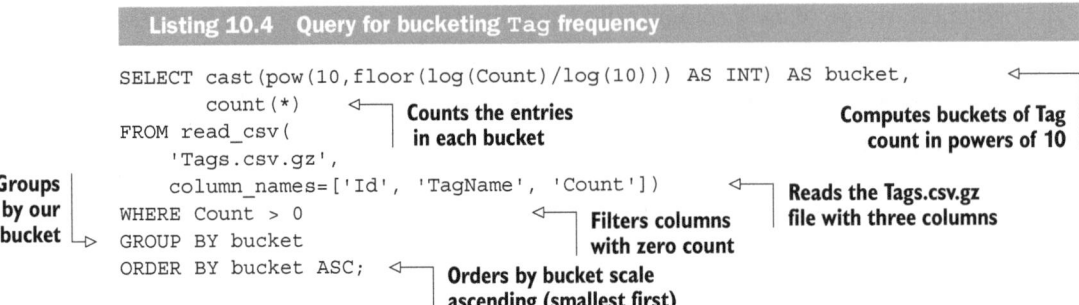

Listing 10.4   Query for bucketing `Tag` frequency

```
SELECT cast(pow(10,floor(log(Count)/log(10))) AS INT) AS bucket,    ◄──────┐ Computes buckets of Tag
       count(*)    ◄──┐ Counts the entries                                   count in powers of 10
FROM read_csv(        │ in each bucket
    'Tags.csv.gz',
    column_names=['Id', 'TagName', 'Count'])    ◄──┐ Reads the Tags.csv.gz
WHERE Count > 0    ◄──┐ Filters columns              file with three columns
GROUP BY bucket       │ with zero count
ORDER BY bucket ASC;    ◄──┐ Orders by bucket scale
                           │ ascending (smallest first)
```

Groups by our bucket

To create our buckets, using the count of 112 as an example, we do the following:

1 We compute the logarithm of each count to the base of 10 (`log(112)/log(10)` `= 2.049`).

2 This gives us the order of magnitude of the count.

3 We use this to get the base integer value and `floor(2.049)` `= 2.0`.

4 We use it again to recompute the power of 10 `pow(10,2.0)` `= 100.0`.

5 We get, as an end result, the original value in powers of 10.

6 We cast these to an integer for the grouping `cast(100.0 as int)` `= 100`.

We can see the result follows a power law distribution (i.e., the number of tags with few uses is high, and fewer tags have a high count), tapering off to only 25 tags with more than 1 million uses. The only exception is rare tags with one mention; there are fewer of them, as expected.

bucket int32	count_star() int64
1	6238
10	23018
100	23842
1000	9126
10000	1963
100000	252
1000000	25

10.1.4 *Loading the data into DuckDB*

To get the Stack Overflow data into DuckDB, we can either create a table first and then ingest the data, or we can create the table on the fly as we read the data. The former approach is more explicit and allows us to define the column names and types, but it requires us to know and spell out the schema of the data beforehand. Then, the

CREATE TABLE statements also need to be adjusted when the file structure or column types change; otherwise, the load will fail. We use CREATE OR REPLACE TABLE so that we can run the imports multiple times for testing without having to drop the table in between.

The latter approach is used in listing 10.5. We choose the relevant column names, with the data types being inferred while reading the CSV files, and we get "what's there."

Let's have a look at the import statements for Users and Posts. You can find the import statements for the other tables in the book's GitHub repository.

Listing 10.5   Creating or replacing the Stack Overflow users table

```
CREATE OR REPLACE TABLE users AS
SELECT *
FROM read_csv(
    'Users.csv.gz',
    auto_detect=true,
    column_names=[
        'Id', 'Reputation', 'CreationDate', 'DisplayName',
        'LastAccessDate', 'AboutMe', 'Views', 'UpVotes', 'DownVotes'
    ]
);
```

Now, in the following listing, we can check the number of rows in the users table with

```
SELECT count(*) FROM users;
```

We will see that we have roughly 20 million users.

Listing 10.6   Creating or replacing the Stack Overflow posts table

```
CREATE OR REPLACE TABLE posts AS
FROM read_csv(
    'Posts.csv.gz',
    auto_detect=true,
    column_names=[
        'Id', 'PostTypeId', 'AcceptedAnswerId', 'ParentId', 'CreationDate',
        'Score', 'ViewCount', 'Body', 'OwnerUserId', 'LastEditorUserId',
        'LastEditorDisplayName', 'LastEditDate', 'LastActivityDate', 'Title',
        'Tags', 'AnswerCount', 'CommentCount', 'FavoriteCount',
        'CommunityOwnedDate', 'ContentLicense'
    ]
);
```

NOTE   The Tags column is a text column that contains up to six Stack Overflow tags wrapped in angle brackets (e.g., —<sql><performance><duckdb>).

We can see the structure of the generated table with

```
`select column_name, column_type from (show table posts);`
```

Meanwhile, we will skip irrelevant fields, like `null`, `key`, `default`, and `extra`:

```
|       column_name        |  column_type  |
|         varchar          |    varchar    |
|--------------------------|---------------|
| Id                       | BIGINT        |
| PostTypeId               | BIGINT        |
| AcceptedAnswerId         | BIGINT        |
| CreationDate             | TIMESTAMP     |
| Score                    | BIGINT        |
| ViewCount                | BIGINT        |
| Body                     | VARCHAR       |
| OwnerUserId              | BIGINT        |
| LastEditorUserId         | BIGINT        |
| LastEditorDisplayName    | VARCHAR       |
| LastEditDate             | TIMESTAMP     |
| LastActivityDate         | TIMESTAMP     |
| Title                    | VARCHAR       |
| Tags                     | VARCHAR       |
| AnswerCount              | BIGINT        |
| CommentCount             | BIGINT        |
| FavoriteCount            | BIGINT        |
| CommunityOwnedDate       | TIMESTAMP     |
| ContentLicense           | VARCHAR       |
|--------------------------|---------------|
| 19 rows                  |    2 columns  |
```

Now we have inserted 58 million posts, which we can check using

```
SELECT count(*) FROM posts;
```

From previous experience, we've found that a good approach for working with large datasets is to first get an overview of the data values in our tables. In chapter 4, we learned about the SUMMARIZE clause. Running it on all columns of the users and posts tables will take a few seconds, and the output is huge, as the tables have a lot of columns, and SUMMARIZE computes a lot of metrics. Let's have a look at some of the columns of the users table and check for the approximate number of unique users, their creation date, and how often they interact with posts by upvoting and downvoting them. You get these statistics without writing a complex query, as shown in the following listing.

Listing 10.7   Summarizing a subset of columns

```
SUMMARIZE (
    SELECT Id, Reputation, CreationDate, Views, UpVotes, DownVotes
    FROM users
);
```

Here are the results of summarizing the most interesting user attributes:

column_name varchar	column_type varchar	max varchar	approx_unique varchar	avg varchar
Id	BIGINT	21334825	20113337	11027766.241
Reputation	BIGINT	1389256	26919	94.752717160
CreationDate	TIMESTAMP	2023-03-05	19557978	
Views	BIGINT	2214048	7452	11.630429738
UpVotes	BIGINT	591286	6227	8.7674283438
DownVotes	BIGINT	1486341	2930	1.1697560125

If you want to follow along without creating and ingesting the CSV files, use the Stack Overflow example data from MotherDuck (see chapter 7) by running the following:

```
ATTACH 'md:_share/stackoverflow/6c318917-6888-425a-bea1-5860c29947e5'
  AS stackoverflow`;
```

10.1.5 Fast exploratory queries on large tables

Now that we have our tables loaded, we can run a few more queries to see what kind of data is available and how quickly we can get results. Let's say we're a Stack Overflow analyst and want to check to see who are top users and whether they're still active. And if they aren't, perhaps we can come up with a way to persuade them to come back to the platform! We can find the top users by reputation along with their last login time by writing the following query.

Listing 10.8 Top users by reputation

```
.timer on

SELECT DisplayName, Reputation, LastAccessDate
FROM users
ORDER BY Reputation DESC
LIMIT 5;
```

The query finishes in only 0.126 seconds for 20 million rows to analyze, which is quite fast:

DisplayName varchar	Reputation int64	LastAccessDate timestamp
Jon Skeet	1389256	2023-03-04 19:54:19.74
Gordon Linoff	1228338	2023-03-04 15:16:02.617
VonC	1194435	2023-03-05 01:48:58.937
BalusC	1069162	2023-03-04 12:49:24.637
Martijn Pieters	1016741	2023-03-03 19:35:13.76

```
Run Time (s): real 0.126 user 2.969485 sys 1.696962
```

If you're familiar with Stack Overflow, you won't be surprised to find the legend that is Jon Skeet in top place. However, Jon has been using Stack Overflow for a long time, so he's had ages to accrue that reputation.

It will be difficult for anyone to exceed his total reputation score, but perhaps he has more competition when it comes to the reputation `rate`. We can compute this by working out the number of reputation points per day on the platform, which will help us identify people who are gaining reputation points faster but don't yet have a high total reputation. We can compute this score by dividing `reputation` by the number of days from today to `createdAt` so that our result gives us a reputation `rate` per day, as shown in the following listing.

Listing 10.9   Top `users` by reputation `rate` per day

```
.timer on
SELECT DisplayName, reputation,
       round(reputation/day(today()-CreationDate)) as rate,
       day(today()-CreationDate) as days,
       CreationDate
FROM users
WHERE reputation > 1_000_000
ORDER BY rate DESC;
```

Computes reputation rate, dividing the reputation by the number of days since the user's creation date ←

Computes the number of days since the user's creation date ←

Only considers users with a reputation of more than 1 million ←

Orders by rate, in reverse order ←

Jon drops into second place on this measure, with Gordon Linoff taking the top place. Reputation on Stack Overflow also accrues when people upvote your past answers, and the more useful the answers you have given are, the more likely it is that people will upvote them over time:

DisplayName varchar	reputation int64	rate double	days int64	CreationDate timestamp
Gordon Linoff	1228338	294.0	4181	2012-01-11 19:53:57.59
Jon Skeet	1389256	258.0	5383	2008-09-26 12:05:05.15
VonC	1194435	221.0	5396	2008-09-13 22:22:33.173
BalusC	1069162	211.0	5058	2009-08-17 16:42:02.403
T.J. Crowder	1010006	200.0	5059	2009-08-16 11:00:22.497
Martijn Pieters	1016741	197.0	5164	2009-05-03 14:53:57.543
Darin Dimitrov	1014014	189.0	5360	2008-10-19 16:07:47.823
Marc Gravell	1009857	188.0	5380	2008-09-29 05:46:02.697

```
Run Time (s): real 0.006 user 0.007980 sys 0.001260
```

We can turn that result into a bar chart using the `bar` function, which takes a value, a minimum and maximum value, and the width of the bar, returning a string with the bar rendered as black blocks. To make the query more readable, we can turn our existing query into a common table expression (CTE) using `WITH` and then use the `bar` function in the outer query, as shown in the following listing.

Listing 10.10 Computing bar charts of the top `users` by reputation rate per day

```
WITH top_users as (
    SELECT
        DisplayName,
        Reputation,
        round(reputation/day(today()-CreationDate)) as rate,
        day(today()-CreationDate) as days,
        CreationDate
    FROM users
    WHERE Reputation > 1_000_000
)
SELECT DisplayName, Reputation, rate, bar(rate,150,300,35) AS bar
FROM top_users
ORDER BY rate DESC;
```

Wraps the same query as before

Uses a named CTE, top_users, to refer back to later

Uses the bar() function on rate with a minimum of 150, a maximum of 300, and a width of 35

Selects data from top_users CTE

As promised, the `bar` function will create an ASCII art chart for us:

DisplayName varchar	Reputation int64	rate double	bar varchar
Gordon Linoff	1228338	294.0	███████████████████████████████
Jon Skeet	1389256	258.0	███████████████████████████
VonC	1194435	221.0	███████████████████████
BalusC	1069162	211.0	██████████████████████
T.J. Crowder	1010006	200.0	█████████████████████
Martijn Pieters	1016741	197.0	█████████████████████
Darin Dimitrov	1014014	189.0	████████████████████
Marc Gravell	1009857	188.0	████████████████████

So those are our top users.

Next, we want to get an understanding of how much activity there is on the platform and whether it's changing over time. We are going to do this by querying the posts table, which has 58 million rows. In the following listing, we will compute the total number of posts, the average view count, and the maximum number of answers for each of the last 10 years by grouping the results accordingly.

Listing 10.11 A query for yearly activity on Stack Overflow

```
SELECT
    year(CreationDate) AS year,
    round(count(*)/1000000,2) as postM,
    round(count_if(postTypeId = 1)/1000000,2) as questionM,
    round(count_if(postTypeId = 2)/1000000,2) as answerM,
    round(count_if(postTypeId = 1)/count_if(postTypeId = 2),2) as ratio,
    round(avg(ViewCount)) as avgViewCount,
    max(AnswerCount) as maxAnswerCount
FROM posts
GROUP BY year
```

The count of posts (questions and answers) in millions

The count of questions in millions

The count of answers in millions

The average view count of posts

The maxAnswerCount of posts

The ratio between questions and answers

Grouping by the year

```
ORDER BY year DESC          ←┐  Sorting years in descending
LIMIT 10;          ←┐         │  order (latest first)
                    Showing the
                    last 10 years
```

The statistics of the last 10 years on Stack Overflow look like this:

year int64	postM double	questionM double	answerM double	ratio double	avgViewCount double	maxAnswers int64
2023	0.53	0.27	0.26	1.03	44.0	15
2022	3.35	1.61	1.74	0.93	265.0	44
2021	3.55	1.55	2.0	0.78	580.0	65
2020	4.31	1.87	2.44	0.77	847.0	59
2019	4.16	1.77	2.39	0.74	1190.0	60
2018	4.44	1.89	2.55	0.74	1648.0	121
2017	5.02	2.11	2.9	0.73	1994.0	65
2016	5.28	2.2	3.07	0.72	2202.0	74
2015	5.35	2.2	3.14	0.7	2349.0	82
2014	5.34	2.13	3.19	0.67	2841.0	92

| 10 rows | | | | | | 7 columns |

```
Run Time (s): real 5.977 user 7.498157 sys 5.480121 (1st run)
Run Time (s): real 0.039 user 4.609049 sys 0.078694
```

Even when computing these statistics across 58 million rows, the query only takes a few seconds to run for the first run and only 40 milliseconds for the subsequent run after the data had been loaded from disk.

We don't have complete data for 2023 in this dataset, so we can't compare the full data for that year. The total number of posts (the sum of questions and answers) asked has been falling steadily since 2014. The ratio of questions to answers has also gotten worse, as there are more questions than answers as of the last 2 years. The view count of newer posts is also smaller due to their relatively short existence. The maximum number of answers per post is slightly decreasing over the years too, as older questions had more time to collect answers.

10.1.6 *Posting on weekdays*

We're curious when people use the platform. Do they only use it to answer questions at work, or do they use it on the weekend as well?

This question was also asked by Evalina Gabova in her Stack Overflow Analysis (https://evelinag.com/exploring-stackoverflow/). Let's see if we can reproduce Evalina's analysis.

Here is a query that shows us the questions for the sql tag, grouped by day of the week, with the frequency and a bar chart.

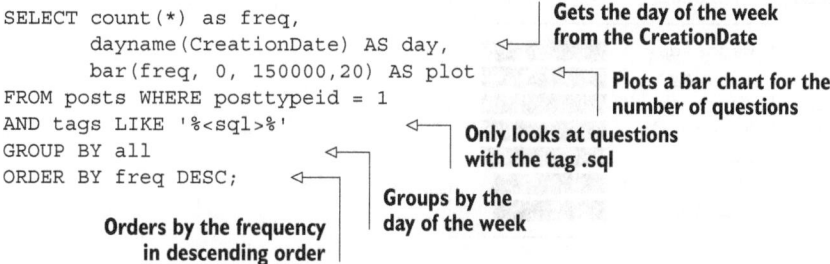

Listing 10.12   Query for asking questions about SQL on weekdays

```
SELECT count(*) as freq,                      Gets the day of the week
       dayname(CreationDate) AS day,          from the CreationDate
       bar(freq, 0, 150000,20) AS plot        Plots a bar chart for the
FROM posts WHERE posttypeid = 1               number of questions
AND tags LIKE '%<sql>%'                       Only looks at questions
GROUP BY all                                  with the tag .sql
ORDER BY freq DESC;
                                              Groups by the
       Orders by the frequency                day of the week
         in descending order
```

We see that most questions are posted on weekdays, especially during the middle of the week, and the least on weekends. That could indicate that people mostly deal with SQL for work and ask questions during their work time:

```
|  freq   |    day     |           plot            |
|  int64  |  varchar   |          varchar          |
|---------|------------|---------------------------|
| 119825  | Wednesday  | ████████████████████████  |
| 119514  | Thursday   | ████████████████████████  |
| 115575  | Tuesday    | ███████████████████████   |
| 103937  | Monday     | █████████████████████     |
| 103445  | Friday     | █████████████████████     |
|  47390  | Sunday     | ██████████                |
|  47139  | Saturday   | █████████                 |
```

Run Time (s): real 0.303 user 2.780285 sys 0.010856

Processing the 23.5 million questions took only 0.3 seconds before a result was computed.

But what if we look at a different tag? Rust is a relatively new programming language that isn't as ingrained in companies as SQL. When do people ask questions about Rust?

Listing 10.13   Query for asking questions about Rust on weekdays

```
SELECT count(*) as freq,
       dayname(CreationDate) AS day,
       bar(freq, 0, 10000,20) AS plot
FROM posts WHERE posttypeid = 1
AND tags LIKE '%<rust>%'
GROUP BY all
ORDER BY freq DESC;
```

The questions are evenly distributed throughout the week, with a slight drop on the weekend:

```
| freq  |    day    |    plot   |
| int64 |  varchar  |  varchar  |
|-------+-----------+-----------|
|  5205 | Wednesday | ████████  |
|  5167 | Tuesday   | ████████  |
|  5160 | Thursday  | ████████  |
|  5054 | Monday    | ████████  |
|  5009 | Friday    | ████████  |
|  4784 | Sunday    | ███████   |
|  4667 | Saturday  | ██████    |
```

We should also note that there are between 10 and 20 times fewer questions asked about Rust than SQL!

10.1.7 *Using enums for tags*

When you're using DuckDB with larger datasets, you might sometimes choose to do optimizations that wouldn't be necessary on a smaller dataset. An example of this in the Stack Overflow dataset is the way that tag names assigned to posts are stored and processed.

DuckDB has the concept of *enum types*, which represent a fixed set of named values that are stored internally as integers. This is more efficient for storage and processing than large amounts of string values. You can read more about it in the enum documentation (https://duckdb.org/docs/sql/data_types/enum.html).

You can create enums as a type based on a list of values like this.

Listing 10.14 Example of creating an enum type

```
CREATE TYPE weekday AS enum (
    'monday', 'tuesday', 'wednesday',
    'thursday', 'friday', 'saturday', 'sunday'
);
```

The values are accessible via their string representation (e.g., as 'saturday' or in a typed way as saturday::weekday). The enum type itself can be referred to with the NULL value (e.g., null::weekday).

There are several functions for operating on enums:

- enum_code(enum_str)—This returns the numeric code of the enum.
- enum_range(null:enum_type)—This returns all values of the enum type as a list.
- enum_first, enum_last, *and* enum_range_boundary—These are for the first, the last, or a range of values.

DuckDB enums are automatically cast to string types whenever necessary. This allows enum values to be used in any string function and comparisons between enum and string values.

Although we have a tags table, up to six tags can also be stored in a post. Each tag is wrapped in angle brackets (e.g., <sql><duckdb><performance>), which means the post has the tags `sql`, `duckdb`, and `performance`. This isn't particularly efficient for analytical querying, and it makes it difficult to search `posts` for multiple tags.

That's why we want to convert that column into a set of values that makes it easier to handle. For instance, we can use a list of strings, or we can use an enum type, which is more efficient, as previously mentioned, and also allows us to use the enum functions built into DuckDB.

To convert the `tags` column in our `posts` table into a list of enums, we need to follow a series of intermediate steps. We're going to start by creating an enum type from the values in the `tags` table in the following listing.

Listing 10.15 Creating an enum type for `tags` from the `tags` table

```
CREATE TYPE tag AS enum (SELECT DISTINCT tagname FROM tags);
```

We can get a list of the enums by running the following query.

Listing 10.16 Selecting a few of the enum values

```
select enum_range(null::tag)[0:5];
```

This shows us a few known and lesser-known tags:

```
┌─────────────────────────────────────────────┐
│       enum_range(CAST(NULL AS tag))[0:5]     │
│                    varchar[]                 │
├─────────────────────────────────────────────┤
│ [textblock, idioms, haskell, flush, etl]     │
└─────────────────────────────────────────────┘
```

Now let's see how we can use this enum in our `posts` table.

We're first going to add an intermediate column for a string array, which we can also use to compare the performance of the enum array.

Listing 10.17 Adding the `tagNames` column

```
ALTER TABLE posts ADD tagNames VARCHAR[];
```

Next, we'll split the tags string (e.g., `'<sql><duckdb><python>'`) into an array of strings by taking the substring after the first character `<` to before the last character `>` to skip the leading and trailing angle brackets and then splitting on the `><` separator between two entries.

Listing 10.18 Populating the `tagNames` column from the `tags` column

```
UPDATE posts                          ⊲─┤ Updates the posts table
SET tagNames = split(tags[2:-2],'><')   ⊲─┐
                                          │ Splits the tags text (except for the first and
                                          │ last 1 character) on >< into an array
```

```
WHERE posttypeid = 1;                                          ─────┐  **Only considers questions**
-- Run Time (s): real 51.120 user 61.063576 sys 2.088018           │  **(i.e., posttypeid is 1)**
```

As you can see from the run time, this update takes over a minute because we have a lot of rows (23.5 million) to process. Now we're ready to add our new enum type `tag`, which we had populated by the values from the `tags` table.

Let's now add the `tag` enum array to the `posts` table.

Listing 10.19   Adding the `tagEnums` column

```
ALTER TABLE posts ADD tagEnums tag[];
```

So our `posts` table now looks like this:

```
| column_name      | column_type    |
| varchar          | varchar        |
|------------------|----------------|
| Id               | BIGINT         |
| PostTypeId       | BIGINT         |
| AcceptedAnswerId | BIGINT         |
| CreationDate     | TIMESTAMP      |
| Score            | BIGINT         |
| ViewCount        | BIGINT         |
| Body             | VARCHAR        |
| Title            | VARCHAR        |
| ...              |                |
| Tags             | VARCHAR        |
| tagNames         | VARCHAR[]      |
| tagEnums         | ENUM(tag)[]    |
```

We can assign the string array to the enum array, and DuckDB will automatically cast the values to the enum type, as shown in the following listing. That's really helpful and user friendly.

Listing 10.20   Populating the `tagEnums` column from the `tagNames` column directly

```
UPDATE posts SET tagEnums = tagNames
WHERE posttypeid = 1;
```

If we want additional transformations on the values (like capitalization or changing hyphens to spaces in the tag names), we could use a list transform function to convert the values of the string array to entries in an equivalent enum array. We can do that by using a `list_transform` function on each element of the `tagNames` list and passing in a lambda function that casts each element to the appropriate enum type:

```
SET tagEnums = list_transform(tagNames, x -> upper(x)::tag)
```

By keeping the string array around, we can compare the behavior and performance of a list of strings and a list of enums. For example, the following queries count the number of posts with the `tag` named `java`, which gives us 1.9 million rows.

```
SELECT count(*)
FROM posts
WHERE postTypeId = 1
  AND tags LIKE '%<java>%';
```

Running this query on 28 million rows takes 0.3 seconds, which is already pretty good, but let's see if we can do better with the next approaches.

```
SELECT count(*)
FROM posts
WHERE postTypeId=1
  AND list_contains(tagNames, 'java');
```

This time, we use list_contains on the tagNames column.

The `list_contains` operation has a runtime of 0.24 seconds, which is .06 seconds (20%) faster than the string comparison.

```
select count(*)
from posts
where postTypeId=1 and list_contains(tagEnums, 'java');
```

With an execution time of 0.17s, we've achieved another 30% (0.07 second) speed improvement by using the enums, which almost halves the total execution time. However, this is less relevant at these short run times. You should see similar small improvements on your machine. So for these simple count operations, the difference is negligible, but for more complex queries, the enum type can be more efficient and easier to work with.

Let's have a look at one more query, which should be faster after this optimization. To count the top-ranking tags along with their score, we can write the following query, which uses the string-based `tags` column.

```
SELECT tag,
       count(*), sum(score) AS score
FROM (
    SELECT unnest(split(p.tags[2:-2],'><')) as tag,
```

Counts the number of posts and sums their score by tag

```
        p.score AS score
    FROM posts p WHERE p.posttypeid = 1
)
GROUP BY ALL
ORDER BY score DESC LIMIT 10;
```

Splits the tags text (except for the first and last character) on >< into an array and then unnests it into individual rows

Uses the score column of each post

Only considers questions with the posttypeid of 1

That query takes 6.7 seconds and returns the following results:

tag varchar	count_star() int64	score int128
javascript	2479793	5214097
python	2112946	5154237
java	1889685	4280171
c#	1583813	3790940
android	1399966	3241732
c++	789658	2166603
html	1167672	1995072
php	1456223	1793966
jquery	1033102	1684906
git	147408	1662800
10 rows		3 columns

```
-- Run Time (s): real 6.698 user 60.197508 sys 0.197970
```

What is the performance if we use the enum field instead?

Listing 10.25 Statistics for the top 10 tags using the `tagEnums` column

```
SELECT tag, count(*), sum(score) AS score
FROM (
    SELECT unnest(p.tagEnums) as tag,
           p.score AS score
    FROM posts p
    WHERE p.posttypeid = 1
)
GROUP BY ALL
ORDER BY score DESC LIMIT 10;
-- Run Time (s): real 3.546 user 31.661123 sys 0.072986
```

Turns the tagEnums list into individual rows, with one per entry

This one is almost twice as fast at 3.5 seconds.

So we see that for more complex operations that operate on many values of the list of values, the change in representation matters. With these kinds of optimizations, we need to invest more effort upfront—both in terms of preparation and storage—to achieve better performance later on. This is worthwhile when the analytics query is run many times (e.g., for dashboards or reports) but less so if it's a one-off operation. The preparatory work also needs to be integrated into your data processing pipelines to ensure the correct shape of data for your queries.

10.2   Query planning and execution

In the large datasets we are working with in this chapter, efficient query execution is more crucial than ever. DuckDB's query execution engine is designed to be fast and efficient, using modern hardware and the latest database research and implementation techniques to achieve this goal.

Let's look a bit at how DuckDB processes our queries internally and make use of EXPLAIN and EXPLAIN ANALYZE to see which operations and operators our queries are turned into and how we can optimize them. The steps of the execute process are shown in figure 10.3.

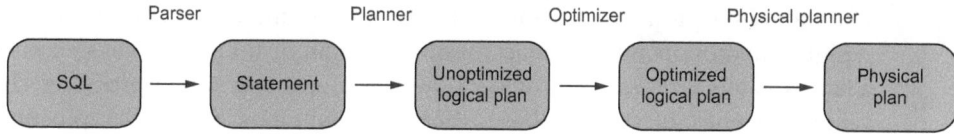

Figure 10.3   Query processing pipeline

10.2.1   Planner and optimizer

Once DuckDB has parsed an SQL query using its flexible parser derived from Postgres, it transforms the resulting abstract syntax tree (AST) through several stages. In the *parse phase*, the system can detect syntactic errors, like misspelled keywords or missing parentheses.

Initially, the *binder* resolves elements like tables, views, types, and column names. Here, the processing checks to see if the used elements (tables, columns, and types) exist in the database and whether they are correctly used. Following that, the *plan generator* converts this into a basic logical query plan consisting of logical query operators, such as scans, filters, and projections.

During the planning process, the database system uses statistics from stored data and indexes, which assist in various operations, such as type transformations, join order optimizations, and subquery flattening. After these optimizations, an *optimized logical query plan* is created. Ultimately, the planner refines this logical plan into physical operations best tailored to the environment, considering statistics, caching, and other factors.

10.2.2   Runtime and vectorization

DuckDB's runtime operates on a vectorized and parallelized architecture based on its columnar storage nature. DuckDB's storage format stores the data in *row groups* (i.e., horizontal partitions of the data). Horizontal partitioning of data is a strategy for sharding data, in which each partition has the same schema and holds a specific subset of the data. A row group in DuckDB's database format consists of a maximum of 122,880 rows. Each row group contains the required information about each column.

This column-centric approach offers numerous advantages, especially when selecting columns or filtering, scanning, and sorting data. It also allows the CPU to keep the processing of an operator in-memory, optimize CPU branch prediction, and have all required data in CPU caches.

A main difference compared to row-based engines lies in DuckDB's fine-tuning for efficient data operations, rather than disk storage or data transfer (I/O) optimizations. In the execution runtime, every data type is represented as a vector or compact array of values. These typed vector implementations are optimized for various data types and values (numbers, strings, and arrays), simplifying data selection and processing by employing compression, metadata, and additional indexes.

As data flows through the system, these vectors seamlessly transition between plan operators in a push-based manner. The execution model is centered on a pipeline design, wherein operators can act as sources, sinks, or both. DuckDB's execution parallelizes batch processing through a "morsel" approach, which processes chunks of values (batches of 2,048 values) through a number of parallel pipelines, with parallelism-aware operators at the start and end of each pipeline. Figure 10.4 shows different morsels passing through different pipelines of the runtime.

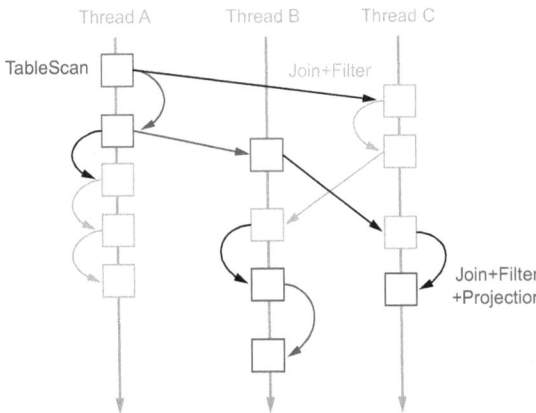

Figure 10.4   Morsel runtime

In addition, DuckDB also uses vectorized computation, which employs single instruction, multiple data (SIMD) to process multiple values in a single CPU instruction. This is not to be confused with the data vectors.

10.2.3 *Visualizing query plans with Explain and Explain Analyze*

The query plan the optimizer and planner creates is also accessible to you. You can prefix each SQL statement with EXPLAIN to see the tree of operators your original query was transformed into:

```
EXPLAIN
SELECT  year(CreationDate) AS year, count(*),
        round(avg(ViewCount)), max(AnswerCount)
FROM posts
GROUP BY year
ORDER BY year DESC LIMIT 10;
```

A visualization of the resulting query plan is reproduced as follows. We can see that our query has been turned into the following operators (as well as some internal operators that are used for data compression and decompression):

- ORDER BY and LIMIT → TOP_N
- SELECT → PROJECTION
- GROUP BY → Perfect_Hash_Group_By
- SELECT + FROM → SEQ_SCAN with estimated cardinality (EC)

The plan is executed *bottom up*; it starts with the SEQ_SCAN of the stored data and then applies operators on the chunks of results from previous ones. When run, the physical plan looks like this:

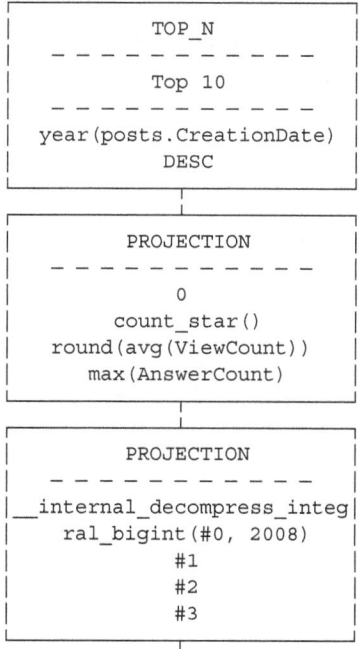

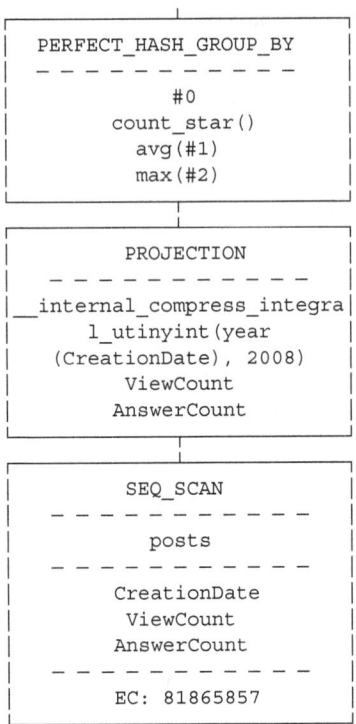

Run Time (s): real 0.003 user 0.001378 sys 0.001833

With EXPLAIN ANALYZE, our query is not just planned but executed as well so we can
see the actual time, resources, and number of rows that were processed:

```
EXPLAIN ANALYZE
SELECT  year(CreationDate) AS year, count(*),
        round(avg(ViewCount)), max(AnswerCount)
FROM posts
GROUP BY year
ORDER BY year DESC LIMIT 10;
```

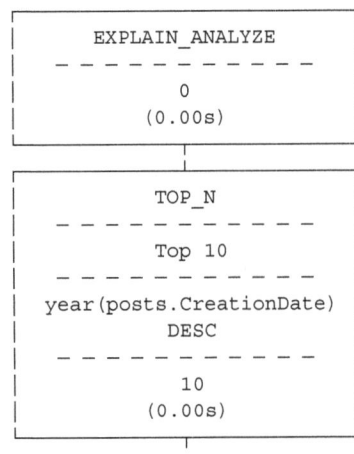

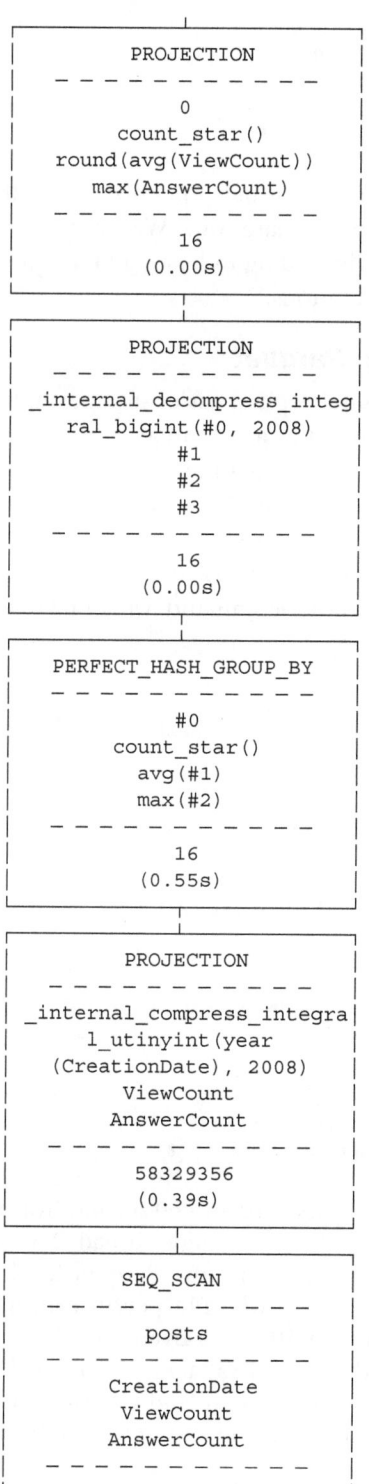

```
|   — — — — — — — — — |
|         58329356        |
|         (0.98s)         |
|                         |
```

```
Run Time (s): real 0.199 user 1.367440 sys 0.379777
```

This helps us identify (especially for slow queries) which operators need the most time as well as which ones return the most intermediate rows. We can use that information to optimize our queries—for instance, by adding indexes, adding query hints, using subqueries, or changing the order of operations.

10.3 *Exporting the Stack Overflow data to Parquet*

We can export our tables to Parquet files for safekeeping, easier storage, and processing in other ways. As we discussed before, Parquet as a columnar format compresses better, includes the schema, and supports optimized reading with column selection and predicate pushdown. We want to see here how long these exports take, what optimizations we can apply, and how to export whole databases.

Supported compression formats for Parquet are UNCOMPRESSED, SNAPPY, and ZSTD. To export the users table, we can run the following command, which takes about 10 seconds for the 28 million rows.

Listing 10.26 Exporting the `users` table to Parquet

```
COPY (FROM users)
TO 'users.parquet'
(FORMAT PARQUET, CODEC 'SNAPPY', ROW_GROUP_SIZE 100000);
-- Run Time (s): real 10.582 user 62.737265 sys 65.422181
```

And then for the posts table, the statement looks like the following code and takes roughly 60 seconds for 58 million rows.

Listing 10.27 Exporting the `posts` table to Parquet

```
COPY (FROM posts)
TO 'posts.parquet'
(FORMAT PARQUET, CODEC 'SNAPPY', ROW_GROUP_SIZE 100000);
-- Run Time (s): real 57.314 user 409.517658 sys 334.606894
```

> **NOTE** We saw that the serial export takes between 10 and 60 seconds for our tables, which is a write output of about 70 MB/s on a single thread. To optimize write performance, you can also choose to write the Parquet file in a multithreaded fashion; DuckDB will then create one file per thread. This improves the performance on our system with 10 CPUs from 10 to 1.7 seconds for the user table and 57 to 11 seconds for the post table. We could also choose to sort the data before exporting it, which could lead to faster querying of sorted fields when the Parquet file is read, as you can see in the following listing.

Listing 10.28   Exporting the `users` table to Parquet in multithreaded fashion

```
COPY (
    SELECT *
    FROM users
    ORDER BY LastAccessDate DESC
) TO 'users.parquet'
(FORMAT PARQUET, CODEC 'SNAPPY', PER_THREAD_OUTPUT TRUE);
```

We also exported the other tables but won't include the `COPY` commands here for brevity's sake. You can find those commands in the book's GitHub repository. Once all the exports are done, we'll have the following files on our disk:

```
6.9G comments.parquet
4.0G posts.parquet
2.2G votes.parquet
734M users.parquet
518M badges.parquet
164M post_links.parquet
1.6M tags.parquet
```

> **NOTE** These Parquet files are available on the S3 bucket (s3://us-prd-moth-erduck-open-datasets/stackoverflow/parquet/2023-05/) and can be read from there.

Out of curiosity, we're going to compare the performance of reading the users' data from the CSV and Parquet files to see which is quicker. Let's start with the Parquet file, as shown in the following listing.

Listing 10.29   Reading the row count of users from a Parquet

```
SELECT count(*) FROM read_parquet('users.parquet');
```

This gives us a result of `19942787` in subsecond (0.008s) time. Querying the CSV file, on the other hand, takes considerably longer.

Listing 10.30   Reading the row count of users from a CSV

```
SELECT count(*) FROM read_csv_auto('Users.csv.gz');
```

The result is the same, but it takes about 7 seconds to get there. So reading the row count from the Parquet file is almost 1,000 times faster than the CSV file!

This isn't a fair fight because the Parquet file can use its metadata to provide the answer, rather than having to scan the whole file. Having that metadata is one of the big benefits of the Parquet file format and is why we tend to prefer it to CSV files.

You can also export your whole database as Parquet files into a target folder. This saves you from calling the export commands individually and automatically adds files for creating the table schema and loading the data back in with a single `import` command.

Listing 10.31   Exporting the whole database to Parquet

```
EXPORT DATABASE 'target_directory'
(FORMAT PARQUET);
```

In addition to the Parquet files, this will create two SQL files, `schema.sql` and `load.sql`, which will be used for creating the database schema and executing the load, when you import the data again with

```
IMPORT DATABASE 'source_directory';
```

In the schema.sql file tables, views and enums are created, as shown in the following listing.

Listing 10.32   The contents of schema.sql

```
CREATE TABLE posts(Id BIGINT, PostTypeId BIGINT, AcceptedAnswerId BIGINT,
  CreationDate TIMESTAMP, Score BIGINT, ViewCount BIGINT, Body VARCHAR,
  OwnerUserId BIGINT, LastEditorUserId BIGINT, LastEditorDisplayName
  VARCHAR, LastEditDate TIMESTAMP, LastActivityDate TIMESTAMP, Title
  VARCHAR, Tags VARCHAR, AnswerCount BIGINT, CommentCount BIGINT,
  FavoriteCount BIGINT, CommunityOwnedDate TIMESTAMP, ContentLicense
  VARCHAR
);
CREATE TABLE "comments"(Id BIGINT, PostId BIGINT, Score BIGINT, "Text"
  VARCHAR, CreationDate TIMESTAMP, UserId BIGINT, ContentLicense VARCHAR);
CREATE TABLE badges(Id BIGINT, UserId BIGINT, "Name" VARCHAR, Date
  TIMESTAMP, "Class" BIGINT, TagBased BOOLEAN);
CREATE TABLE users(Id BIGINT, Reputation BIGINT, CreationDate TIMESTAMP,
  DisplayName VARCHAR, LastAccessDate TIMESTAMP, AboutMe VARCHAR,
  "Views" BIGINT, UpVotes BIGINT, DownVotes BIGINT);
CREATE TABLE tags(Id BIGINT, TagName VARCHAR, Count BIGINT,
  ExcerptPostId BIGINT, WikiPostId BIGINT);
CREATE TABLE votes(Id BIGINT, PostId BIGINT, VoteTypeId BIGINT,
  CreationDate TIMESTAMP);
```

And in the load.sql file, the data is loaded from the Parquet files, as shown in the following listing.

Listing 10.33   The contents of load.sql

```
COPY posts FROM 'parquet/posts.parquet' (FORMAT 'parquet',
  ROW_GROUP_SIZE 100000, CODEC 'SNAPPY');
COPY "comments" FROM 'parquet/comments.parquet' (FORMAT 'parquet',
  ROW_GROUP_SIZE 100000, CODEC 'SNAPPY');
COPY badges FROM 'parquet/badges.parquet' (FORMAT 'parquet',
  ROW_GROUP_SIZE 100000, CODEC 'SNAPPY');
COPY users FROM 'parquet/users.parquet' (FORMAT 'parquet',
  ROW_GROUP_SIZE 100000, CODEC 'SNAPPY');
COPY tags FROM 'parquet/tags.parquet' (FORMAT 'parquet',
  ROW_GROUP_SIZE 100000, CODEC 'SNAPPY');
```

```
COPY votes FROM 'parquet/votes.parquet' (FORMAT 'parquet',
  ROW_GROUP_SIZE 100000, CODEC 'SNAPPY');
COPY post_links FROM 'parquet/post_links.parquet' (FORMAT 'parquet',
  ROW_GROUP_SIZE 100000, CODEC 'SNAPPY');
```

As we can see in this Stack Overflow example, even medium-sized datasets are no problem for DuckDB. We can import, query, process, and export them in very reasonable times on a single machine with the memory and CPU resources of a modern laptop or desktop (e.g., 4–10 cores and 8–64 GB RAM). It doesn't fail or abort with out-of-memory errors, and it doesn't take hours to process the data.

But can we go bigger, say *billions* of records?! The New York City taxi dataset is the go-to dataset for seeing whether new database systems can handle big data, and we're going to explore that in the next section.

10.4 Exploring the New York Taxi dataset from Parquet files

The New York City taxi dataset we use in this example (https://mng.bz/qODE) is published and maintained by the NYC Taxi & Limousine Commission. This dataset contains taxi trip records and includes pickup and drop-off dates, times, and locations; trip distances; itemized fares; rate types; payment types; and driver-reported passenger counts. The data is published in Parquet format, with one Parquet file for each month, starting in January 2009, and is continuously updated.

Over the years, many articles have been written explaining how to load and query the dataset in R, Python, Spark, Redshift, SQLite, and other databases. Just search *SQL Analysis New York Taxis* on your favorite search engine to find some of them.

At the time of writing, the dataset contains over 1.7 billion rows, consisting of 175 Parquet files of 28 GB in size. We have collected all the Parquet files and put them in an S3 bucket (s3://us-prd-md-duckdb-in-action/nyc-taxis/), kindly hosted by MotherDuck.

This section of the large data exploration will focus on using Parquet files as sources for querying and show that DuckDB can use predicate and projection pushdown to optimize the queries on these files without actually populating a database. You could use this approach when doing a one-off analysis of data stored on a cloud storage bucket, such as S3 or Google Cloud Storage. For instance, you can use it to analyze access or download logs of your website or application.

For these amounts of data, it is beneficial to move the query computation to where the data lives and only transfer the results over the network. If you have the files downloaded onto your local machine, you can execute DuckDB there. Otherwise, it is sensible to run DuckDB on a cloud instance that is as close to the data as possible. In our case, with the Parquet files on S3, that can be an EC2 instance in the same region as the S3 bucket or a hosted service, like MotherDuck. If not, you would have to pay both the egress costs and network transfer time and latency for reading the files to your local machine when executing queries that cannot be satisfied by the Parquet metadata alone.

10.4.1 *Configuring credentials for S3 access*

The objects on the aforementioned bucket are publicly readable, so you can access them directly from DuckDB without any extra setup. But if you want to try this out with your own S3 bucket, which you probably don't want to make accessible to the world, you can configure your S3 credentials by creating a temporary or persistent secret (available from duckdb version `0.1.0`) of `TYPE S3`.

The `REGION` is the region of your bucket, while the `KEY_ID` and `SECRET` are the credentials for accessing the bucket, shown in the following listing.

Listing 10.34   Creating the S3 secret

```
CREATE [PERSISTENT] SECRET (
    TYPE S3,
    KEY_ID 'AKIA...',
    SECRET ''Sr8VSfK...',
    REGION 'us-east-1'
);
```

The `httpfs` extension is used to access files on S3, which is auto-loaded by DuckDB when necessary. In case it is not automatically loaded for you, you can do so manually, as shown in the following listing.

Listing 10.35   Installing and loading the `httpfs` extension

```
INSTALL httpfs;
LOAD httpfs;
```

Now we can access the Parquet files directly without any extra setup just by specifying the filename or URL in the `FROM` clause of a statement.

10.4.2 *Auto-inferring file types*

To count the number of records in a Parquet file, you can write a query like the following to compute the row count of a Parquet file:

```
SELECT count(*)
FROM
's3://us-prd-md-duckdb-in-action/nyc-taxis/yellow_tripdata_2022-06.parquet';
-- 3,558,124 rows in 600 ms
```

Despite reading a huge file, it finishes in 600 milliseconds because the query uses the metadata of the file to compute the answer. Under the hood, this query is converted to the following `read_parquet` function call:

```
SELECT count(*)
FROM read_parquet(
's3://us-prd-md-duckdb-in-action/nyc-taxis/yellow_tripdata_2022-06.parquet'
);
-- 3,558,124 rows
```

Inference from filename extensions works automatically when we want to process data from a single file or URL or from a glob-wildcard pattern that matches multiple files, like this:

```
SELECT count(*)
FROM 's3://us-prd-md-duckdb-in-action/nyc-taxis/yellow_tripdata_*.parquet';

-- 1,721,158,822 rows in 11s
```

But if we want to load a more specific set of files, for example, to find trips in June 2021 and June 2022, we need to call the underlying `read_parquet` function ourselves:

```
SELECT count(*)
FROM read_parquet([
's3://us-prd-md-duckdb-in-action/nyc-taxis/yellow_tripdata_2021-06.parquet',
's3://us-prd-md-duckdb-in-action/nyc-taxis/yellow_tripdata_2022-06.parquet'
]);
-- 6,392,388
```

The queries we've seen so far have all been counting numbers of records, and they return a result quickly because they're able to use Parquet metadata to compute the answer and don't need to read the actual data.

The metadata of a Parquet file, as already mentioned in chapter 5, contains information about the number of rows, the schema (column names and types), and the mininum values, maximum values, and nullability of each column. Let's have a look at that metadata.

10.4.3 Exploring Parquet schema

Before we start querying the Parquet files, let's have a quick look at the structure of the data they contain. Throughout this book, we've learned about various functions we can use to do this. We're going to use the `parquet_schema` function here since this gives us control over the fields rendered, and since we're mostly interested in the name and type, this is exactly what we need:

```
FROM parquet_schema(
's3://us-prd-md-duckdb-in-action/nyc-taxis/yellow_tripdata_2022-06.parquet')
SELECT name, type;
```

The output of this query is as follows:

name varchar	type varchar
schema	
VendorID	INT64
tpep_pickup_datetime	INT64
tpep_dropoff_datetime	INT64
passenger_count	DOUBLE
trip_distance	DOUBLE

```
| RatecodeID            | DOUBLE     |
| store_and_fwd_flag    | BYTE_ARRAY |
| PULocationID          | INT64      |
| DOLocationID          | INT64      |
| payment_type          | INT64      |
| fare_amount           | DOUBLE     |
| extra                 | DOUBLE     |
| mta_tax               | DOUBLE     |
| tip_amount            | DOUBLE     |
| tolls_amount          | DOUBLE     |
| improvement_surcharge | DOUBLE     |
| total_amount          | DOUBLE     |
| congestion_surcharge  | DOUBLE     |
| airport_fee           | DOUBLE     |
|                                    |
| 20 rows                 2 columns  |
```

We can see all the types of information relevant to a taxi trip and their data types, like the passenger count, pickup and drop off locations, and, of course, the amount that the trip costs!

> **NOTE** If the Parquet files you're reading from have different schemas, you can use the union_by_name = true option of read_parquet to combine them into a single result. Nonexistent or differently named columns will be filled with NULL values.

10.4.4 *Creating views*

We probably don't want to type (or more likely copy–paste) that wildcard string of all the Parquet files. If we're planning to do a lot of analysis on the data, it probably makes sense to create a DuckDB database that materializes the contents of the Parquet files into tables. If we want to do ad hoc analysis instead, we can create a view over the Parquet files.

A view in DuckDB is not physically materialized but instead runs the underlying query each time queries on the view are executed. It is integrated into the query planning and optimization of the outer query as a whole, much like with common table expressions (CTE). The benefit of defining a view in this case is that it provides us a shorthand for querying the data rather than having to write out the full location of the files on S3 each time. Views also allow for stable interfaces to the data so that if the underlying data changes, the view can be updated to reflect that change without having to change the queries that use the view.

We can create a view by running the query shown in the following listing.

> **Listing 10.36 Creating a view across multiple files**

```
CREATE OR REPLACE VIEW allRidesView AS
FROM 's3://us-prd-md-duckdb-in-action/nyc-taxis/
    yellow_tripdata_202*.parquet';
```

To keep the amount of data read from S3 reasonable, we only include the files from 2020 onward, which is still 118 million rows. But if you want to query all the data, feel free to expand the wildcard to include more of the files.

This should return immediately because it's not reading any data—it's only defining the view. The view covers roughly 118 million rows, so it's not a small dataset, but it's also not huge.

10.4.5 Analyzing the data

To get an overview of the data values and their distribution as well as test the read performance of DuckDB while retrieving data from S3, we'll use the following query, using SUMMARIZE again.

Listing 10.37   The SUMMARIZE command

```
.timer on
SUMMARIZE allRidesView;
```

This query needs to read the actual data to get all the statistics information, so it will take a bit for it to return a result. Even when running the query on an AWS EC2 instance close to the data, it took more than 30 seconds to produce the result from the 118 million rows of data:

column_name varchar	column_type varchar	min varchar	max varchar	approx_uniq varchar
VendorID	BIGINT	1	6	4
tpep_pickup_datetime	TIMESTAMP	2001-01-01	2098-09-11	59777057
tpep_dropoff_datetime	TIMESTAMP	2001-01-01	2098-09-11	60115892
passenger_count	DOUBLE	0.0	112.0	12
trip_distance	DOUBLE	-30.62	389678.46	14254
RatecodeID	DOUBLE	1.0	99.0	7
store_and_fwd_flag	VARCHAR	N	Y	2
PULocationID	BIGINT	1	265	264
DOLocationID	BIGINT	1	265	265
payment_type	BIGINT	0	5	6
fare_amount	DOUBLE	-133391414	998310.03	17618
extra	DOUBLE	-27.0	500000.8	671
mta_tax	DOUBLE	-0.55	500000.5	82
tip_amount	DOUBLE	-493.22	133391363	9064
tolls_amount	DOUBLE	-99.99	956.55	3897
improvement_surcharge	DOUBLE	-1.0	1.0	5
total_amount	DOUBLE	-2567.8	1000003.8	36092
congestion_surcharge	DOUBLE	-2.5	3.0	16
airport_fee	INTEGER	-2	2	5
19 rows				

```
Run Time (s): real 33.907 user 586.582679 sys 8.706259
```

As we can see, there are trips with negative distances, so it might make sense to filter those out before doing any further analysis.

Let's redefine our base view to exclude trips with negative distances so our following analysis and queries will not be skewed by those outliers.

Listing 10.38   Creating a filtering view

```
CREATE OR REPLACE VIEW allRidesView AS
FROM 's3://us-prd-md-duckdb-in-action/nyc-taxis/yellow_tripdata_202*.parquet'
WHERE trip_distance > 0;
```

If we read only one column of the data, `trip_distance`, it will be faster, only taking about 3 to 4 seconds, as shown in the following listing.

Listing 10.39   Summarizing on a single column

```
.timer on
.mode line
SUMMARIZE (SELECT trip_distance FROM allRidesView);
```

The result in line mode now looks like this and gives us detailed information about the column `trip_distance`, on which we are able to estimate whether we are dealing with sane data or not as well as whether we should filter out outliers:

```
column_name = trip_distance
    column_type = DOUBLE
            min = 0.01
            max = 389678.46
  approx_unique = 13114
            avg = 5.430654112761637
            std = 536.0306563795983
            q25 = 1.093394143132663
            q50 = 1.8271836758492157
            q75 = 3.389607008136687
          count = 115976028
null_percentage = 0.0%
Run Time (s): real 3.033 user 49.924611 sys 1.228218
```

Aside from the more sensible aggregation results, we can see that about 2 million rows have been filtered out because they had negative distances.

Using SUMMARIZE

Since DuckDB version 0.10.0, `SUMMARIZE` has been capable of being used as a source for a `SELECT` statement, so you can write

```
SELECT column_name, column_type, count, max FROM SUMMARIZE allRidesView;
```

if you're only interested in a few of the columns. At the time of writing, it still computes the rest of the column statistics, though, so there is no time saved.

If we only execute certain aggregation operations that are available as metadata in Parquet, we can get results even faster, taking less than a second.

Listing 10.40 Aggregations on single column

```
SELECT min(trip_distance),          ⟵┐  Uses various aggregate
       max(trip_distance),           │  functions on the same column
       avg(trip_distance),
       stddev(trip_distance),
       count(trip_distance) AS nonNull,        Computes the percentage of NULL
       count(*) as total,                      values by dividing the count of non-
       1-(nonNull/total) AS nullPercentage  ⟵┘ null values by the total count of rows
FROM allRidesView;
```

We see the same results as before in the output but at a fraction of the time, as we don't need to read the actual data:

```
min(trip_distance) = 0.01
   max(trip_distance) = 389678.46
   avg(trip_distance) = 5.430654112761703
stddev(trip_distance) = 536.030656379596
             nonNull = 115976028
               total = 115976028
        nullPercentage = 0.0
Run Time (s): real 0.747 user 7.789698 sys 0.682236
```

With the advanced SQL features in DuckDB that allow you to apply computation on multiple columns, we can also compute the same aggregations on all columns at once, as shown in listing 10.41.

For the average and standard deviation, we only apply the aggregation to the numeric columns that contain the words `distance`, `amount`, `tax`, `surcharge`, or `fee`, once as a regular expression filter and once as a lambda function (for demonstration purposes). We can even post-process the results, including rounding them as needed. You can learn more about this feature at Star Expressions (https://duckdb.org/docs/sql/expressions/star) in the documentation.

Listing 10.41 Aggregations on multiple columns

```
.mode line                       │ Counts
SELECT count(*),        ⟵┘  all rows         Computes the minimum and
       min(columns(*)), max(columns(*)),  ⟵ maximum values of all columns
       round(avg(columns('_(distance|amount|tax|surcharge|fee)')),2),  ⟵┐
       round(stddev(                                                     │
           columns(c ->
             c SIMILAR TO '.+(distance|amount|tax|surcharge|fee)')),2)
FROM allRidesView;
```

Uses a lambda function for each column name with the regular expression operator **SIMILAR TO** and computes the standard deviation for all matching columns

Computes the Average value of all columns that contain the words distance, amount, tax, surcharge, or fee

You can see in the output that the aggregations are applied to all columns at once, which is much faster than applying them individually; it only takes roughly 7 seconds:

```
count_star() = 115976028
                        min(allRidesView.VendorID) = 1
              min(allRidesView.tpep_pickup_datetime) = 2001-01-01 00:03:14
             min(allRidesView.tpep_dropoff_datetime) = 2001-01-01 00:16:31
                 min(allRidesView.passenger_count) = 0.0
                    min(allRidesView.trip_distance) = 0.01
                       min(allRidesView.RatecodeID) = 1.0
              min(allRidesView.store_and_fwd_flag) = N
                   min(allRidesView.PULocationID) = 1
                   min(allRidesView.DOLocationID) = 1
                   min(allRidesView.payment_type) = 0
                   min(allRidesView.fare_amount) = -2564.0
                         min(allRidesView.extra) = -27.0
                       min(allRidesView.mta_tax) = -0.5
                     min(allRidesView.tip_amount) = -493.22
                    min(allRidesView.tolls_amount) = -91.3
         min(allRidesView.improvement_surcharge) = -1.0
                   min(allRidesView.total_amount) = -2567.8
         min(allRidesView.congestion_surcharge) = -2.5
                      min(allRidesView.airport_fee) = -2
                        max(allRidesView.VendorID) = 6
              max(allRidesView.tpep_pickup_datetime) = 2098-09-11 02:23:31
             max(allRidesView.tpep_dropoff_datetime) = 2098-09-11 02:52:04
                 max(allRidesView.passenger_count) = 112.0
                    max(allRidesView.trip_distance) = 389678.46
                       max(allRidesView.RatecodeID) = 99.0
              max(allRidesView.store_and_fwd_flag) = Y
                   max(allRidesView.PULocationID) = 265
                   max(allRidesView.DOLocationID) = 265
                   max(allRidesView.payment_type) = 5
                   max(allRidesView.fare_amount) = 998310.03
                         max(allRidesView.extra) = 113.01
                       max(allRidesView.mta_tax) = 53.16
                     max(allRidesView.tip_amount) = 1400.16
                    max(allRidesView.tolls_amount) = 956.55
         max(allRidesView.improvement_surcharge) = 1.0
                   max(allRidesView.total_amount) = 998325.61
         max(allRidesView.congestion_surcharge) = 2.75
                      max(allRidesView.airport_fee) = 2
               round(avg(allRidesView.trip_distance), 2) = 5.43
                 round(avg(allRidesView.fare_amount), 2) = 14.74
                   round(avg(allRidesView.mta_tax), 2) = 0.49
                 round(avg(allRidesView.tip_amount), 2) = 2.65
                round(avg(allRidesView.tolls_amount), 2) = 0.45
      round(avg(allRidesView.improvement_surcharge), 2) = 0.43
                round(avg(allRidesView.total_amount), 2) = 21.58
       round(avg(allRidesView.congestion_surcharge), 2) = 2.3
                round(avg(allRidesView.airport_fee), 2) = 0.09
            round(stddev(allRidesView.trip_distance), 2) = 536.03
              round(stddev(allRidesView.fare_amount), 2) = 157.03
                round(stddev(allRidesView.mta_tax), 2) = 0.08
```

```
               round(stddev(allRidesView.tip_amount), 2) = 3.18
              round(stddev(allRidesView.tolls_amount), 2) = 1.9
    round(stddev(allRidesView.improvement_surcharge), 2) = 0.29
             round(stddev(allRidesView.total_amount), 2) = 157.38
    round(stddev(allRidesView.congestion_surcharge), 2) = 0.72
               round(stddev(allRidesView.airport_fee), 2) = 0.32
Run Time (s): real 6.813 user 82.841430 sys 7.124035
```

10.4.6 Making use of the taxi dataset

Now let's imagine we're a city planner in New York who wants to understand the way that people are navigating the city. From our previous queries on trip distances, we've learned that there's quite a big difference in the types of journeys being taken. Some of them look like road trips, while others are very short shuttle runs. We can drill down into the data to see how it varies across the years by running the following query. The query computes the average distance, the fare amount, and the fare amount per distance per year between 2020 and 2024. The year is taken from the pickup time.

Listing 10.42   Trip data yearly aggregation

```
SELECT year(tpep_pickup_datetime) AS year,
       round(avg(trip_distance)) AS dist,
       round(avg(fare_amount),2) AS fare,
       round(AVG(fare_amount/trip_distance),2) AS rate,
       count(*) AS trips
FROM allRidesView
GROUP BY year
HAVING year BETWEEN 2020 AND 2024    ⟵  Restricts the years used in the query to between
ORDER BY year;                            2020 and 2024, which must be done in the
                                          HAVING clause, as the year is the grouping key
```

We've restricted the years used in the query because some year's entries had wrong date values, notably 2098, 2028, 2001, and 2008. The results of running the query are as follows:

| year | dist | fare | rate | trips |
int64	double	double	double	int64
2020	4.0	12.49	7.57	24316408
2021	7.0	13.42	7.09	30496201
2022	6.0	14.69	8.47	39081642
2023	4.0	19.15	9.82	22080786

```
Run Time (s): real 1.831 user 22.398789 sys 3.331710
```

We can see that the average fare is going up over time because the value of money decreases due to inflation. We also notice a further dip in 2020, which most likely was caused by the COVID-19 pandemic. In our full analysis of the dataset, a similar dip could be observed in the mid-2010s when ride services like Uber and Lyft came onto the scene. You can explore this period with the shared database.

We can also look into the average passenger count over time. In the following listing, we'll focus on journeys longer than 10 miles with fewer than 10 passengers.

Listing 10.43   Taxi trips per passenger count

```
SELECT passenger_count, count(*)
FROM allRidesView
WHERE passenger_count <10
GROUP BY passenger_count
ORDER BY count(*) DESC;
```

The output of this query shows a power law distribution, with most trips having only a single passenger:

passenger_count double	count_star() int64
1.0	5366688
2.0	1580495
3.0	370175
4.0	193333
5.0	149485
0.0	118751
6.0	102836
8.0	65
7.0	60
9.0	40
10 rows	2 columns

```
Run Time (s): real 0.897 user 7.388453 sys 0.862978
```

This only scratches the surface of what kinds of queries can be run with these datasets, but we wanted to focus more on examining the performance of queries on these data volumes than on digging deeper into use cases. As you learned in previous chapters, you can go ahead and build apps, APIs, or dashboards on top of those kinds of datasets and sources, or you can just analyze them in a notebook and output the results for further processing.

Summary

- Using the SUMMARIZE clause to get an overview of a dataset is a good way to start exploring a dataset.
- Converting strings to enums is a useful technique for speeding up queries.
- DuckDB's modern analytical architecture utilizes vector representations and intra-query parallelism.
- During execution, SQL queries are turned into execution plans, which can be inspected with EXPLAIN.

- Datasets located in cloud buckets should be analyzed from machines close to where they are stored to avoid network transfer costs and latency.
- DuckDB can use predicate and projection pushdown to optimize queries on Parquet files without actually populating a database.
- DuckDB's ability to use Parquet metadata when reading files is extremely useful when working with large datasets, as it avoids reading data over the network that is not needed for the query.
- Column expressions within the SELECT clause allow us to apply multiple aggregations to many columns at once.
- DuckDB can comfortably query datasets that contain hundreds of millions, or even billions, of records.

Conclusion

11

Thank you for accompanying us on our journey through *DuckDB in Action*. We hope you have learned a lot about DuckDB and how it can be used to make your day-to-day data engineering life more productive and enjoyable. We're glad we could share our excitement and passion for the power and usefulness of DuckDB and empower you to use it to solve your data engineering problems and to build amazing data products. In this chapter, we will summarize what we have learned, mention the areas we did not cover, and discuss the future of data engineering with DuckDB.

11.1 What we have learned in this book

We looked at how to get started with DuckDB, how to install it, and how to use the CLI and the Python API. Next, we illustrated how easy it is to load data from CSV, JSON, and Parquet files and then analyze it with DuckDB using SQL—even without creating tables for the data. We also explored how to use DuckDB via the Python APIs, both for SQL and fluent queries, and how tightly and efficiently it integrates with pandas DataFrames.

We learned how to make the most out of DuckDB with SQL, from the basics to more advanced features like window functions and CTEs. As part of our SQL explorations, we highlighted all the goodies that DuckDB adds to the standard SQL language, like support for JSON, nested data structures, advanced joins, and flexible selection, grouping, and aggregation.

To demonstrate how to integrate DuckDB into your data architectures, we built data pipelines with dbt, dltHub, and Dagster. On the application side, we used Streamlit and Apache Superset to visualize data from DuckDB directly.

In the last chapter, we looked at the specifics of handling large datasets, including performance considerations.

11.2   *Upcoming stable versions of DuckDB*

With the release of the book, you should soon have the first stable version in your hands: DuckDB 1.0. Our work is based on 0.10.0, the latest prerelease version at the time of writing, which is meant to stabilize all features, APIs, and formats as well as to be compatible with version 1.0. These versions are meant to handle database version format changes automatically and be backward compatible (and, in parts, even forward compatible), which will also extend to the MotherDuck service.

11.3   *Aspects we did not cover*

Even with the breadth of the book, we could not cover everything in the vast ecosystem of DuckDB. Since the focus of the book is on being an introductory and practical guide, we did not cover the internals of DuckDB, how it is implemented, and how it works under the hood. There is much more to learn about the architecture, the query execution engine, the indexing capabilities, the storage layer, and the vectorized execution model.

We touched a little bit on that in chapter 10, but there is much more to explore in the DuckDB source code, blog posts, videos, and documentation. Hannes and Mark have also been interviewed in several podcasts (see https://www.youtube.com/watch?v=pZV9FvdKmLc and https://www.youtube.com/watch?v=f9QlkXW4H9A) where they dive into the details of DuckDB, which you can listen to for more insight.

We mostly used the CLI and the Python API throughout the book and cover access from Java in the appendix. However, DuckDB also has APIs for C, R, Rust, Go, JavaScript, and many other languages, so you can use DuckDB in your favorite environment. Please consult the documentation for more details: https://duckdb.org/docs/api/overview.

Another area we didn't dive deeper into is performance optimizations and considerations. Fortunately, DuckDB performs really well out of the box, so you rarely have to worry about performance, but there are still many things you can do to optimize your queries and your data to make the most out of DuckDB. Feel free to consult the documentation (https://mng.bz/7d2g) and additional blog posts, such as "Perf is not Enough" (https://motherduck.com/blog/perf-is-not-enough/) by Jordan Tigani.

The documentation also provides great content about DuckDB's extension framework. Extensions can be written in both C++ and Rust. Speaking of extensions, there are already many useful extensions, including the spatial index (https://duckdb.org/docs/extensions/spatial.html), which has a lot of capabilities, similar to PostGIS, and can be used to build advanced geospatial applications.

DuckDB provides an information schema, aligning with the classic SQL catalog, but also provides various table functions for accessing current configurations and ways to change it. These are covered on the "DuckDB_% Metadata Functions" documentation page (https://mng.bz/maWM). DuckDB Labs and MotherDuck list over 50 partners that integrate DuckDB into their products and services, so there is a lot for you to explore, according to your needs.

11.4   *Where can you learn more?*

The DuckDB docs (https://duckdb.org/docs) are a great place to start. They are very comprehensive and cover all aspects of DuckDB in great detail. The same is true for the MotherDuck documentation (https://motherduck.com/docs).

There are a few YouTube channels run by either MotherDuck and DuckDB people or individuals, which have a number of tutorials, talks, and presentations on DuckDB and MotherDuck. For quick answers from an active community, check out the DuckDB Discord (https://discord.duckdb.org/) and the MotherDuck Community Slack (https://slack.motherduck.com/).

If you want to contribute to DuckDB, you can find the source code on GitHub (https://github.com/duckdb). There you can also raise bugs and feature requests.

11.5   *What is the future of data engineering with DuckDB?*

We think DuckDB is a very promising technology that will play a prominent role in the future of data engineering. DuckDB is a very versatile tool that can be used in many different scenarios, from local analysis of medium-sized datasets to large-scale data processing in the cloud close to where your data lives. With the growth of local data from health monitoring, home automation, and other personal information systems, efficient processing of private data on your own devices will become more relevant.

Given its similarity to SQLite, we think DuckDB will be used in many places SQLite is used today. That includes applications, games, browser, phones, IoT and edge devices for analytics, data aggregation, prefiltering, and serving data to other systems and end users.

An interesting business use case is the long tail of cloud data warehouses, like BigQuery, Redshift, Snowflake, and so on. Most users of these systems don't have petabytes of data to analyze and process but, rather, gigabytes or terabytes, which can be handled by DuckDB at a fraction of the cost and resource usage—and with much less complexity.

Some potential areas of innovation that will be interesting to watch include the integration in generative AI use cases, like adding efficient embedding vector storage and indexing and supporting streaming data processing. Given the DuckDB team's focus on usability, we're also looking forward to their ideas on making SQL and data processing even more flexible, accessible, and user friendly. As part of that work, we would expect more composability so that every aspect of the system can be queried and combined flexibly.

And now it's your turn to shape the future of data engineering with DuckDB! Happy Quacking!

appendix
Client APIs for DuckDB

This appendix covers

- Alternative client APIs for DuckDB
- When and where those APIs are useful
- A word on concurrency
- How to ingest large amounts of data through client APIs
- A showcase of the Java Database Connectivity integration

So far, we've focused on either the DuckDB CLI or the Python integration. The former is not only the easiest and fastest way to bring up a DuckDB database and use it but also the smoothest way of teaching DuckDB without having to install a lot of things. The latter just follows naturally, as many of the analytics use cases of DuckDB are rooted in the broader Python world.

There is only so much you can put into one book, however, so the look we are taking at integrations in this appendix will be more concise. If you're interested in other integrations, we assume you are familiar with concepts like the classpath for Java and are aware of dependency management for both Java and R.

A.1 *Officially supported languages*

DuckDB provides support for the following languages:

- *C*—DuckDB implements a custom C API following the SQLite C API to a large extent. The API is contained in the `duckdb.h` header. In addition, a full wrapper for the SQLite API is provided, which can be used to relink existing SQLite programs against DuckDB. The C API is distributed as `libduckdb`.

- *C++*—DuckDB is written in C++, so an integration follows quite naturally. It is distributed as `libduckdb` too. It's worth mentioning that you want to use this API for providing any user-defined functions (UDFs) that should be vectorized.

- *Java*—As explained in this appendix, DuckDB provides a JDBC driver (`org.duckdb:duckdb_jdbc`) through Maven central, which bundles the DuckDB binaries for each major operating system and can run as part of your Java programs.

- *Julia*—This integration will run in the same process as the Julia client and fully supports the `DBInterface` interface. DuckDB provides native Julia DataFrames, which let you seamlessly continue your analytic work in a scientific language. The integration is delivered as a `DuckDB` package.

- *Python*—As shown throughout the book, DuckDB integrates well with the Python ecosystem, allowing you to run analytics directly in your Python programs and notebooks and even seamlessly interact with Pandas DataFrames. The integration is delivered as the `duckdb` package.

- *Node.js*—An API modelled along the SQLite API is available. It's noteworthy that the API exposes Apache Arrow integration for zero-copy ingestion of data.

- *R*—The official `duckdb` package provides an implementation of R's DBI Interface and all of its methods. As with Julia, the package is optimized for efficient data transfer. Any DuckDB table can be mapped directly onto an R DataFrame and vice versa. The DuckDB R integration also works well with `dbplyr` and `dplyr`, two packages that are somewhat similar to the relational API offered in Python for the safe, programmatic query construction.

- *Rust*—The Rust API is an idiomatic and ergonomic wrapper for Rust around the C-API and can be installed via crates.io.

- *Swift*—The Swift API enables developers on Swift platforms to harness the full power of DuckDB using a native Swift interface. The API is not only available on Apple platforms but on Linux too, opening up new opportunities for the growing Swift on server ecosystem.

- *ODBC*—The *Open Database Connectivity* (ODBC) is a C-style API that provides access to different flavors of database management systems (DBMSs). The ODBC API consists of the driver manager (DM) and the ODBC drivers. DuckDB supports ODBC version 3.0.

Both the WebAssembly (WASM) and Arrow Database Connectivity (ADBC) integrations are worth a special mention:

- *WASM is a binary instruction format for a stack-based virtual machine and ships with all four major browsers: Firefox, Chrome, Safari, and Edge.* DuckDB can be compiled to WASM and will run natively in your browser. There, it can be used as an interactive Web shell or programmatically through JavaScript, which is also how MotherDuck provides a web-based interface to their DuckDB backend.
- *Arrow Database Connectivity (ADBC), similarly to ODBC and JDBC, is a C-style API that enables code portability between different database systems.* The main difference between ADBC and ODBC/JDBC is that ADBC uses Apache Arrow as an efficient columnar format to transfer data between the database system and the application. DuckDB has an ADBC driver that takes advantage of the zero-copy integration between DuckDB and Arrow to efficiently transfer data. The ADBC driver is available for C++ and Python.

A.2   A word on concurrency

In this book, we focused on data processing and only briefly touched on application development in chapter 9 with Streamlit. Most interactive applications will provide concurrent access to themselves. This might be through multiple threads in a multithreaded environment, such as Java, or within event loops on a single thread.

DuckDB offers two configurable options for concurrency:

- A single process can both read and write to the database.
- Multiple processes can read from the database, but none of them can write, as the database is in read-only mode for all of them.

This does not mean you can't use DuckDB in concurrent, interactive applications; you just need to be aware of the limitations. When using the first option, DuckDB supports multiple writer threads using a combination of multiversion concurrency control (MVCC) and optimistic concurrency control, but all within that single writer process.

If your application does not span multiple processes, it can safely access one shared in-memory or file-based database under the following rules:

- As long as there are no write conflicts, multiple concurrent writes will succeed.
- Appends will never conflict, even on the same table.
- Multiple threads can also simultaneously update separate tables or separate subsets of the same table.
- Optimistic concurrency control comes into play when two threads attempt to edit (update or delete) the same row at the same time. In that situation, the one thread attempting the update will fail with a conflict error.

What will not work without restriction is a typical microservices architecture, in which your orchestrator will scale your application up and down by starting new processes or stopping existing ones, while accessing the same underlying files. Such a scenario is limited to using read-only access to the same DuckDB files or read–write access to different separate DuckDB files.

A.3   *Use cases*

Many applications we all use on a daily basis on our phones embed a relational database: SQLite.

It can be found in

- Every Android device
- Every iPhone and iOS device
- Every Mac
- Many television sets and set-top cable boxes
- Many automotive multimedia systems

SQLite itself claims to be the "most widely deployed and used database engine," with an estimated 1 trillion SQLite databases in active use (see https://www.sqlite.org/mostdeployed.html). DB-Engines, a website that regularly ranks databases for their popularity, usually finds it in the top 10.

With an API mostly compatible with SQLite, you can swap out SQLite for DuckDB for your example in your next iOS application. By incorporating DuckDB into your application, even in read-only mode, you can benefit from its data-ingestion capabilities. Instead of using some arbitrary API to process CSV files, you can use DuckDB consistently to query all supported formats and use the results directly in your application through SQL, as explained in chapter 5. The same holds true for read-only DuckDB databases, against which you can run hardcoded or dynamically generated queries.

Whether your typical online transaction processing (OLTP) application should make use of DuckDB as a primary storage is debatable. While DuckDB supports transactional semantics and several thousand writes per second, it's not designed for typical transactional workloads with many small operations. In guaranteed single-process deployments, this will work similarly to other applications with this style, using SQLite or H2, a Java-based, embedded, in-process database. DuckDB is explicitly designed for online analytical processing (OLAP) and will definitely shine in those use cases.

Maybe a hybrid approach better suits your needs. The following is a personal example.

I run a page tracking my sports activities. All tracking data is maintained and inserted via a handful of scripts, and after updating, the website is statically regenerated using a Python Flask application. While this is a hobby project, this approach scales for bigger setups. The source code can be found here: https://github.com/michael-simons/biking3.

A.4   *Importing large amounts of data*

Using prepared SQL statements, where data is bound to named or indexed parameters, is the preferred method of inserting data into relational databases. This is not only because using parameters prevents most cases of SQL injections but also for performance reasons. These statements have the same shape and don't require repeated parsing and planning by the database, and their execution plans can be cached. Prepared statements exist in all standardized client APIs, such as JDBC and the database connectivity in C++, but they are not the best option for bulk loading data into DuckDB.

Your go-to approach should actually be ingesting data from inside DuckDB via the methods we learned in chapters 3, 4, and 5: `read_csv`, `read_json`, and `read_parquet` with direct inserts into tables as necessary. If this is not possible, both the JDBC driver and the C++ client offer an appender, which directly writes into the corresponding tables. The JDBC driver additionally offers import and export via Apache Arrow.

A.5   *Using DuckDB from Java via the JDBC Driver*

The Java Database Connectivity (JDBC) API is one of the oldest specifications on the Java platform, and a client—or a *driver*, in JDBC lingo—exists for almost every database. JDBC itself is closely tied to the SQL standardization efforts and relational databases. So of course, DuckDB offers a JDBC driver too.

This section is not an introduction to Java, JDBC, or dependency management on the JVM. We will have a look at the structure and the peculiarities of the DuckDB JDBC driver, what it is capable of, and what it is not. If you want to use the JDBC driver to ingest large amounts of data, we will cover that too.

The Maven coordinates for the DuckDB JDBC driver are `org.duckdb:duckdb_jdbc:0.10.0`. In a project based on the Maven build system, you would declare a dependency on the driver as follows.

> **Listing A.1   Maven dependency declaration for DuckDB JDBC**

```
<dependency>
    <groupId>org.duckdb</groupId>
    <artifactId>duckdb_jdbc</artifactId>
    <version>0.10.0</version>
</dependency>
```

> **NOTE** We suggest including the driver in the `compile` scope, in contrast to `provided`, so that you are able to explicitly unwrap a generic JDBC `Connection` into a dedicated `DuckDBConnection` for accessing some of its specific methods.

For Gradle, another build system for Java, the declaration also uses the `compile` scope:

```
dependencies {
    compile 'org.duckdb:duckdb_jdbc:0.10.0'
}
```

To keep things as simple as possible, we are not using any build- or dependency-management systems in the following examples. Our examples are all single-class programs that don't require any dependencies apart from the JDBC driver.

You can download duckdb_jdbc-0.10.0.jar directly from Maven central, using the link in the listing. The listing utilizes cURL, a command-line tool for accessing web resources, to download the JAR file. This needs to be done only once, and you can, of course, use any other tool (or your browser) for that purpose.

The filename of our first example is simple.java. The example requires Java 17 and can be run with the following incantation directly from the source file, without explicit compilation:

```
curl -OL https://repo1.maven.org/maven2/org/duckdb/duckdb_jdbc/\
0.10.0/duckdb_jdbc-0.10.0.jar
java -cp duckdb_jdbc-0.10.0.jar simple.java
```

All example source code is available in the book repository (https://github.com/duckdb-in-action/examples/tree/main/a1). There is no need to manually enter the code.

On the outside, the DuckDB JDBC driver looks like any other JDBC driver. It provides an implementation of the `java.sql.Driver`, the `java.sql.Statement`, and the `java.sql.PreparedStatement`. It does not support callable statements, the retrieval of generated keys, or some other details of the JDBC spec. When in doubt, you will need to read its sources to check if the API you want to use is supported, or just try it out.

The JAR file is quite large—for version 0.10.0, it's about 65 megabytes. The reason for this is actually quite simple. Looking into the JAR file with unzip -l duckdb_jdbc-0.10.0.jar reveals that the driver ships the DuckDB binaries for all major operating systems.

The files beginning with libduckdb_java are the actual native DuckDB binaries:

```
Archive:  duckdb_jdbc-0.10.0.jar
  Length      Date    Time    Name
---------  ---------- -----    ----
        0  02-13-2024 13:20   META-INF/
       64  02-13-2024 13:20   META-INF/MANIFEST.MF
       24  02-13-2024 13:20   META-INF/services/java.sql.Driver
     3297  02-13-2024 13:20   org/duckdb/DuckDBAppender.class
     2581  02-13-2024 13:20   org/duckdb/DuckDBArray.class
    20549  02-13-2024 13:20   org/duckdb/DuckDBArrayResultSet.class
     2699  02-13-2024 13:20   org/duckdb/DuckDBColumnType.class
      812  02-13-2024 13:20   org/duckdb/DuckDBColumnTypeMetaData.class
    11017  02-13-2024 13:20   org/duckdb/DuckDBConnection.class
    24447  02-13-2024 13:20   org/duckdb/DuckDBDatabaseMetaData.class
      676  02-13-2024 13:20   org/duckdb/DuckDBDate.class
     2289  02-13-2024 13:20   org/duckdb/DuckDBDriver.class
      ...
 48822768  02-13-2024 13:26   libduckdb_java.so_linux_amd64
 87819276  02-13-2024 14:54   libduckdb_java.so_osx_universal
 24764928  02-13-2024 14:54   libduckdb_java.so_windows_amd64
 44872680  02-13-2024 14:55   libduckdb_java.so_linux_arm64
---------                     -------
206440213                     33 files
```

The JDBC driver will load the native DuckDB library for your operating system into the Java process, thus staying true to the fact that DuckDB is an embedded, in-process database. So what we said about concurrency in the beginning of this appendix applies here as well. An instance of the DuckDB driver and database can safely be accessed from several threads inside a Java program and several instances of a `java.sql.Connection` at once. It is not possible for several Java processes to use the same DuckDB database file in write mode at once. In that case, they would be limited to read-only mode.

A.5.1   Understanding the general usage pattern

The general usage pattern for the DuckDB JDBC driver is no different from other JDBC drivers. The JDBC URL for DuckDB is `jdbc:duckdb:` for a pure in-memory database that will not be saved to disk when the Java process ends. The following code acquires a connection, creates a JDBC statement, executes a query returning all DuckDB settings, prints them, and then exits. Just using an available database function here allows us to focus on the relevant parts for understanding how to use the JDBC driver.

Asking the `DriverManager` to get a connection for a JDBC URL is the standard way to acquire a JDBC connection. Of course, we are using a DuckDB URL.

Listing A.2   `simple.java`

```java
import java.sql.DriverManager;
import java.sql.SQLException;

class simple {

    public static void main(String... a) throws SQLException {

        var query = "SELECT * FROM duckdb_settings() ORDER BY name";
        try (
                var con = DriverManager
                    .getConnection("jdbc:duckdb:");
                var stmt = con.createStatement();
                var resultSet = stmt.executeQuery(query)
        ) {
            while (resultSet.next()) {
                System.out.printf("%s %s%n",
                    resultSet.getString("name"),
                    resultSet.getString("value"));
            }
        }
    }
}
```

The connection is wrapped in a "try-with-resources" block so that it will be automatically closed.

Our query will be executed here; a ResultSet is a resource and needs to be closed too.

You need a Statement to execute queries, which we acquire in the same block to close it after usage too.

We iterate the result set and print its contents.

The first few lines when running this Java program look like this on the author's machine. Remember, you need to run the program like this: `java -cp duckdb_jdbc -0.10.0.jar simple.java`, from our example repository using at least Java 17:

```
Calendar gregorian
TimeZone Europe/Berlin
```

```
access_mode automatic
allocator_flush_threshold 134.2MB
allow_unsigned_extensions false
arrow_large_buffer_size false
autoinstall_extension_repository
autoinstall_known_extensions true
autoload_known_extensions true
binary_as_string
```

A.5.2   *Using multiple connections from several threads*

Here we answer the following question: Could you safely use DuckDB inside one instance of your Java application that might use multiple threads to respond to multiple concurrent http requests? In short, yes, you totally can. We are, however, not building a backend for a web application here but demonstrating this by using a few threads. In a proper application, you would most likely not create a new connection in each thread but use a JDBC connection pool instead. Frameworks like Spring Boot or Quarkus do this for you automatically. While not included in this book, we confirmed successfully that DuckDB indeed works fine in any of those frameworks with the respective connection pools. What we recreate in the following text is similar to how multiple concurrent requests against a web application would eventually end up as concurrent queries running in one DuckDB instance.

The following program will save the database to a file named readings.db; hence, it uses the following JDBC URL to retrieve a connection: jdbc:duckdb:readings.db. It will create a readings table on the main thread and then spawn 20 new threads that insert readings with random values.

This example shows that while only one process can open a DuckDB file, it is no problem to use multiple threads in that process to access it for reading and writing.

Listing A.3   `using_multiple_connections.java`

```java
import java.sql.Connection;
import java.sql.DriverManager;
import java.sql.SQLException;
import java.sql.Timestamp;
import java.time.LocalDateTime;
import java.util.concurrent.Executors;
import java.util.concurrent.ThreadLocalRandom;
import java.util.concurrent.TimeUnit;
import java.util.concurrent.atomic.AtomicInteger;

import org.duckdb.DuckDBConnection;

class using_multiple_connections {

    private static final AtomicInteger ID_GENERATOR = new AtomicInteger(0);
    private static final String DUCKDB_URL
        = "jdbc:duckdb:readings.db";        ⟵   The DuckDB URL that will
                                                 create a readings.db

    public static void main(String... a) throws Exception {
```

```
var createTableStatement = """
    CREATE TABLE IF NOT EXISTS readings (
        id           INTEGER NOT NULL PRIMARY KEY,
        created_on TIMESTAMP NOT NULL,
        power        DECIMAL(10,3) NOT NULL
    )
    """;
```

This statement ensures the target table exists. → (points to `"""`)

```
var executor = Executors.newWorkStealingPool();
try (
    var con = DriverManager
        .getConnection(DUCKDB_URL);
    var stmt = con.createStatement()
) {
    stmt.execute(createTableStatement);
    var result = stmt
        .executeQuery("SELECT max(id) + 1 FROM readings");
    result.next();
    ID_GENERATOR.compareAndSet(0, result.getInt(1));
    result.close();

    for (int i = 0; i < 20; ++i) {
        executor.submit(() -> insertNewReading(con));
    }
    executor.shutdown();
    executor
        .awaitTermination(5, TimeUnit.MINUTES);
}


    }
}
```

The connection is created on the main thread and closed when the try block ends. ← (points to `.getConnection(DUCKDB_URL);`)

A java.sql.Statement opened in the try block as well to get it cleaned up after usage. ← (points to `var stmt = con.createStatement()`)

Retrieves the largest value of the id column so far → (points to `var result = stmt`)

Creates 20 tasks, each executing the given method in parallel ← (points to `for (int i = 0; i < 20; ++i) {`)

Makes sure the program does not terminate until all tasks are finished ← (points to `executor`)

This program creates 20 tasks that are submitted to an executor, which uses a thread pool with as many threads as available processors. Which task do they run? It turns out they run the static method `using_multiple_connections::insertNewReading`, which is shown in listing A.4. The method is called with the original connection. Inside the method, we turn this connection into a `DuckDBConnection`, using the typesafe JDBC approach by unwrapping the class. The `DuckDBConnection` now can be duplicated, which is equivalent to calling `DriverManager.getConnection("jdbc:duckdb:readings.db")` again, but much faster. The method then inserts a single row with a random value and handles the resources correctly. Checked SQL exceptions are caught and rethrown as runtime exceptions to be handled outside, which is a common pattern in Java.

Listing A.4 `using_multiple_connections::insertNewReading`

```
static void insertNewReading(Connection connection) {
    var sql = "INSERT INTO readings VALUES (?, ?, ?)";
    var readOn = Timestamp.valueOf(LocalDateTime.now());
    var value = ThreadLocalRandom.current().nextDouble() * 100;
```

```
        try (
            var con = connection                              Unwraps into a
                .unwrap(DuckDBConnection.class)   ◄───   specialized connection
Duplicates ├──▷   .duplicate();
            var stmt = con.prepareStatement(sql)   ◄──┐  Gets a
        ) {                                            │ java.sql.PreparedStatement
            stmt.setInt(1, ID_GENERATOR.getAndIncrement());│ that can be parameterized
            stmt.setTimestamp(2, readOn);
            stmt.setDouble(3, value);
            stmt.execute();
        } catch (SQLException e) {
            throw new RuntimeException(e);
        }
    }
```

Running this program with `java -cp duckdb_jdbc-0.10.0.jar using_multiple_connections.java` will create `readings.db` in the same directory, populated with a `readings` table and at least 20 rows. If you run a SELECT on the table, ordered by the millisecond timestamp at which the records have been created, you can see that the ID values do not have the same order. This indicates that the insert statement did actually run asynchronously:

```
java -cp duckdb_jdbc-0.10.0.jar \
  using_multiple_connections.java
duckdb readings.db -s ".maxrows 6" -s "FROM readings ORDER BY created_on"
```

id int32	created_on timestamp	power decimal(10,3)
0	2024-02-10 18:15:58.457194	73.185
4	2024-02-10 18:15:58.457272	24.159
2	2024-02-10 18:15:58.457432	46.807
.	.	.
.	.	.
.	.	.
16	2024-02-10 18:15:58.462457	55.934
18	2024-02-10 18:15:58.462785	1.298
19	2024-02-10 18:15:58.46287	55.559
20 rows (6 shown)		3 columns

You can use all SQL constructs supported by DuckDB over JDBC. The main APIs for your SQL statements are `java.sql.Statement` and `java.sql.PreparedStatement`. Use the latter if you want to parameterize your statements. If you find yourself looking for a fluent query builder similar to the relational API in DuckDB's Python package or to what R offers, you can have a look at jOOQ (https://www.jooq.org), which is an open source project that bridges SQL and the Java world. I've used it with great success (and fun!) in many projects.

A.5.3   *Using DuckDB as a tool for data processing from Java*

In chapter 5, we used DuckDB to explore data without using DuckDB's persistent storage. This is, of course, possible not only from the DuckDB CLI or the Python client but also from Java. For some formats, such as Parquet, it's a great solution: Java cannot deal with Parquet files without using external libraries. The libraries that exist for dealing with Parquet in Java oftentimes depend on Apache Hadoop, Apache Spark, or Apache Avro—great products, but ones that come with a huge number of dependencies. If you prefer a project without that many dependencies, you can simply use DuckDB.

We have a list of Parquet files in the a1/weather folder of our example repository that contain weather data scraped from Wikipedia (https://en.wikipedia.org/wiki/ List_of_cities_by_average_temperature). We want to list these weather stations in our Java program by name and the yearly temperature value. Instead of writing a lot of Java code to load and inspect the files one by one, we can just ask an embedded DuckDB instance to do this for us. The method presented in the following listing opens an in-memory connection, selects the data of interest, and creates our list. The method itself is part of the using_the_appender.java file. The whole program will be shown later.

The query we are using here does a lot of things that normally would require a considerable amount of code and at least one additional library. It reads all Parquet files in the weather folder by using a glob in the FROM clause (weather/*.parquet) and then extracts one value from the `Year` column per `City` (the source does contain the temperature in Celsius and Fahrenheit). As with previous data sources, data quality varies, and the query also makes sure the temperature value can actually be read as a numeric value. The rest of the code then boils down to the ceremony Java requires for JDBC, as shown in the following listing.

> **Listing A.5**   `using_the_appender::weatherStations`

```
private record WeatherStation(String id, double avgTemperature) {
}

static List<WeatherStation> weatherStations() throws SQLException {

    var query = """
            SELECT City AS id,
                    cast(replace(
                      trim(
                        regexp_extract(Year,'(.*)\\n.*', 1)
                      ), '-', '-') AS double)
                    AS avgTemperature
            FROM 'weather/*.parquet'
          """;
    var weatherStations = new ArrayList<WeatherStation>();      ◁── Keeps all the resources
    try (                                                            in the try block
        var con = DriverManager
```

```
            .getConnection("jdbc:duckdb:");
        var stmt = con.createStatement();
        var resultSet = stmt.executeQuery(query)
    ) {
        while (resultSet.next()) {
            var id = resultSet.getString("id");
            var avgTemperature = resultSet.getDouble("avgTemperature");
            weatherStations.add(new WeatherStation(id, avgTemperature));
        }
    }

    return weatherStations;
}
```

⟵ **Iterates the date and creates objects as desired from it**

A.5.4   *Inserting large amounts of data*

You already know by now how to ingest data with DuckDB "from the inside," essentially treating CSV, Parquet, or JSON files as tables and relying on DuckDB's machinery to insert batches of data efficiently. But what about data that was created as part of another process and never written to a file? A Java-based service might run all kinds of computations, maybe calling other services while doing so. It could be wasteful to write large results first to a file and then ingest them.

Normally, you would use an instance of `java.sql.PreparedStatement` and its batch processing capabilities to do so. We already used a prepared statement in listing A.4 for a single insert, and the batch usage would look similar. While nothing prevents you from using it as a batch insert, it would be slower than necessary with the DuckDB JDBC driver.

For our example, we will use the list of weather stations created in the previous section. In early 2024, a challenge had taken the hearts—but especially the minds—of the Java community by storm: the One Billion Row Challenge, also known as 1BRC, run by Gunnar Morling (see https://github.com/gunnarmorling/1brc). The task of this challenge was to write a Java program that read a CSV file, calculated the minimum, average, and maximum temperature values per weather station, and emitted the results in a specific format.

The original challenge was based on a CSV file with one billion rows, which can, of course, read via DuckDB directly, but we want to have the data available in DuckDB's native table format for processing. So we tasked ourselves to create a DuckDB database with a configurable number of rows in one table derived from the weather stations from the previous section.

We will use the `org.duckdb.DuckDBAppender` to directly write data into the table. To get a hold of an instance of that class, we must again unwrap the generic JDBC connection into a `DuckDBConnection`, which will let you create an appender that writes directly into a table. The following method is also part of the bigger program `using_the_appender.java`. It creates one connection, persisting data into `weather.db`, and unwraps the generic JDBC connection into `DuckDBConnection` to access its specialized methods. The `DuckDBConnection` is used to create an appender for the `weather` table, to which many rows are appended.

Listing A.6 `using_the_appender::generateData`

```
import java.sql.DriverManager;
import java.sql.SQLException;
import java.util.concurrent.ThreadLocalRandom;
import org.duckdb.DuckDBConnection;

static void generateData(int size) throws SQLException {

    var stations = weatherStations();
    var numStations = stations.size();

    try (var con = DriverManager.getConnection("jdbc:duckdb:weather.db")
        .unwrap(DuckDBConnection.class)
    ) {
        var rand = ThreadLocalRandom.current();
        long start = System.currentTimeMillis();
        try (var appender = con.createAppender(
                DuckDBConnection.DEFAULT_SCHEMA,
                "weather")
        ) {
            for (int i = 0; i < size; ++i) {
                if (i > 0 && i % 50_000_000 == 0) {
                    appender.flush();
                }
                var station = stations.get(rand.nextInt(numStations));
                appender.beginRow();
                appender
                    .append(station.id());
                appender
                    .append(station.measurement());
                appender.endRow();
            }
        }
    }
}
```

> The generic connection must be unwrapped into a DuckDBConnection to access vendor-specific methods.

> Appenders must be created specifically for one table— here, for the weather table.

The beginning of a new row must be indicated.

> Columns must be appended in the order in which the table columns are defined.

The end of the row must be indicated.

The program, executed with `java -cp duckdb_jdbc-0.10.0.jar using_the_appender.java 1000000000`, takes about 10 minutes on my machine to create a 2.4 GB database file containing a billion randomized rows.

DuckDB takes roughly 3 seconds to compute the answer to the One Billion Row Challenge, as shown in the following listing.

Listing A.7   Solving the 1BRC with SQL

```
.mode line
WITH src AS (
    SELECT id AS station_name,
           MIN(measurement) AS min,
           CAST(AVG(measurement) AS DECIMAL(8,1)) AS mean,
           MAX(measurement) AS max
    FROM weather
```

```
    GROUP BY station_name
)
SELECT '{' || ARRAY_TO_STRING(
        LIST(station_name || '=' || CONCAT_WS('/', min, mean, max)
          ORDER BY station_name), ', ')
     || '}' AS "1BRC"
FROM src;
```

The abbreviated output looks like this:

```
1BRC =  {Abha=-33.5/18.0/71.7, Abidjan=-22.1/26.0/75.0, .. }
Run Time (s): real 3.051 user 29.247171 sys 0.033100
```

A.6   *Additional connection options*

The DuckDB JDBC driver doesn't support any URL parameters, but instead, it uses connection options. In read_only.java, we demonstrate the available options. Here, we're using a read-only connection so that multiple processes can access the same database and streaming JDBC result rows. The program uses a similar query to the preceding one to solve the One Billion Row Challenge and formats the output in Java code, as shown in the following listing.

Listing A.8   `read_only.java`

```java
import java.sql.DriverManager;
import java.sql.SQLException;
import java.util.Locale;
import java.util.Properties;

import org.duckdb.DuckDBDriver;

class read_only {

    public static void main(String... args) throws SQLException {

        var properties = new Properties();
        properties.setProperty(
            DuckDBDriver.DUCKDB_READONLY_PROPERTY, "true");
        properties.setProperty(
            DuckDBDriver.JDBC_STREAM_RESULTS, "true");

        var query = """
            SELECT id AS station_name,
                   MIN(measurement) AS min,
                   CAST(AVG(measurement) AS DECIMAL(8,1)) AS mean,
                   MAX(measurement) AS max
            FROM weather
            GROUP BY station_name
            ORDER BY station_name
            """;
        var url = "jdbc:duckdb:weather.db";

        try (
            var con = DriverManager
```

Options for JDBC are passed via a Properties object.

Uses the available constants on the DuckDBDriver class and doesn't hardcode the names as strings

```
                .getConnection(url, properties);        ◄─┐  The properties object
        var stmt = con.createStatement();                 │  needs to be passed to
        var result = stmt.executeQuery(query)             │  the driver manager.
    ) {
        boolean first = true;
        System.out.print("{");
        while (result.next()) {
            if(!first) {
                System.out.print(", ");
            }
            var station = result.getString("station_name");
            var min = result.getDouble("min");
            var mean = result.getDouble("mean");
            var max = result.getDouble("max");
            System.out.printf(
                Locale.ENGLISH, "%s=%3.2f/%3.2f/%3.2f",
                station, min, mean, max);
            first = false;
        }
    }
    System.out.println("}");
    }
}
```

While the pure DuckDB solution runs in about 3 seconds, the Java program takes about 26 seconds, which is astonishingly good, as it includes the following:

- Compiling the Java program into byte code
- Loading the JDBC Driver and the native DuckDB code
- Loading the 2.4 GB database file
- Doing the aggregation
- Streaming and formatting the results

The baseline timing for the original One Billion Row Challenge setup was around 5 minutes. In 2024, the winning program solved the challenge in about 300 milliseconds—however, with beautiful, hand-optimized code.

Nevertheless, the One Billion Row Challenge and our own experiments here demonstrate one thing: Java is not slow, and neither is database interaction with Java. If you are familiar with Java or have an existing codebase in which you need some analytics of medium to relatively large data volumes, using DuckDB from Java is a feasible approach.

Summary

- DuckDB can be used from a plethora of different languages.
- Most languages are supported by DuckDB or DuckDB Labs with official extensions.
- There's usually a mechanism to directly map a table into the host languages on platforms that support DataFrames.

- Prepared statements should only be used for handling parameterized queries, not for batch loading.
- If possible, use an SQL-based import from the inside. Otherwise, look for a dedicated mechanism, such as an appender or the Arrow import, and export in the language of your choice.
- A single DuckDB file can only be accessed from one process in write mode or from many in read-only mode.
- A process can access a single DuckDB resource from many threads in both write and read-only mode at once.

index

V

VARCHAR type 101, 118, 139
vectorization 243–244
vectorized query engine 3
views, creating 254–255

W

WASM (WebAssembly) 266
weakly typed database system 118
weekdays, posting on 236–238
WHERE clause 23, 53–54, 71, 78–81, 181
window functions 69–78
   accessing preceding or following rows in
     partition 77–78

framing 74
named windows 75–77
partitioning 72–74
Windows, installing DuckDB CLI 13

X

xidel 225

Y

YAML (YAML Ain't Markup Language) 173

Z

ZSTD format 248